Plane Insanity

A Flight Attendant's Tales of Sex, Rage and Queasiness at 30,000 Feet

Elliott Hester

ST. MARTIN'S PRESS ❦ NEW YORK

www.stmartins.com

"Payback for a Condescending Jerk" originally appeared in the *San Francisco Chronicle*.

The remaining stories originally appeared on Salon.com except: "Escape from New York," "Fly Boys and Girls," "Anatomy of a Carry-On Bag," "Good Ole Airplane Sustenance," "Pass the Defibrillator Please," "Beer and Loathing in Caracas," "The No-Show," "Miguel Mendoza: Playboy of the Skies," and "Membership Has Its Privileges," which have never before been published.

Design by Susan Walsh

Library of Congress Cataloging-in-Publication Data

Hester, Elliott Neal.
    Plane insanity : a flight attendant's tales of sex, rage and queasiness at 30,000 feet / Elliott Neal Hester.—1st ed.
        p. cm.
    ISBN 0-312-26958-7
    1. Hester, Elliott Neal. 2. Flight attendants—United States—Anecdotes. I. Title.
    HD8039.A43 H47 2001
    387.7'42'092—dc21
    [B]
                                                          2001041898

First Edition: January 2002

10 9 8 7 6 5 4 3 2 1

Plane Insanity *was written, edited, and sent to press prior to the tragic events of September 11, 2001. As victims rest in peace, why can't we learn to live in it?*

Contents

Acknowledgments

This book would not have been possible without the guidance, encouragement, and desperately needed meals courtesy of my agent, Faith Hamlin. If every struggling author had a representative like Faith, book publishing would be a far less intimidating concept. Jennifer Enderlin, my editor, approached this project with the kind of wide-eyed enthusiasm that authors dream of. (I hope her uncle—a retired airline pilot—will still speak to her after reading chapter three.) I am forever indebted to Don George. During his cyber-editing days, Don hired me to write the on-line travel column from which this book bloomed. Last and definitely not least, I'd like to thank Jean Hester, my mom. Years ago, after reading an essay I wrote about a girl in my sixth-grade class, my mom looked down at me, beaming. "You should be a writer when you grow up," she said.

Well, Mom, I finally became a writer. Forgive me for not growing up.

Bad trips are wonderful as long as they happen to other people. We all love travel misadventure stories, partly because they make us laugh, but mainly because they could have happened to us and didn't—at least not this time around.

—Douglas McArthur
The Globe and Mail, Toronto

Introduction

I never wanted to be a flight attendant.

I never fantasized about slinging chicken and beef at thirty thousand feet. Never dreamed of wearing a polyester-wool uniform, working fourteen-hour days, being cussed at by business flyers, puked on by kids, swung on by air ragers, poked by the elderly and subjected to the rueful drone of pilots reminiscing about simpler days when they flew C-130 military cargo planes and had yet to sign an alimony check. I never aspired to any of this. At least not until freezing my ass off in the winter of '85.

That January, during one of the nastiest subzero streaks in Chicago's history, I worked outside as a part-time baggage handler for a second-rate airline at the world's busiest airport. Relegated to the graveyard shift, I'd show up at the O'Hare ramp dressed in layered clothing suitable for the Alaskan Ididerod: long underwear, polypropylene sweats, extra-thick wool army fatigues, a turtleneck pullover, heavy sweater, three-quarter-length parka, insulated work boots, insulated gloves, an insulated jock strap and a wool skull cap. When the temperature really plummeted, I put on a ski mask and goggles.

For a moment, try to imagine me on the airport tarmac, dressed in the aforementioned igloo wear and standing beneath the belly of a Boeing 727. Imagine a night when the windchill factor knocks the temperature down to 64 degrees below zero. Imagine crystals of my own frozen breath, clinging around the mouth hole of my ski mask as

I turn to the luggage cart, bend forward, lift a forty-pound piece of passenger luggage and toss it onto a belt loader that angles up to the 727's cargo compartment. Imagine a gust of ice-cold wind rushing up my pant leg, past the insulated jockstrap—instantly reducing my testicles to the size of cocktail peanuts. Imagine my aching back, after I've lifted and tossed the 527th passenger bag of the night. Now try to imagine the condition of *your* Samsonite, my 528th, once I've snatched it from the baggage cart, raised it above my head and slammed it onto the belt loader in an act of primal fury.

On one such night—as arctic winds roared up my pant leg, as yet another piece of luggage flew from my frostbitten fingers—I looked up, squinted through my ski goggles and gazed upon a flight attendant through an airplane window. She was sitting in a passenger seat, sipping something warm and steamy from a Styrofoam cup. Waiting, no doubt, for the throng of passengers with whom she would soon fly away to Mexico City. She looked down at me and waved. It was a short, sad wave. The kind of wave offered by an inmate's wife, when visiting hours have ended at Rikers Island.

Perhaps it was the late hour (1 A.M.), or the muscle fatigue (everything—including my glutes—ached), or the fact that hypothermia was about to set in—whatever the reason, I stood there, shivering, mesmerized by the look of pity on her face. A look that, in turn, made me feel sorry for myself. That's when the cold, hard hand of common sense reached out and slapped me in the face.

Why the hell was I slaving on the frozen airport tundra with a bunch of guys like Vic and T-Bone, when I could be working *inside* the airplane with long-legged coworkers named Audrey and Monica and Priscilla Jean? Why was I still living in Chicago, the Siberia of the Midwest, when I could be based in Miami or Los Angeles? There was nothing to keep me here in the Cold and Windy City. No wife. No illegitimate kids. No mortgage payments. I suddenly realized that this was my chance to get out of town before I found myself stuck in an O'Hare-area suburb, buried beneath a familial snow drift from which I could never dig out.

A few months after this bone-chilling epiphany, I found myself at the headquarters of a major U.S. airline, immersed in a five-week flight-attendant training program.

Simply put, training was five weeks of hell. Five weeks of sharing a dormitory room with four male trainees—one snored like a drunken cartoon character, another argued with his mother in his sleep. Five weeks of listening to Stalinist lectures about the common good of the company and the importance of teamwork. Five weeks of practicing airplane evacuation procedures, of contemplating the great complexities of in-flight food service, of performing mouth-to-mouth resuscitation on truncated mannequins, of worrying about being kicked out for one of a variety of indiscretions. (One of my roommates crashed and burned for laughing too loud in the hallway.) It was five long weeks of sympathizing with more than fifty women who were forced to wear prodigious amounts of makeup. "Lipstick should be bright enough to be seen from across a large room." This lipstick mandate—held as near to the hearts of airline grooming instructors as the Second Amendment to NRA devotees—left some women feeling like circus clowns.

"I can't wait till the day I get off probation," I heard one of them say. "This crap is coming right off."

Jasmine, one of only a handful of African-American trainees, was forced to dye her red hair black. The grooming coordinator, an alleged style expert who hailed from the trend-setting metropolis of Waxahachie, Texas, apparently believed that a black woman with natural red hair was a walking fashion faux pas. Even if this particular black woman had the freckles to match.

The grooming coordinator managed to spread her ignorance beyond racial boundaries as well. Compelled to have her white locks homogenized to a more "appropriate" shade, Cynthia, a platinum blonde from Los Angeles, found herself at the mercy of an inexperienced airline stylist. After a screw-up in chemical application, the green-haired Californian was last seen running from the training center in tears.

Because hair and makeup issues rarely concern men, I managed to escape the scrutiny of the backwoods grooming Gestapo. Nevertheless, I learned to buff my fingernails to a luster that would make Richard Simmons proud. Although I failed one or two exams, screwed up the meal service during "simulated flight," and got caught kissing a horny coed (her redneck townie boyfriend would have shot us both had he known what happened the following night), I matriculated from the Charm Farm and was shipped off to New York.

That's where I began earning my stripes as an in-flight bartender/referee/therapist.

Human behavior is rarely more incomprehensible than when witnessed on an airplane at thirty thousand feet. Passengers have been known to freak out or act up for a variety of reasons: turbulence, fear of flying, too much alcohol, not enough sense, or because they're stuck for hours in a crowded metal tube equipped with smelly lavatories, lousy food and seats best suited for Danny Devito and family. These conditions can turn even the most sophisticated travelers into airborne newborns that flight attendants, despite our best efforts, have difficulty trying to appease.

In sixteen years of flight service, I've flown to nearly one hundred destinations in twenty-three countries and seen more than my share of in-flight theatrics. I once saw a drunken couple puke on each other until they looked as if they'd emerged from a pool of oatmeal. I watched a smug-faced man receiving high-altitude fellatio from a woman he'd just met on the flight. I witnessed a daring heist in which five hundred thousand dollars was stolen from a 727. I've seen full-blown airplane brawls, passenger stampedes, a flight attendant in the midst of a nervous breakdown, passengers in various stages of undress, and stressed-out flyers attempting to open the emergency exit six miles above the Atlantic.

Having dealt with these problems for nearly two decades, having ducked punches and calmed nerves and gazed sullenly as yet another passenger whipped out his willy and peed in front of startled frequent flyers, I've come to the conclusion that at least 2 percent of the traveling public is certifiably insane (the percentage is slightly higher for airline crew). With approximately 650 million people traveling annually on U.S. airlines and more than one hundred thousand flight attendants to serve them, many of us, at one time or another, will be caught in the grip of plane insanity.

The narratives appearing on the following pages are lowlights from my sixteen-year career in the air. All names have been changed (and in many cases, locations) to grant privacy to passengers and crew, and to make identifications as difficult a task as trying to clear customs at Miami International Airport.

If you question the veracity of these stories, simply pack this book in a carry-on bag and take it on your next flight. After the attendants finish with the food and beverage service, once they've disappeared behind the galley curtain to gobble up the leftover entrées, get up from your seat (even if the seat belt sign is on), walk to the galley and poke your head through the curtain. Be afraid. Be very afraid. But after they realize you don't want another Coke and that you want to give *them* something instead, the daggers will fall from their eyes. Show the book, point to a story and ask, "Has this ever happened to you?" As my colleagues begin to flip through the pages, you will hear the unbridled chuckle of commiseration. Mechanical delays, flight cancellations, boarding fiascoes, ballistic passengers—the stories are as wild and as varied as the crew members who tell the tale. From our perspective, the majority of flights reach their destination without major incident. But the remaining trips are rife with drama and absurdity—the likes of which will make you shake your head and sigh.

So welcome aboard, my frequent-flying friend. The plane is packed, the skies will be turbulent and you're stuck in a center seat in the next-to-last row of coach. To your left, a screaming infant squirms upon the lap of an indifferent mother. A businessman the size of a sumo wrestler is wedged into the seat on your right. You're cramped, hungry, suicidal. There's a foul stench drifting overhead. That's when you notice the guy in back just pushed his bare foot between the seats so that it's stretched out on *your* armrest—bunions, toe-jam and all. The flight attendants have faces like prison guards. The captain's P.A. announcements drive spikes through your skull. You can't sit back, can't relax, can't enjoy the friggin' flight because it's thirty minutes past departure time, the hydraulic system is busted and the airplane is still at the gate, waiting for mechanics who are threatening to go on strike. Forget about your connection in Chicago. Better pray your luggage doesn't get lost. This ain't no flight through the friendly skies, my friend.

This is the flight from hell.

American fined for flight urinating

AMSTERDAM, Netherlands, Aug. 5 (Associated Press) – Two intoxicated men, including one American, were fined $480 for urinating on passengers and airplane seats while aboard separate flights to Amsterdam, officials said Thursday.

The two incidents happened over the past two weeks on flights by the same airline. Police would not name the carrier or the men, in line with privacy regulations.

While waiting 26 hours in Cairo on July 25 for a flight to the Dutch capital, a Norwegian man consumed excessive amounts of whiskey and vodka, military police spokeswoman Marcha Muller said.

"Once airborne, the man felt the urge to relieve himself and dampened the three nearest seats," Muller said.

A few days later on July 29, an American passenger drank eight cans of beer while airborne before letting down his pants, stumbling through the aircraft with a glass of ale in his hand and finally urinating over three seats and his neighbor's sleeve.

Flight attendants overpowered the man, pulled up his trousers, and alerted authorities at Amsterdam's Schiphol Airport, where military police are responsible for security.

Dutch military police fined the two men $480 each for unruly behavior. The airline intends to press charges against the American for cleaning costs and disrupting fellow travelers with his "shocking behavior," Muller said.

Reprinted with permission of The Associated Press, 1999.

1 Something Smelly in the Air

Speed and altitude notwithstanding, flying in a commercial jet is not much different than riding in a Greyhound bus. You pay a higher-than-expected round-trip fare, inch sideways down a narrow aisle, toss your carry-on in the overhead, squeeze into a tiny seat next to a stranger whose ass is as wide and unruly as the Australian outback, then try to read, sleep, or stare out the window until you pull into the terminal in Boise or Detroit. Despite advertising campaigns that suggest a level of comfort and attention one might expect aboard the *Queen Elizabeth II*, air travel, in its purest main-cabin form, is little more than public transportation. Greyhound at thirty thousand feet. Amtrak with wings.

As with most forms of public transportation, your travel experience is affected as much by the staff as the passengers sitting near you. At times, your seatmates can have an even greater impact. We've all sat next to someone who talked until our eardrums bled, who laughed obnoxiously while watching the in-flight movie or yammered on the telephone until we harbored thoughts of homicide. We've all endured the frequent-flying Goober who sucks his teeth, clips his dirty toenails (toenail shrapnel can be as foul as it is deadly), picks his nose unmercifully, or falls asleep and either drools from one corner of his mouth or snores with the vigor of a drunken wildebeest.

The more unfortunate among us have suffered worse. On one crowded flight or another, I've been victimized by flatulence—the stealthy, gaseous, repeated break of wind from a businessman who should never have eaten that burrito. An SBD (silent but deadly) can be a pungent emission, but it's far more civilized than the eye-opening trumpet blast from less conscientious cheeks.

Flatulence, be it an SBD or a blaring tribute to Herb Alpert, is as short-lived as the crossing of a garbage truck at a busy intersection. You can wait for the pungency to pass (pun intended). You can breathe through your mouth for a little while. Or you can live in denial, like many passengers, pretending you can't smell a thing. But if your seat-mate is suffering from a different kind of body odor, if the stench of dirty dishrags and rotten eggs seeps from his armpits like a noxious gas, you might find yourself praying for a cabin depressurization—just so the oxygen masks will drop.

Not long ago, as our Boeing 767 was ready to depart JFK for Paris, a couple of peevish passengers confronted me and my crew. "We refuse to fly under these conditions," said a man approaching with his wife. Like a growing number of middle-aged American travelers, they were dressed in brightly colored sweat suits, brand new Nike athletic shoes and fanny packs that hung from their waists like decorative sashes. It wasn't clear whether they were preparing to fly to Paris or work as road monitors at the New York Marathon.

The purser turned to address them. "What conditions?" she asked.

"It's that group of rowdy Frenchmen," he replied. "They . . . they . . ." The man couldn't seem to find the right words so his wife interjected. "They stink!" she said, with a sneer.

The purser and I exchanged a glance and went back to investigate. Sure enough, as soon as we approached the middle of the main cabin, we stopped dead in our tracks and gagged. The funk was alive. It came at us like a mugger in broad daylight. Bold. Brutal. Uncompromising. The stench of old gym shoes and exotic cheese. The reek of bottled sweat.

The purser's face became a rictus of horror. Looking at her, one would think she had just walked into her bedroom to find her husband in bed with another woman, or perhaps another man. Had she been a new flight attendant on probation, a look like that could have easily gotten her fired. "Inappropriate facial expression," that's what the company calls it. (I know of one probationary flight attendant who lost her job because she rolled her eyes after a passenger made a sexist remark.)

Inappropriate looks and all, the crew huddled in the first-class galley, trying to figure out what to do. Like reluctant bloodhounds, the purser and I had traced the stench to a cluster of fifteen or twenty Frenchmen. They were laborers: grim-faced, rough-handed, dressed in worn jeans and work boots as if they'd just finished a six-week stint on an oil rig. They spoke easily among themselves as if emitting the redolence of tulips instead of moldy Gouda cheese.

The two passengers in sweat suits weren't the only ones who were offended. During my very brief stay in the coach cabin, I noticed many tortured faces. Several victims blinked at me as if sending a Morse Code plea for help. An elderly woman fanned her frowning face with an in-flight magazine. A man coughed repeatedly into his fist and threw a dirty look my way. Others cursed beneath their breath. A few passengers turned their heads or pinched their nostrils—one guy even draped his head with a blanket. They tried anything to escape the inescapable aroma of hard-working Frenchmen who smelled as if they hadn't bathed since Bastille Day.

Inside our flight attendant manual—the Bible of rules, regulations and step-by-step procedures that govern every activity from passenger boarding to emergency evacuations—there is a section dedicated to "Passenger Acceptance." Here, the airline provides a list of those who are forbidden on an aircraft: barefoot passengers; infants less than a week old (unless their parents have a physician's note giving approval to fly); intoxicated passengers; those with communicable diseases; those who are clothed in such a way as to offend other passengers; violent, obnoxious and rowdy passengers; anyone carrying an unauthorized firearm—concealed or otherwise. The list goes on and on.

About halfway down the no-go list, somewhere between handcuffed criminals who refuse to cooperate with their escort, and people who appear to be under the influence of drugs, there's an entry that came in handy on the JFK–Paris flight. It says the airline reserves the right to refuse passage to anyone with an offensive body odor. No joke. The words are right there, written in black and white. If the ghastly smell is the result of a physical handicap or disability, the passenger is allowed onboard and his fellow voyagers will simply have to grin and bear it. But if someone stinks because of ineffective or nonexistent personal hygiene, if that someone could use a quadruple swipe of Right Guard or a dusting of Dr. Scholl's, the airline has the right to dismiss him on the spot—even if religious or cultural beliefs are cited for the offense.

Luckily, I do not speak French. Once the crew came up with a strategy, one of several French-speaking flight attendants was dispatched to the main cabin. In a very low voice, she told a couple of guys in the group that passengers were complaining about their *parfum*. The offending men were offended, of course. But not as much as a plane full of pinched-nosed passengers. The accused threw their hands in the air and mumbled in French about the inherent stupidity of Americans (the French-speaking flight attendant made us aware of this later). But when they were told the plane would not leave until the smell had been eliminated, they rose like troopers and marched to the jet bridge where a quick-thinking gate agent had amassed twenty bars of soap and an assortment of underarm deodorant. When the men returned from an airport bathroom, smelling fresh as a dirty street hosed down from the night before, the plane took off. The flight was about fifteen minutes late—a delay that most passengers appreciated.

It's not always so easy to get putrid passengers to freshen up, however. Once, while boarding a flight from Caracas to Miami, I caught the foul stench of a couple whose collective funk could fuel the warhead of a nuclear stink bomb. While loading oven racks in the galley of a 757, I looked up from a cluster of half-frozen chicken dinners and noticed two passengers moving toward me down the aisle. They were the first to board. The fact that no passengers followed was not unusual. Perhaps they were pre-boards, I thought. Perhaps age or physical disability made it necessary for them to come aboard ahead of everyone else. But they were in their early thirties and showed no apparent signs of disability. There were no children with them, either.

The reason no one followed, I soon discovered, was that both of them stank to high heaven.

First, I noticed a slight shift in air quality, as if the door to the Detroit Lion's locker room had opened just a crack. As they approached, the door flew wide open and I staggered backward as if I'd been shot.

Suddenly, I was a small boy inhaling a big-city pile of doggie doo. A police diver hit by a pungent stench before splashing into a swamp in search of decomposing bodies. My head ached. My nostrils burned. I thought I was going to wither and die.

By the time I came out of the lavatory the two passengers had settled into seats 30-A and 30-B. Several pissed-off passengers were waiting for me in the galley. They bombarded me with threats: "You better do something *right now*, goddammit!" and "I paid too much money to sit next to these pigs." But the most telling comment came from a man who spoke in a slow Southern accent. He shook his head, sucked his teeth and said: "Smells like somethin' crawled up their asses and died."

I snatched the interphone and conferred with the purser. She told me to tell the couple to come to the front of the aircraft. I argued, insisting that dirty work like this falls under the domain of purser duty. "You're in charge of the cabin," I said. "This is why you guys get extra pay." But the purser was busy with another problem in first class. Besides, the galley was filling with passengers trying to escape the fallout. If I stalled any longer we might have a riot on our hands.

With all the composure I could muster, I approached the aroma-challenged (is that the politically correct term?) couple. I held my breath, speaking from a constricted diaphragm that made my voice sound hoarse. It was like trying to speak after inhaling a joint when you didn't want the smoke to escape. "Excuse me folks," I said. "But ahhh . . . the purser . . . she ahhh . . . she needs to speak with you in the front of the aircraft."

"The who?" the man asked.

"The purser. She's the flight attendant in charge of the cabin." Aside from the caustic odor, they seemed like pleasant people. They were dressed in clean casual clothes and smiled as I spoke.

"What does she want?" he said.

"She wants to . . . well . . . It's like this . . ." I was running out of air so I threw caution to the stench and blurted out the truth. "To be perfectly blunt, sir, the passengers are complaining . . . they say your body odor is offensive . . . you need to speak to the purser and try to rectify the problem."

Like a swimmer who'd been under a few seconds too long, I took a huge gulp of air and immediately wished I hadn't. The couple exchanged a look and threw at me a gaze that could have melted steel.

"We are not moving!" the man said defiantly.

After a visit from the gate agent and the captain, after we threatened to call airport security, after impatience nearly gave rise to a passenger revolt, the couple finally grabbed their bags and walked to the front of the aircraft, leaving thirty rows of gagging humanity in their wake. Before leaving the airplane, however, they bestowed upon us a parting comment. The final insult voiced by drunks, obnoxious jerks, and yes, the indelibly stinky—as they are tossed from an aircraft: "We're never flying this airline again."

Hallelujah!

2 Payback for a Condescending Jerk

Dressed in black, ponytail dangling imperiously from behind his up-turned head, he sauntered to his first-class seat with the unspoken arrogance of a passenger who had already arrived. He was rife with self-importance, the quintessential traveler with an attitude. But an hour after takeoff he would be whimpering like a child, cradled in my reluctant embrace.

Allow me to explain.

I'm not the type of flight attendant portrayed in television commercials. For one thing, I'm a man. You'll rarely see a male attendant fluffing up some businessman's pillow or pulling a blanket to his chin while sappy theme music lifts the hearts and tugs at the purse strings of 10 million viewers. Tall, black and bald, a little rough around the edges, I'm the kind of guy you'd expect to see scoring touchdowns for the Jets, instead of serving chicken and beef inside of them. As is the case with the passenger dressed in black, appearance can sometimes belie the man.

Bound for Miami from Chicago, our 727 carried fewer than fifty passengers in the main cabin and only three in first class. The service would be completed in no time. A piece of cake. Or so I thought.

Ensconced in a vast leather seat that could scarcely contain his ego, the man in black snickered pretentiously into the in-flight telephone. He crossed his stockinged feet on the bulkhead and bragged about his self-owned business to the unreceptive couple across the aisle. He made sexual innuendoes to the female flight attendant who was assigned to work first class. Her vexation prompted an interphone call. I picked up in the aft galley and listened while she recounted his behavior and asked for my support.

The moment I left my position in the aft galley, the aircraft began to encounter "light" turbulence. The Aeronautical Information Manual (AIM)—the pilot handbook of flight information and procedures developed by the Federal Aviation Administration—lists four specific categories of turbulence (light, moderate, severe, and extreme) and the resulting conditions that occur inside the airplane.

During light turbulence, "occupants may feel a slight strain against seat belts or shoulder straps. Unsecured objects may be displaced slightly, food service may be conducted and little or no difficulty is encountered in walking."

In response to her call for backup, I teetered up the aisle, entered the first-class cabin and observed the man in black. He was reclining luxuriously in seat 3-A. One hand absently preened his glossy ponytail, the other held a full glass of champagne. Noting that his seat belt was unfastened, even though the "fasten seat belt" sign was illuminated, I politely asked him to buckle up. He threw at me a look that was both hostile and dismayed. *How dare you instruct me*, the look said. *I am a first-class passenger, a man to be regarded*, the look said. He turned his head away, dismissing my presence and my request. His seat belt was still unfastened when I left.

About halfway through the main-cabin dinner service, the turbulence intensified. There was a thunderstorm ahead, and apparently no way to steer completely clear of it. The aircraft began vibrating in harsh, rhythmic thumps, as if it were a speed boat traversing a choppy sea. Drinks spilled. Meal trays fell to the floor. A woman shrieked and then fell silent. One male passenger tightened his seat belt and stared at me wide-eyed like a foot soldier awaiting the lieutenant's command. (During moments like these, even the most condescending passenger will bestow upon flight attendants a level of respect that is usually reserved for priests and emergency room practitioners.)

The captain's voice crackled over the P.A. system instructing flight attendants to suspend the meal service—we had progressed to "moderate" turbulence. During this condition AIM says: "Occupants feel definite strains against seat belts or shoulder straps. Unsecured objects are dislodged. Food service and walking are difficult."

With the help of another flight attendant, I moved a wobbling two-hundred-pound liquor cart and stowed it in the aft galley. Less than ten seconds after strapping into my jump seat, the interphone rang again. With an edge of panic in her voice, the first-class attendant asked me to come up. The esteemed man in black needed assistance.

I climbed out of my seat harness and made the long, arduous trek to first class. I walked with my feet spread wide to provide better balance—a technique flight attendants pick up after a few weeks on the job. It's sort of like walking on a patch of ice that moves left to right and up and down while you try not to fall in a passenger's lap. Which brings me to a question that has caused concern since the first flight attendants were hurled at the heavens. If the seat belt sign is illuminated during turbulence—an indication that it's dangerous for *anyone* to walk around the cabin—why are flight attendants required to walk up and down the aisle to make a safety check? Are we immune to midair turbulence that might splatter ordinary passengers against the ceiling? Were we hired because of some immunity to the forces of gravity? As I staggered toward the first-class cabin to help out Mr. Asshole, the paradox occupied my thoughts.

Each time the aircraft lunged I stumbled, caught myself, and started again. For thirty rows I clutched seat backs, braced my knees against armrests, pressed my hands against overhead bins.

Only once did my feet leave the ground.

By the time I reached the first-class cabin, the man in black had been stripped of his grandiose demeanor. He was doubled over in his seat—head between his legs, arms wrapped around his chest, seat belt pulled as tight as humanly possible.

"Jesus!" he shouted, having developed an impromptu relationship with Christ. "When is this shaking going to stop!"

I stood there, smirking. The fact that I was standing beside him—being visibly jiggled around by turbulence—seemed to shift his fear into overdrive. He took one look at me and screamed like an eight-year-old girl. For one brief moment I felt a poetic justice. After all, the guy was a pompous twerp and had been less than a gentleman to a female member of my crew. But he looked up at me with tortured eyes. Eyes that begged for forgiveness. Eyes that were caught in the head-lights of self-induced doom.

I released a great breath and buckled up in the empty seat beside him. With one arm slung around his shoulder, I proceeded to whisper straightforward assurances: "Don't worry," I said. "I've been through much worse than this. We'll clear this turbulence before you know it."

Finding no comfort in this rhetoric, he uttered a request that quick-ened my heterosexual heart.

"Hold me?" he said.

"What!"

A look of disbelief must have registered on my face because he fol-lowed with a more urgent plea: "Please, please hold me!"

In more than sixteen years of flight service I have wiped the tears of grieving passengers while listening to tales of loss, separation and betrayal. In my own arms I have carried aboard men with no legs and children with dead eyes, and deposited the brittle frames of elderly women into waiting wheelchairs. But no one, no matter how distressed or decrepit, has ever asked to be held. I've asked planeloads of good-looking women if I could wrap my arms around *them*, but few have allowed me that indulgence.

To the man who posed this question it was impossible to say no. Through exacerbating turbulence I held him. When he began to cry I held him tighter. I could feel his heart beating in my chest, his wet tears spreading across the front placket of my uniform shirt. In a spate of self-flagellation, he apologized for being rude, for being obnoxious, for being that which he vowed never again to be.

Suddenly, as if snatched by a huge demonic child, the aircraft began to shudder. During "severe" turbulence AIM asserts the following: "Oc-cupants are forced violently against seat belts . . . Unsecured objects are tossed about. Food service and walking are impossible. At this point the aircraft may be temporarily out of control." We had not yet expe-rienced "severe" turbulence, but I steeled myself for the possibility.

Strapped in by our seat belts—with his black-clad torso stretched across the seat divider—we rode the bumps like mismatched partners in a circus rodeo. The aircraft dipped, veered a little to the left, leveled, rose celestially, and then shook some more.

My seatmate drove his sobbing face deeper into my chest. I felt as if he was trying to crawl inside for cover. As repentance poured from him, as his last shred of composure was lost to a flatulent decree, the turbulence began to ease. And with it eased the death-grip on my shoulders.

Meal service resumed, the episode was forgotten and the plane landed right on schedule. But the passenger in 3-A had become a different man. Black garb wrinkled and mussed, ponytail hanging limply from behind his downcast head, he shook my hand one final time and exited the aircraft as if each unsteady step was his first.

3 Flying the Queasy Skies

During the final twenty minutes of a nine-hour all-nighter from Rio de Janeiro to Miami, I came face to face with an unspeakable horror. It was about 5 A.M. The cabin was dark, save for a few passenger reading lamps and a dim glow from the main-cabin galley where I was busy completing the liquor inventory.

As I locked the last of the service carts, a young kid stumbled into the galley. He was about eight years old, with big doll-like eyes that blinked sluggishly beneath his wrinkled brow. He frowned and held his belly in both hands.

"What's the matter?" I asked.

"I don't feeeeel good," he said. He spoke in a soft, reedy voice that would have melted the hearts of my female coworkers had they not disappeared into the lavatories to freshen up before landing. My heart—made cold and hard by too many close calls with queasy kids—didn't melt, however. It didn't even begin to defrost. Instead, I took two steps backward, worried that the kid would puke on my shoes.

"Where are your parents?" I demanded.

"Sleeeeeping."

"Do you need to go to the bathroom?" (I said this while nodding vigorously and pointing to the nearest lavatory.)

"Nooooo."

"Hmmmm. . . . I guess your tummy hurts, huh?"

"Yesssss," he said.

I sat him on the jump seat while I searched for some ginger ale to help settle his stomach. He stared sullenly into space, rocking, both arms wrapped around his tiny waist. By the time I turned to give him the glass of ginger ale, his eyes seemed to have grown to twice their original size. There was a look of blatant surprise on his face—the comical expression of a boy who, upon hearing his father tumble down the stairs, suddenly remembered where he'd left his toy fire engine. His eyes grew even wider. His lips pursed. His cheeks swelled to Dizzy Gillespie proportions. But this kid was preparing to blow something other than air into a trumpet.

In all my years as a flight attendant, I've seen more than my fair share of air sickness. I once saw a drunken couple take turns barfing into each other's laps, as if playing a sickly version of "Can You Top That." I watched a Catholic priest vomit into the face of his secular seatmate. I watched a teenage girl open the seatback pocket in front of her and proceed to fill it with the contents of her stomach. I watched a queasy businessman splatter the last row of passengers after an ill-fated sprint toward the lavatory.

In one particularly memorable episode that triggered a chain reaction of in-flight regurgitation, I watched the volcanic eruption of a bloated vacationer who'd eaten three servings of airplane lasagna. After witnessing this spectacle (and inhaling the pungent odor that wafted through the cabin in its wake) more than two dozen passengers leaned into the aisle and puked. Gallons of heavy liquid splashed onto the carpet; even if you closed your eyes you could not escape the sound. Or the smell.

I still get queasy just thinking about it.

Throughout all these years of high-altitude nausea there is one consolation, however. Though I've dumped enough airsick bags to fill an Olympic-size pool, though my olfactory gland has been violated far beyond the limits of rational expectation, though I've sprinkled more puke-absorbent coffee grounds than the folks at Maxwell House would care to know, I had never been splattered by a single drop of vomitus.

But now, an eight-year-old kid with bulging eyes and a high-octane stomach was aiming his nozzle directly at me.

In the split-second that I realized he was about to explode, I dove to one side like a stuntman in a Schwarzenegger flick. I hit the floor, rolled once, and came to rest against the aft right-hand exit door. From this relatively safe vantage point, I watched the action unfold in a semi-detached, slow-motion blur.

Just before the kid convulsed, he managed to cover his mouth with both hands. But this maneuver seemed to cause more harm than good. Thin sheets of ejecta shot between his tiny fingers and splattered the face of all four galley ovens. His head proceeded to swing side to side in a 180-degree assault that covered the galley in a yellowish-orange slime.

I stared at him with a mixture of awe and repulsion. It was as if he had become one of those rapid-fire lawn sprinklers with the rotating mechanical head. *The Lawn Boy 2000: We guarantee maximum saturation or your money back!* The stuff just kept coming and coming and coming.

After what seemed like an eternity, the kid finally ran out of juice. With a half-hearted swipe of his sleeve, he wiped his chin and turned to look at me. His eyes had returned to normal size. But now they were heavy, weighed down by guilt and embarrassment. His spew-covered hands began to tremble as tears ran tracks down his reddened cheeks.

Watching this display of raw kiddie emotion, my hardened heart loosened a bit. I staggered to my feet and moved toward the kid, fighting the stench that was beginning to make me dizzy, stepping between pools of ooze that covered much of the galley floor. As I approached, he began to cry in earnest. Big boo-hoo sobs. Crocodile tears. He sat there, bawling, covered from head to toe in liquefied airplane cuisine.

Overcome by a sudden paternal urge to pat him on the shoulder, but unable to find an adequate dry spot, I reached out with one finger and sort of ruffled his hair a bit. He looked up at me wearing an expression that, for a moment, tugged at the heartstrings of forgiveness. Then the unthinkable happened.

Much like that infamous scene from *The Exorcist*, the kid looked right into my eyes and let loose a Linda Blair pea-soup blast that covered me from the knees down to the tips of my uniform shoes. I stood there, motionless, feeling the molten bile seep through my socks and into the gaps between my toes.

Before I could throttle the kid he leapt from the jump seat and disappeared into the darkened cabin.

4 The Heist

It happened on a sun-baked taxiway as our 727 prepared to depart the Caribbean island of Curaçao. And although I was right there, in the middle of the action—along with a planeload of passengers and six fellow crew members—I still can't believe it. I still can't believe we wuz robbed.

A few moments before our plane departed for Miami, I performed my part in the routine safety demonstration. I stood in front of a hundred people who stared at me like artists marooned at an accounting seminar. First, I displayed my trusty seat belt extension. I inserted the metal clip into the buckle and pulled the loose end to tighten the belt. Next, I lumbered down the aisle, holding the emergency information card high above my head. For one absurd moment I felt like one of those half-naked women who prance around the boxing ring, holding up a piece of cardboard between rounds. The two teenage boys sitting near me must have thought I looked pretty funny. They pointed at me, sniggering. When I donned the life vest and blew into the tubes located at both shoulders, the boys could no longer contain themselves. They broke out in laughter that brought tears to their eyes.

I walked up to them after removing the life vest.

"You guys enjoy the show?" I said.

"Yeah," said the bolder of the two. "I thought it was hilarious."

Holding the life vest in one outstretched arm, I let it dangle in front of his face. "Do you think you'll be laughing if you actually have to use this after takeoff?"

There was a sudden shift in attitude. The cocky kid stared at the life vest and must have caught a glimpse of his own mortality. His shoulders slumped. His chin fell to his chest. Satisfied, I headed for my jump seat.

Of the four flight attendants onboard, two were assigned to the jump seat near the forward entry door. The other attendant and I were to occupy the seat attached to the emergency door at the rear of the plane.

After the captain made his departure announcement, the engines roared, the plane lurched forward and the aircraft began to roll down the taxiway. Some passengers dozed, others flipped impatiently through magazines. I talked quietly with Patricia, the flight attendant seated beside me, because this is what flight attendants do when we're sitting on a double jump seat, our bodies smushed together like the turkey sandwiches we serve.

According to Patricia, a flight attendant we both knew had been bequeathed a large sum of money from an old woman who used to live next door to him. As a child, he would wave to the old woman on his way to school. Nothing more. Just a kid, an old woman and a friendly ritualistic wave. When she died years later, she left a small fortune to the man who once brightened her mornings. The windfall allowed him to retire from the airline and go into business with his father.

I sat there in the jump seat, vowing to wave at elderly people more often and more vigorously, when suddenly the hydraulic breaks screamed and the aircraft came to an unexpected halt.

From my seat at the rear of the aircraft, I saw the cockpit door swing open. Our captain—a short, no-nonsense, ex-military type who looked like Napoleon wearing a less impressive uniform—marched down the aisle at a gait that made everyone nervous. His face was expressionless, a mask of professional indifference that aroused more suspicion than it averted. I turned to Patricia. She threw a look at me. Something was definitely wrong.

As the captain approached, we unbuckled our seat harnesses and stood nervously. By now, the passengers were stirring in their seats. Like waves closing behind the wake of a passing speedboat, dozens of worried faces splashed into the aisle.

In a hushed voice, the captain spoke to Patricia and me. "The forward cargo door indicator light came on," he said. "I'm going to go check it out."

Even though the engines were running, he opened the aft emergency door (a definite breach of procedure), pulled a lever that lowered the stairs and a moment later he was gone. After this incident, he would be called before the chief pilot to explain why he had broken the rules. As it turned out, the captain is a commuter. Though he is based in New York, he lives somewhere below the Mason–Dixon line. Shutting down the engines would eat precious time, and he did not want to miss his connecting flight home (this I learned later from the flight engineer).

Like angry sirens, the engines screamed into the cabin. Passengers winced, covering their ears with both hands. Just then, I noticed a passenger with both arms flailing. Apparently, he'd been trying to get our attention for a few seconds. He was seated next to a window on the left side of the aircraft. As I approached the passenger began pointing out the window. "Just before the plane stopped, we saw a guy run underneath the airplane," he said. "He just ran underneath and disappeared." Several passengers nodded their heads in agreement.

A gentleman sitting on the opposite side of the plane chimed in. "Yeah, and we saw a guy come from under this side of the airplane. He ran off carrying a bag."

Were we in danger? Was this some kind of terrorist act? Patricia stared at me, but before I could run to the cockpit and alert the first officer, a first-class passenger came running down the aisle. Behind the thick lenses of his wire-frame glasses, his eyes were wide with panic. They were also vaguely familiar.

"Someone ran off with my bag," he told me in a winded voice. "It was in the cargo bin. I . . . I just looked out the window and saw someone running away with it."

I grabbed the man by his shoulders in an attempt to settle him down. That's when I remembered who he was. Over the years I'd seen him on one flight or another, sitting in a first-class seat, chatting with flight attendants he knew by name. He was an air courier for one of the best-known companies in the money transportation business. Air couriers like him are responsible for accompanying large sums of cash and negotiable bonds. But the money is stowed in the cargo hold, not in the airplane cabin.

Here's how large sums of cash are flown from one location to the next: Moments before an airplane departs, an armored truck pulls alongside the aircraft. Gun-toting officers dump the bags of cash into the cargo hold, then watch carefully as the airline ground crew closes the hatch and the aircraft pulls away from the gate. The operation runs in reverse at the point of arrival.

Suddenly everything was clear.

The captain came back up the stairs with a puzzled look on his face. "The cargo door is wide open," he said. "How the hell did that—"

I interrupted, relaying the new facts. His eyes narrowed and he rushed down the stairs again. I went after him. The courier followed. The three of us stood beneath a smoldering Caribbean sun, mouths open, heads shaking, unable to believe our eyes. We were staring into an open cargo compartment that was missing one rather important piece of luggage.

According to the courier, there were two money bags. One was filled with unmarked bills in small denominations; the other held negotiable bonds and other monetary instruments. Apparently, the thief crept onto the taxiway and ran alongside the aircraft as it rolled toward the runway. There were two cargo compartments, both on the right side of the aircraft. He knew exactly which one to open and exactly how to open it. He also knew which of the two bags to take. It was definitely an inside job, and the suspect was long gone.

After reporting the incident to airport authorities, the crew readied the airplane for a late departure. Realizing the plane would not wait, and knowing there was nothing he could do in Curaçao, the courier decided to join us. He had some very bad news to share with his superiors back home.

"Exactly how much money was in the bag?" I whispered while escorting the courier to his seat.

His beleaguered gaze fell upon me. In that one dismal moment I felt about as bad as he looked. "Almost five hundred thousand dollars," he said.

This, according to Patricia, was the same amount bequeathed to the flight attendant who once waved to an old woman on his way to school. A hefty sum by any standard; way too much for an airline and a courier to let slip through their fingers.

I laid a heavy hand on his shoulder and then returned to my jump seat, wondering if the loss would be deducted from his paycheck.

Epilogue: The Curaçao bandit, along with two accomplices—one of whom was an airport employee—were caught within a month, after they embarked upon a conspicuous, on-island spending spree. To the best of my knowledge they're still in prison.

5 Escape from New York

It was supposed to be a simple turnaround—an easy same-day sequence from New York to Chicago and back. Two hours flight time in either direction. A three-hour wait at O'Hare. The return flight would nose up to LaGuardia at 4:30 P.M., leaving me plenty of time to catch the 5 P.M. Carey bus to Forty-second Street. From there I would take the subway to Union Square, walk east to Sixth Street and Second Avenue, climb four flights of stairs to my closet-size apartment and pass out in a sagging twin-size bed.

But Murphy's Law was in full effect that day. A day that began without any sleep for yours truly. A day cursed with foul weather. A day mired in disbelief. A day that, in retrospect, was as laughably underestimated as when Odysseus and his men dipped their oars into the sea, thinking they'd be gone for a little while. We would experience two mechanical breakdowns, a change of aircraft, de-icings, a minor passenger revolt, foul language and the breakdown of union solidarity. It was enough to fuel the premise of a made-for-TV movie. A miniseries, even. But for myself, my crew and 150 seething passengers, the drama was too real to be believed.

And like I said, I hadn't had any sleep.

The lack of sleep was my fault. I had been out at a nightclub until 5 A.M., but for reasons more noble than you'd expect. Believe it or not, I was working. Pulling yet another six-hour shift behind the upstairs bar at Nell's—New York's most happening night spot during the cocaine-crazed epoch of the late 1980s. During these first years of my flying career, when survival was predicated upon a $16,000 annual airline salary and a helluva lot of leftover airplane food, it became necessary to take a second job. So I poured martinis and screwdrivers for Manhattan's beautiful people who swarmed past the velvet ropes like squadrons of flies—the kiss-kiss, hug-hug, I-just-buzzed-in-from-Paris variety.

After counting my cash drawer at the end of my six-hour shift, I ducked into the men's room and changed into my flight attendant uniform. Unlike Clark Kent upgrading to his Superman duds, my uniform made me look like Clark Kent. The polyester pants clung to my legs with the tenacity of Saran Wrap. An ill-fitting jacket drooped from my shoulders. Not surprisingly, I crept up the back stairs, hoping to slip out unnoticed. I was tired. My feet hurt. Needles jabbed my eyeballs every time I blinked. Caught in a ray of artificial light that cut through the darkness of the upstairs lounge, my silver wings glinted on the breast of my uniform jacket. I stared at the floorboards, moving quietly toward the exit.

Up ahead, there was a murmur of voices. The late-night susurrus of a gathering wound down to its essence. I stopped, looked up, sighed. Right there in front of the polished oak bar—the same bar from which I had deployed hundreds of late-night libations—stood a group of nightclub regulars. Diehards. Party troopers. They were sipping the last of their drinks, planning to hit an after-hours club or plotting a way to get laid. Men in black suits and ponytails whispered into the ears of slouching model types who were too drunk or too high to dodge the truckload of bullcrap being dumped upon them. Or maybe it was the other way around. As I approached, they all seemed to turn at once—twenty puppet heads jerked by a single puppet string. They stared wide-eyed and open-mouthed, as if Scotty had just beamed me down from the U.S.S. *Enterprise*.

There was a sudden burst of laughter, followed by drunken whispers and a couple of spilled drinks. In this world of black miniskirts and sculpted goatees, of too many vodka tonics and a couple more lines of cocaine, the sudden appearance of a man in uniform—crisp, clean, freshly shaven, the faintest trace of Tartar-Control Crest on his breath—was the ultimate in late-night incongruity.

The crowd parted as if I were infected with the mange, as if I were a nervous cop ready to shoot the first slimy bastard that flinched. They were a gang of jeering eyes, mocking as I hurried through the gauntlet. Before I could get through the door, however, before shame and embarrassment and a complete lack of coolness caused me to drop the flight bag that hung from my shoulder like a woman's purse, a single voice rang out. It was a man's voice—gruff, sarcastic, laced with insult and innuendo.

"Coffee, tea or me, baby?"

Twenty black-clad groovers burst out in laughter. I rushed out the door, thighs chafing helplessly inside my freshly laundered polyester pants.

Despite the cold, it was a relief to be outside. Snowflakes dusted my shoulders like the dandruff that plagued me back in the days when I had hair. Judging by the accumulation on the street, it had probably been snowing all night. Standing there on the sidewalk in an ankle-deep drift, a shiver ran through my body. I'd worn a leather motorcycle jacket to the club (forgetting to pack my company trench coat in the process), but decided to leave it in the nightclub's prep room. Black leather and zippers have a tendency to pique the ire of airline supervisors. Besides, I wasn't planning on being outside too long.

I looked both ways down snow-covered Fourteenth Street, waiting for an on-duty taxi. Several passed by, all with passengers, so I turned up the collar of my uniform jacket and waited.

A moment later a man approached. Judging by the way he staggered, the guy was roaring drunk. He stumbled down the sidewalk and stopped a few feet behind me. I could feel him staring. I spun around and stared into his eyes, wondering what was about to transpire. We stood in the falling snow, stock-still, like actors who'd forgotten their lines. When his eyes locked on the set of silver wings pinned to my jacket, he nodded and frowned.

"You work for the airlines," he said, in an accusatory voice. It was 5:30 A.M. on a cold, dark, desolate street in New York. I was trying to get to the airport, and this guy wanted to voice a complaint.

"Yeah," I said.

"Which one?" he demanded.

From the corner of my eye I saw a taxi turn onto Fourteenth Street. The "on-duty" light cut through the darkness, shining like a beacon of escape. I stepped from the curb to flag the taxi; it fishtailed before stopping. After tossing my flight bag into the car, I turned to look at the man. Dressed in a full-length coat, fists jammed into the pockets, he swayed in the snow as if driven by a melody that only he could hear.

"You morons lost my luggage!" he screamed. He stood there, swaying in the snow, yelling insults as we drove away.

When dressed in civilian clothes, I am rarely hassled on the streets of Manhattan. Put me in a flight attendant's uniform, however, and the freaks come out of the woodwork. It's like wearing a blinking neon sign of approachability. *Hey! Look at me, I work for an airline! Want to let out your frustrations? Did you have a problem on your most recent flight? Come on, talk to me. I'm paid to be friendly on the airplane, but I'm even easier to talk to on the street!*

Once I was waiting on a crowded subway platform, dressed in uniform, on my way to JFK, when some guy tapped me on the shoulder and said, "Aye . . . where you goin'?" Just like that. As if he were talking to someone he'd known all his life. "Aye . . . where you goin'?" He sounded as if he just walked out of an audition for the part of a street thug on *The Sopranos.* Had he not stared at me with a homicidal glint in his eye, I probably would have told him to get lost. Instead, I grinned sheepishly and told him I was going to Brussels.

"Brussels?" he said, spitting out the city as if it tasted as bad as the sprouts. "Where da hell is that?"

If circumstances had been different, I would have left Nell's in civilian clothes and changed in a men's room at LaGuardia. But time was short. I needed to be in front of an airport computer, inputting my sign-in code in less than (I checked my watched and grimaced) twenty minutes.

Though there was hardly any traffic, the taxi moved up Fourteenth Street at about ten miles per hour. The streets were slippery, the driver complained. "We're gonna have to take it slow."

So we crept toward LaGuardia Airport. One long work day behind me, another looming ahead, no chance for rest in between. I was exhausted from the long night, demoralized by the "Coffee, tea or me" insult, and pissed off because my tips had been lousy. A good portion would be spent on the twenty-five dollar cab ride, when under more favorable time constraints, a couple of subway tokens would have done the trick. A sharp pain at the base of my skull began to quicken—tap, tap, tapping across the arc of my brain like the feet of a dancer working out the kinks in his routine. I tried to sleep, but couldn't. Thought about calling in sick, but knew I shouldn't. Because the cab reeked of day-old pastrami, I held my breath instead.

If nightclubs are dungeons of hipness and depravity, airport flight operations areas are vacuums of squeaky-clean proficiency. By now, the black-clad groovers from Nell's were either passed out in bed next to a complete stranger or working on another gin and tonic. Yet here in the real world, throngs of flight attendants—well-groomed and well-slept—were hovering over neat banks of computers and chatting beneath fluorescent lights powerful enough to blind an outfielder at Shea Stadium. Dot matrix printers fired like machine guns, spitting out hard copies of crew lists and trip sequences. A television morning-show anchor chirped in the distance. The harsh voice from an overhead speaker summoned flight attendant Fredrickson to the supervisor's office.

While rushing through this bastion of early-morning activity, I returned a volley of good mornings from familiar faces—men and women I had flown with last week, last month, last year—before finally finding an unoccupied computer and signing in.

The cold readout on the computer screen screamed at me in silence. I was late! Twenty-six minutes late to be exact. My crew was already onboard. Passenger boarding had already commenced. By now Crew Scheduling had telephoned my apartment and put out an APB. Chances are they'd already assigned a stand-by flight attendant to fill my position. But there was plenty of time to get to the gate before departure. Being late for a flight is one thing. Getting slapped with a "missed trip" would put me in a world of trouble.

I rushed down the stairs, past the security checkpoint, up the terminal and headed toward the departure gate, all the while knowing

my supervisor would later receive a computer-generated message informing her that I was late again. I'd face another demerit, which would
put me one step closer to termination. I carried this in the tight ball
of my stomach, as I rushed past the flight attendant who plucked
boarding passes from a long queue of Chicago-bound passengers.
"About time," she said, through bright teeth clenched in a smile. I
grinned sarcastically, weaving past sleepy passengers who moved down
the jet bridge like mummies heading to the grave.

Each seat in first class was occupied by a man. Frequent-flyer upgrades, all twelve of them. They wore crisp white shirts, thin-knotted
ties, and the early-morning grimace of corporate go-getters on their
way to conquer the world. The aisle was clogged with more business
types. Suits. Business dresses. No jeans. I introduced myself to the
purser who was squeezing back and forth through the procession to
serve pre-departure orange juice to first-class passengers. Slowly, I
worked my way to the back of the aircraft, pausing while people
stowed bags, helping occasionally, and finally stumbling into the galley
to face my replacement.

She was loading the ovens, doing what I should have been doing
for the last thirty minutes.

"You the number two?" she said, her voice crisp as farm-fresh lettuce.
I nodded. She stopped loading the ovens for a minute to give me a
dirty look. "Thanks for showing up," she said.

She then slammed the oven rack into place, grabbed her bag, waited
for the aisle to clear and gave me one last dirty look before storming
off the aircraft.

I looked at the other flight attendant as if to ask what I had done.

"She was hoping you wouldn't show up," she said. "After Crew
Scheduling told her she was going to Chicago, she called her boyfriend.
He lives there, apparently. He was going to meet her at O'Hare and
take her to lunch."

"Believe me," I said. "I wish she was working instead of me."

"Ditto. By the way, my name is Martha."

I shook Martha's hand, introduced myself, and loaded the remaining
oven racks.

Ten minutes later the aircraft pushed back from the gate. Martha, myself, the two flight attendants up front, and a full load of 150 passengers were finally on our way to Chicago.

Or so we thought.

I sat on the jump seat, started a conversation with Martha and immediately wished I hadn't. She bombarded me with stories about an ex-husband and ex-boyfriends, all of whom were "assholes."

It's amazing how revealing flight attendants can be while sitting on a jump seat. I've listened while coworkers spilled their guts about adulterous affairs, financial incompetence, incarcerated loved ones and a variety of personal problems that I wouldn't care to share with someone I'd just met.

For reasons that continue to mystify me, one male flight attendant once told me that he and his redneck buddies used to get up close and personal with farm animals.

"You got to be real quiet, see," he said. "Then you sneak up behind her and . . ."

"Stop it!" I said, not wanting to hear the details about copulation with a frightened goat.

And now at six-thirty in the morning, after I'd been busting my ass behind the bar all night, after spending damn near half my tips on cab fare, after being teased for performing a job that most people associate with the feminine persuasion, my colleague, Martha, a complete stranger until now, was blabbering about a drunken boyfriend who once slapped her in the face.

"You know," I said, cutting her off at the point in the story where her father called to say he was going to kill the no-good son of a bitch. "We've been sitting here way too long." I looked at my watch. Then I looked out the window. It was ten minutes to seven. Snow was falling like crazy. We'd been sitting still on the taxiway, halfway between the gate and the runway, for about twenty minutes.

According to the captain's previous P.A., six or seven airplanes were lined up ahead, waiting for clearance from Air Traffic Control. If we stayed out here much longer our aircraft would need to be de-iced.

And wait we did. The snow fell. The planed idled. Martha's father sped up the turnpike with murder in his heart and a 12-gauge in his pickup. Finally, after thirty minutes of waiting we got the bad news: "Aaaaaaah . . . ladies and gentlemen," the captain's voice crept out of the speakers in that hesitating, good-ole-boy delivery. "We . . . aaaaaaah . . . we're experiencing a problem with the . . . aaaaaaah . . . hydraulic system. We're going to have to return to the gate and let maintenance take a look at it. Remember . . . aaaaaaah . . . safety is our number one concern."

Judging by the collective growl from the passengers, it didn't seem as if safety was their number one concern. They wanted to get to Chicago, dammit! There were business meetings to attend. Regional sales figures to scrutinize. Flight connections to be made. As we rolled back to the gate, the first sentiments of frustration were captured in one man's outspoken reference to Jesus Christ. But his Jesus had a middle name. It started with an *F*.

Some passengers slept while mechanics worked on the problem. Most who stayed awake shook newspapers in front of their faces or flipped through magazines without seeming to notice what was written there. A few fidgeted uncomfortably in their seats. Maintenance assured us that the problem was routine, that the wait should be no longer than about twenty minutes. But when twenty minutes stretched to thirty, and thirty to forty, Mr. Jesus F. rang his flight attendant call button.

Angela, the flight attendant who had smirked at me while plucking tickets, emerged from the front of the aircraft and walked to the rear as if strolling through her garden on a lovely summer's day. She stopped, looked down and appraised Jesus F. Her face suddenly bore the squint of a horticulturist who had come upon a weed in a thicket of begonias.

"Can I help you sir?" she said.

"We've been waiting here for forty goddamn minutes," he shouted. "How much longer is it going to take? This is ridiculous!" His voice was harsh, bestial. He growled at Angela, jerking open the eyelids of several passengers in the process. Angela was unmoved.

"Hydraulic problems are not ridiculous, sir." Her voice was calm, reassuring, the voice of a doctor telling a patient the tumor is benign. "The plane is broken," she continued. "Our mechanics are trying their best to fix it, but it's taking a bit longer than expected. Do you want them to rush, overlook some critical detail maybe? Would you rather they sign off the paperwork now, because *you're* in a hurry, only to have the hydraulic system fail mid-flight?" Angela paused, waiting for an answer she knew would never come. "There's nothing ridiculous about a disabled aircraft, sir. Especially when it's attempting to take off in a snowstorm."

Angela clicked off the call light, adding an exclamation mark to a rebuttal that left Jesus F. slouched in his seat. She then strolled to the back to shoot the breeze with us, smiling, patting passenger's shoulders and handing out a few pillows along the way.

"So what happened to you, did you oversleep?" she said. I looked up at Angela, awed by the manner in which she had handled Jesus F.

"No," I said, smiling. "I underslept."

Just then the interphone rang. I picked up the handset and listened to the deflated voice of our purser. She relayed a message from the captain which had been relayed to him by the mechanics who received the bad news from our brain trust at maintenance headquarters in Omaha. A spare part would have to be flown in. It would arrive in four, maybe five hours. Even then, there was some doubt as to whether the problem could be fixed in a timely fashion. For now, the plane was "out of service." This would translate into a two- to three-hour delay for passengers while another aircraft was located.

For airline crew, an out-of-service aircraft conjures up the most hated word in industry vernacular: "reassignment." If the evil lords at Crew Scheduling deemed it necessary, our simple one-day turnaround from New York to Chicago could mutate into a three-day, multileg, "fly your ass all over the country" extravaganza with ten-hour layovers in Cleveland and Des Moines. Inside my tote bag was my flight manual, a toiletry bag and my wadded bartender garb (black jeans and a black T-shirt). That was it. I didn't even have a change of underwear.

I hung up the phone, closed my eyes and felt my head fall back against the jump seat headrest. "Don't tell me," I heard Martha say.

"No . . . you're kidding, tell me you're kidding," said Angela, the cockiness gone from her voice. I turned my head, winked open my good eye and drew a line across my throat with one finger.

When the captain made the announcement, the collective groan from passengers was three times as loud as the previous one. Bags were savagely yanked out of overhead bins, hats and overcoats snatched up like problem children. One by one, passengers tramped off the aircraft, dirty looks shooting from their faces like so many poison arrows. The looks weren't directed at the pilots, of course. As usual during such an exodus, the captain, first officer and flight engineer remained hidden behind the cockpit door. Left out in the elements, flight attendants are the ones who always feel the sting.

"You guys are pathetic," shouted Jesus F., one of the last to leave the aircraft. He turned to look at me while struggling down the aisle with a couple of overstuffed bags.

"We're really sorry," I said.

"Yeah, right!" He threw another look and then he was gone.

Two hours later, a different 727 was at our disposal. Having camped out for the duration in the first-class section of the disabled aircraft, we readjusted our uniforms, grabbed our bags and marched, like an army of seven, toward a new departure gate.

For the second time that day, we boarded passengers for the flight to Chicago. While this was happening, baggage and cargo was unloaded from the disabled aircraft and loaded into the new one. A few passengers, maybe fifteen or twenty, managed to change to Chicago-bound flights on other airlines. Now, as we rolled along the taxiway, more than three hours late, there were a few empty seats in coach.

The snow was falling heavier than before; it blanketed the tarmac, accumulated on the wings. The captain announced once again that several aircraft were waiting to take off ahead of us. A moment later he said that due to heavy snowfall, our aircraft would have to be de-iced. We waited, and waited, and waited some more. The engines idled. Passengers squirmed in their seats. Martha sat next to me on the jump seat, prattling about personal problems: a controlling mother, credit card debt, difficulty in achieving orgasm. She topped it all off by saying how much she hated being a flight attendant.

There is a small, but vocal group of flight attendants whose mission in life is to complain about the job. They gripe incessantly about needy passengers, inhospitable hotel rooms, foreign cultures they don't understand. They whine about having to spend so much time away from home. Martha is one of these people. Put her in a four-star hotel room, and she'll hate the too-firm mattress. Sit her in a renowned Parisian restaurant, and she'll frown because they don't serve hamburgers. Send her on a thirty-hour layover in the world's most exciting city, and she'll wallow in her hotel room, watching CNN because all the good TV programs are in a foreign language. As is the case with most of her kind, Martha lives to bitch. Somehow she's forgotten that spending time away from home was the main reason she signed up for the job.

"If this is such a pain in the ass, Martha, why don't you quit?" I said this venomously, hoping to quash her complaints for the remainder of the day.

Martha did not answer. Her mouth stopped moving for the first time since we'd met. Perhaps she caught a glimpse of herself behind the checkout counter at Wal-Mart.

I closed my eyes, drifted toward the edge of sleep. Before I got there Martha cranked up again. "You know, if we wait here any longer we'll miss our return flight from Chicago. I'm not going to let Screw Scheduling mess up my plans for today. Last week they reassigned me at the end of my sequence . . . I called the union the next day but they were worthless so I decided that from now on—"

"Martha will you please shut up!"

She stared at me as if she'd been slapped. Tears welled in her eyes. She leapt from the jump seat and went into the lavatory, sobbing along the way.

While Martha cried, the captain's voice came over the intercom again. This new aircraft apparently had a mechanical problem. For the second time that morning we returned to the gate. For the second time that morning, mechanics entered the cockpit. Passengers moaned again, a few more defected to flights on other airlines. Finally, some thirty minutes later, the captain announced that this plane was out of service.

By this time the passengers were furious. Having demanded to be booked on another airline, Jesus F. was long gone, but a dozen people took on his abrasive persona. Profanity, the likes of which I hadn't heard since sitting in the bleachers at a Knicks game, was hurled at me like stones. Because Martha was still busy doing whatever it was she was doing in the lavatory, I was the sole airline representative in the rear of the airplane. For the first time in my career, I felt physically threatened. Rather than face the angry mob, I stepped into the other lavatory and locked the door.

When I stepped out moments later, Martha was trailing the last sulking passenger. She threw a look over one shoulder, turned up her nose and looked away.

Once again the crew gathered in the first-class cabin. Once again we drank orange juice, discussed our options, pondered our fate. After some time had passed, the purser decided to check the computer for information about our next move. When she returned, she was frowning.

"We've been reassigned," she said, holding a new sequence printout in front of her. "Our flight leaves in three hours."

Martha snatched the paper from the purser's hand and stood there, in the middle of the first-class aisle, shaking her head in disbelief. "Orlando?" she said. "We're laying over in Orlando?"

Tears welling in her eyes, Martha disappeared into the nearest lavatory. The rest of the crew scattered, heading off to eat lunch, make phone calls or watch TV in operations.

I walked to the back of the disabled aircraft, pulled out my travel alarm clock and drifted off to sleep.

6 The Ferret in First Class

Just after push-back, as our airplane rolled away from the departure gate, I heard a sudden gasp from someone who sat close to where I was standing. I poked my head out the aft galley, wondering what sort of drama was about to unfold. Could it be that one of my colleagues had ripped her pantyhose? Had an infrequent flyer reacted to the news that no meal would be served on the flight? Was an elderly woman ambling up the aisle, unaware that her bare ass was showing? (This actually happened on a flight from Port of Spain, Trinidad. After exiting the lavatory, a stout, wide-bottomed senior headed back to her seat, oblivious to the fact that her stretch pants and panties were hanging around her knees. A female colleague snatched the poor woman by the arm and pulled her back toward the lavatory, but not before three rows of passengers caught glimpses of her blotched and sagging booty.)

I scanned the cabin of the New York–bound plane, but observed none of these atrocities. Instead, I saw a terrified woman who had just leaped from her seat. With one trembling finger, she pointed to the floor. "There!" she said. "There it is!"

It was a cockroach. A common household cockroach. Denizen of seedy tenements and penthouse condominiums alike. One of a breed of more than four thousand cockroach species, the likes of which will thrive long after mankind is annihilated in a hail of meteorites. *La cucaracha.* Virtually unchanged since it first began twitching its antennae some 320 million years ago. One of their kind was just a few feet away from me, scaring the hell out of one of my passengers. I watched dispassionately as the insect scuttled across the matted carpet of our Boeing 727—which just happened to be headed to New York City, cockroach capital of the United States.

Perhaps the cockroach had family there.

"Do something!" the woman demanded. She glared at me as if my uniform was that of an exterminator instead of a mild-mannered fly guy. I arched an eyebrow, raised a patent leather shoe and dropped it on the scurrying critter. Afterward, I locked eyes with the woman who reacted as if I had yanked her from the jaws of death. "Oh . . . thank you," she said, patting her palm against her chest. "I despise roaches." I scanned the cabin, wondering if some insect-rights activist would stand up for the deceased by threatening to sue the airline. Nobody said a word. The masses watched as I placed an airsick bag lengthwise on the floor, kicked the flattened corpse inside and dumped the package into a lavatory trash receptacle.

The slain cockroach was soon to become the topic of conversation. *Is the plane infested? Should we worry about disease?* I could hear the questions even before they left the lips of passengers. Using levity to quash their fears, I turned to face the last three rows. "The roach was not part of an organized gang," I said. "It was a drifter, operating on its own." Laughter broke out. Faint mutterings of cheer rippled through the cabin. But one man watched me with sinister eyes. He saw no humor in my actions or my words. I had just killed a cockroach, a semiconscious act committed by thousands of people every day—in schools, homes, even in kitchens at four-star restaurants—but this guy stared at me as if the initials on my name tag read O. J.

Needless to say, I was not shocked by his reaction. You can't please all of the people all of the time. Someone will always be offended, no matter what you do. Had I allowed the cockroach to live, there would have been at least one inconsolable passenger, and dozens who would look twice when we served the Chicken Kiev.

This wasn't the first time I'd seen uninvited critters in the airplane cabin. Nor was this the first time a passenger had asked me to "do something" about it. In addition to crushing the occasional cockroach, I've swatted flies and moths and mosquitoes, cornered a mouse, downed a couple of dragonflies and fought off a squadron of Caribbean bumblebees that stung two first-class passengers before buzzing away.

During one memorable flight, a dachshund got away from its owner and scurried up the aisle. I chased the paltry pooch into the first-class cabin—charging through the curtains like a bull, freaking out the passengers, frightening the crew—and finally cornered it in the forward entry area. I took him back to coach and demanded that the owner return it to his kennel. The owner acquiesced. But as the kennel door shut and the owner placed it underneath the forward seat, the dachshund began to bark. *Rurr, rurr, rurr . . . rurr, rurr, rurr . . . rurr, rurr, rurr* . . . So pitiful was its whining, so tragic the look in its eyes, the owner begged us to let him hold the dog in his lap. I said no. My colleague said yes. This prompted a heated debate between passengers and cabin crew. As long as the dog was in its owner's arms, he remained quiet. When forced back into his tiny kennel prison, he yelped like a doggie possessed.

If it were up to me, the owner would have been allowed to hold the dog in her arms, if for no other reason than to spare passengers from auditory stress. But the Federal Aviation Administration mandates that carry-on pets are not to be let out of their kennels at any time. If a concerned passenger saw an uncaged pet and reported the incident to the FAA, the airline, believe it or not, could face a possible fine.

Most airlines allow only common household pets—dogs, cats, rabbits, etc—in the passenger cabin. These pets must remain in a kennel underneath the seat. Less common pets such as lizards, ferrets and snakes are deemed unacceptable in the cabin (even when transported in kennels); they must travel in the pressurized cargo compartment with larger animals.

Worried about a pet's chances for survival in the cargo hold, short on cash for shipping fees or merely too stubborn to follow the rules, passengers occasionally smuggle their pets aboard the aircraft. It happens a lot more than you'd think. I once caught a woman with a lizard in her purse; her seatmate screamed after noticing the creature halfway through the flight. A teenager carried aboard a ferret in a hatbox; air holes had been punched in the top. During a flight from Miami to

Caracas, I walked up the aisle and noticed a woman with an aquarium on her tray table. It was a two-, maybe two-and-a-half-gallon tank filled with octopi and tropical fish.

Even more astounding, a colleague discovered a man with a five-foot snake in his backpack. Just before agents closed the door of the airplane, a worried passenger walked up to one of the flight attendants. "That guy's backpack is moving," she said, pointing to a man sitting in a center seat. "It's under the seat in front of him." The attendant approached the man, demanding to know what was in the bag. The nervous man spilled his guts immediately. "It's just a snake," he said, reaching into his backpack to reveal his pet python. Passengers took one look at the snake and screamed. The man laughed. The flight attendant did not. Man and beast were promptly ejected.

As is the case with just about everything else in life, there are exceptions to the airplane animal rule. Take Seeing Eye dogs for example. Service animals such as these are allowed in the cabin without a kennel. Well-trained and unobtrusive, they sit at their owner's feet without making a noise. Truth be told, Seeing Eye dogs are some of the best passengers I've ever had. They don't growl. They don't bark. They don't display any of the tendencies that disgruntled passengers often do.

Joining service animals in the category of privileged four-legged passengers, airlines make exceptions for "celebrity" animals as well. Yes, you heard correctly. Believe it or not, talented beasts are not required to ride with their heathen cousins in the cargo compartment. If the Taco Bell Chihuahua decides to fly from L.A. to Acapulco, for example, it's allowed to sit in a first-class seat next to Meg Ryan and Halle Berry and all the other beautiful people.

Word for word, here's what company regulations say about celebrity animals:

Celebrity Animals are defined as:
- Cats/Dogs that are seen on popular TV programs/ commercials
- Usually travel in the First Class cabin but can travel in any cabin
- Do not require pet kennels to be accommodated in the cabin

A celebrity animal is considered acceptable if the animal is:
- Free of odor and parasites
- Well-mannered and harnessed

Celebrity animals may be seated at the owner's feet during takeoff and landing.

A celebrity animal may travel in a passenger seat provided the following:
- Must be a celebrity animal, not have a celebrity owner
- Animal companion must provide own seat cushion and seat belt adapter for animal to be strapped in seat

I'm not making this up. If you don't believe me, call a major airline.

A few years ago, I had an onboard run-in with a noncelebrity animal. A commoner who didn't even have a boarding pass.

As a long line of passengers filed into our DC-10 aircraft, a sparrow flew in right along with them. It darted through the cabin, back and forth, back and forth, skimming the heads of passengers who were forced to duck repeatedly in both aisles. It was pretty funny, actually. The passengers looked like spectators at a baseball stadium. Each time they ducked it appeared as if they were doing "the wave."

During an elongated fly-by pause, most passengers managed to make it to their seats. That's when my colleague sprang into action. She began chasing the bird up one aisle and down the other, swinging her arms in an effort to shoo it out the door. I stood in back of the aircraft, eyes squinting, arms folded across my chest, praying I wouldn't have to get involved. But when my coworker shot a nasty look my way, I felt a sudden compulsion to join in the chase.

Judging by the laughter that erupted, our bird-chasing efforts provided the kind of onboard entertainment passengers only dream of. Children stared at us with big goofy grins on their faces. Men roared like giddy lions. Women held their sides in fits of silent sniggering. Someone asked, "Do you guys get paid extra for this?"

I made a mental note to mention this to our labor union.

After departure time had come and gone, and the stowaway bird continued to fly sorties through the cabin, the mirth began to fade. Not for lack of comedic activity, mind you. Our "run-through-the-cabin-and-try-to-catch-the-frigging-bird" routine had risen to new heights of hilarity once the rest of the crew joined the act. But many passengers began to focus on a more critical issue. They realized their flight connections in Miami were now in jeopardy.

The clock was ticking. Ten more minutes passed. Twenty. The sparrow flew around and around the cabin, chirping insanely like a wind-up toy with a busted spring. The same passengers who had been laughing at our ineffective efforts were now demanding that something be done. "This is ridiculous," blurted one enraged man. Of course it's ridiculous, you moron. So is your assessment of the situation. (I didn't say this, of course, but I really, really wanted to.) There's a goddamned bird flying inside the goddamned airplane with four goddamned flight attendants running after it. What's more ridiculous than that?

Though cabin crews are trained to handle in-flight childbirth, cabin decompression, onboard fires and emergency evacuations, we are not skilled in the process of removing sparrows from the cabin. We had to wing it.

After cornering the sparrow in the back of the airplane, I grabbed a blanket. Like a high-school jock with a wet towel and a wicked disposition, I snapped the blanket toward (not at) the bird, hoping to coax it out the door. After a couple of near-hits that made bird lovers squirm in their seats, our feathered friend finally flew the coop. Forty-five minutes after scheduled departure, we were on our way, minus one menacing critter.

Which brings me back to what happened after the cockroach incident on the flight to New York. Our plane landed at LaGuardia without additional sightings. But later that night, after drinking way too many Amstels in a sleazy Greenwich Village bar, I found myself staggering past Washington Square Park. Beneath the dim glow of streetlights, I saw movement from the corner of one out-of-focus eye. Although the park was closed to humans at the late hour of 2:00 A.M., it was nevertheless open for rats. Dozens of them. Hundreds maybe. They scuttled around the rim of metal trash cans. Cavorted among tufts of grass. They frolicked across the blighted landscape like children let out for morning recess. I watched with a kind of drunken fascination, wondering what would happen should one of these critters slither its way onto an airplane.

On August 31, 1999, I found out.

A rat was sighted on an Air New Zealand flight from Los Angeles to Auckland, New Zealand, via Papeete, Tahiti. The coarse-haired, pink-tailed, long-snouted stowaway made its presence known in horrifying fashion. At one point during the flight, a business-class passenger felt something on her right leg. The woman lifted the blanket that lay across her lap. There she found the rat—resting comfortably on her right knee.

Words can't describe the chaos that followed.

Seven weeks earlier, on July 6, a similar event took place aboard an Air India flight. This time the plane was preparing to depart Dubai, United Arab Emirates. As the New Delhi, India–bound aircraft rolled down the taxiway prior to takeoff, someone spotted a rat. Passengers and crew evacuated while the airplane underwent fumigation.

Sixteen hours later, the flight finally departed. But the rat was never found.

Canadian Airlines joined the in-flight rat race back on Feb. 17, 1996. This particular rodent was believed to have escaped from a catering container shortly after the plane took off from Hong Kong. Realizing the potential problems a loose rat might create if the plane continued on its eleven-hour flight to Vancouver, British Columbia, the pilot decided to divert the aircraft to Tokyo. Passengers were subsequently booked on other flights. Many were angry, not simply because of the inconvenience but because they suspected the rat was a prank. They were probably right.

The plane, filled with holiday merrymakers, had taken off near the start of the Chinese New Year, which had begun the preceding Monday. That particular year was the "Year of the Rat."

Vomiting woman a travel "nightmare"/drunk air rager acted "disgusting"

TORONTO, Feb. 22 (Ottawa Sun)—Tom Godfrey – An Edmonton woman has been charged in an air rage incident that turned a three-hour flight to Toronto into a nightmare for 100 passengers.

Police said a woman threatened to "kick the ass of a female passenger," stole food off the tray of another, drank and tried to smoke before vomiting on herself.

"People sitting around her had to be moved from their seats," said Insp. John Byrne. "One passenger said he's never seen such loud and disgusting behavior."

Byrne said the pilot radioed police for help as the Air Canada flight approached Pearson Airport on Saturday.

"Our officers were waiting for her," he said. "We had no problem getting her off the plane."

Police said the woman, who was drinking on the flight, was grabbed by crew members when she tried to light a cigarette.

"At one point, she became angry at a female passenger and threatened to kick her ass," Byrne said.

The woman kept yelling at and insulting other passengers.

"Some passengers called her a loudmouth," officers said. "The flight ended up being a nightmare for many."

Byrne said the woman eventually threw up on herself.

"The flight attendants had to subdue her. She was held for police," Byrne said.

Reprinted with permission of Sun Media Corporation, Toronto, Ontario, 2000.

British grandmother gets six months in jail for punching stewardess

LONDON, April 11 (Deutsche Presse-Agentur) – A British court has jailed a 56-year-old grandmother, described as of "impeccable character," for six months for punching an air stewardess after she had drunk duty-free rum and inhaled amyl nitrate with a drag artist she had met on the flight.

Doris Healy had become abusive after drinking and inhaling poppers with a drag artist on a holiday flight to Florida, the Express reported on Tuesday.

Healy lashed out three times at an air stewardess after being asked to sit down and fasten her seat belt as the aircraft came in to land.

Healy, a wife and mother-of-three, was so drunk when the flight finally arrived in Florida that she had to be carried off in a wheelchair. Even then she continued to swear and kick out at crew members and U.S. customs officials.

She broke down in tears at Manchester Crown Court on Monday when the judge told her he had no alternative but to send her to prison.

"I have a duty to protect air crew and passengers—particularly young children—from air rage incidents which occur on flights at least four times a day on British airlines," he said.

Healy told police she believed her drinks had been spiked by the man sitting in the seat next to her before he gave her "poppers," or amyl nitrate, to inhale during the flight.

She said she could not remember anything further until she woke up on the floor of the U.S. immigration office.

Her lawyer said she had previously been of "impeccable" character and was extremely distressed by her appearance in court.

Reprinted with permission of dpa, Deutsche Presse-Agentur GmbH, 2000.

7 When Fists Flew on the San Juan Special

Back in the mid-1980s, when DC-10s roamed the air space between New York and Puerto Rico, when I was new with the airline, when the world lay before me like a virgin wearing nothing but a wicked grin, I worked, on occasion, the most dreaded of all flights: the infamous San Juan Special. The S.J.S. had the dubious distinction of departing from JFK shortly before midnight, seven days a week, 365 days a year. It was always filled to capacity with 295 cut-rate passengers who didn't give a damn about the 3:30 A.M. arrival time. What mattered was the $99 one-way airfare.

Only the hardiest flight attendants remained mentally and physically unscathed after working a typical three-and-a-half-hour flight. The Saturday night departure (a.k.a. the Saturday Night Special) was particularly rough. It seemed there was always a fight, always a problem, always an incident to add to the pages of airline folklore.

On one particularly comical Saturday Night Special, I watched a new flight attendant suffer a nervous breakdown while she collected tickets at the boarding gate. A hoard of overanxious New Yorkers—the likes of whom the poor, naive Texas girl had never seen—descended upon her, trying to board the airplane all at once. From my faraway position at the aircraft end of the jet bridge, I could barely make out her frantic shouts: "Please . . . please, back up," she cried. "Y'all listen to me . . . nooooooo!"

Forgoing my assigned position at the aircraft entry door, I stepped into the jet bridge, looked down the corridor and saw one of the strangest sights of my airline career. The flight attendant was sprinting toward me—arms flailing, knees pumping, big hair splashing around her head like a waterfall gone berserk. A herd of heckling passengers crossed the jet bridge in leisurely pursuit.

"They won't listen to me, they won't listen to me," she cried.

"They won't listen to me, they won't listen to me," mocked a voice from the approaching crowd.

Riotous laughter erupted inside the jet bridge, but from the flight attendant's perspective, the eruption might just as well have come from a volcano. Crazy with panic, she shifted into overdrive. I had no idea a country gal could run so fast wearing three pounds of makeup and two-and-a-half-inch heels. She seemed to be more than ten feet away when she launched herself, flinging her arms and legs around me as if I were a soldier returning from war and she was the expectant fiancée. Sobbing uncontrollably, twin rivers of snot running from her flaring nostrils, she trembled like scrub brush in a cold Siberian breeze.

With the hysterical flight attendant still glued to me, and a smile struggling to blossom on my pseudoserious face, I announced to the passengers that boarding would commence in a moment. They waited impatiently—smirking, rolling their eyes, jostling for position with an elbow or a knee—while a coworker escorted the traumatized flight attendant to a lavatory where she could collect herself. But she never did. The very next day she submitted her resignation and returned home to Texas, where only the cattle stampede.

Such was life on the San Juan Special. The passengers ate you up and spat you out; only the strong survived.

During the beverage service, it was not unusual for a female passenger to demand a can of Coca-Cola. Not for herself, mind you. The high-octane soft drink was to be fed to her infant child. S.J.S. flight attendants have been known to shake their head and sigh while pouring oceans of Classic Coke into baby bottles. I've done so many times myself. To add insult to a very possible long-term injury, the same retro-mommy might request five or six packs of sugar which would be torn open, poured into the baby bottle filled with Coke, and then, like a tit plump with sugar and caffeine and carefully balanced phosphoric acid, the bottle would be jammed into the screaming infant's mouth.

At any time during the flight you might witness a card game with serious money involved. Gold chains flashed on a regular basis. Boom boxes, while not uncommon, had the uncommon habit of blasting music loud enough for everyone to hear. Rumor had it that on one exceptionally rambunctious flight, a group of hookers worked the coach-class lavatories. Passengers who wished to use the lavs for conventional purposes simply had to wait.

Patience never fared well on the San Juan Special, however. Whenever the lavs were occupied, even when alleged hookers weren't on board, passengers sometimes found creative ways to purge their swollen bladders. Once, I saw a man standing absently, a few feet away from the lavatory. Upon closer inspection, I realized he was peeing into a free-standing garbage bag. As if squirted from a figurine in some debauched European fountain, the golden arc of fluid glistened in dim light that, for one fleeting moment, made the lurid scene appear respectable.

Considering the distance between man and bag, the passenger was blessed with remarkable aim and trajectory. Had we been young boys engaged in a peeing contest, I might have been impressed. But we were grown men on a goddamn airplane. I walked up beside him, threw up my hands in exasperation and said, "What the hell are you doing?" He tossed a sidelong glance, nodded his head and smiled the blissful smile of a man who had finally found relief.

On one of my very first Saturday Night Specials, airport security was summoned to the departure gate to break up an airplane brawl. The fight was initiated during the boarding process, by two men who, as children, probably suckled hundreds of Coke-filled baby bottles and pissed liquid sugar well into their thirties.

Here's how the action unfolded.

I watched a nervous-looking gentleman as he placed his new Panama hat in the overhead bin. Noting the tremendous care he bestowed upon the hat—the meticulous placement of it, the way he moved it a few inches to the left, turned it slightly, then moved it a few inches to the right—I couldn't help but smile. This was a man who loved his hat, a man whose hat was as precious as a newborn child. Clearly, this hat was not to be touched by the unsavory hands of strangers. Though the overhead bin was otherwise empty, the man closed it gently, leaving his prize to rest in uncluttered peace.

I was standing at the rear of the airplane, about twenty-five feet away from the hat man, when a heavyset gentleman plopped into the last row of seats. His eyes were red. He stank of liquor. He was sweating and panting and seemed on the verge of collapse. Still, he looked up at me and smiled. "Pssssst, pssssst . . ." he said. "*Yo necesito un vaso con hielo* [I need a glass with ice]." He opened his jacket, pointing somewhat stealthily to a fifth of rum tucked in his breast pocket. "*Yo necesito un vaso con hielo,*" he repeated. "Ahhh, ha, ha, ha, ha, ha . . ."

This was the kind of passenger we occasionally greeted on the Saturday Night Special—a tipsy traveler impressed by his own resourcefulness.

As the final passengers squeezed into the crowded cabin, I noticed a man dragging a heavy carry-on bag along the right-hand aisle of the aircraft. He hurled repeated insults at his wife, who, though she was half the size of her husband, was dragging a carry-on that seemed twice as heavy as his. His wife snapped back at him, delivering a Spanish-speaking retort that sent ripples of laughter through the crowd of nearby passengers. Embarrassed by this public display of female disobedience, the husband flew into a frenzy. He yelled and cursed, berating her with a volley of conjugated verbs that drew ice-cold stares from passengers. In the midst of his tirade, the husband threw open an overhead bin. In one blind movement, he picked up his massive carry-on bag and slammed it in the overhead bin, directly on top of the precious Panama hat.

The hat man sat still in his seat, frozen momentarily by the ramifications of this callous act. When the paralysis finally broke, he leapt to his feet, cursed the assailant, then reached beneath the bag to extract what was left of his hat. To his extreme displeasure, the crown had been completely crushed so that now it was level to the brim. It looked like a broken Frisbee. Like a nest built by druggie sparrows.

The hat man's jaw came unhinged. He began to tremble. His eyes filled with something more complex than rage. Without taking a breath, the hat man spat a fusillade of insults in rapid-fire Spanish. The husband responded with a foul-mouthed blast of his own. Their shouts attracted the attention of everyone on board, including first-class passengers who were poking their heads in the aisle, trying to get a glimpse of the ruckus in the back.

I threaded my way through the crowded aisle, hoping to intervene before things got out of hand. But by the time I reached the two shouting men, the first punch had already been thrown. The hat man had been leveled by a vicious right cross.

A collective gasp seemed to suck the air out of the cavernous DC-10 cabin. Many of the 295 passengers and ten crew members froze in their places. There was no sound. The seconds floated by like Goodyear blimps. Like a heavyweight champion refusing to be beaten by a ten-count, the hat man rose slowly from the floor. He massaged his chin for a moment, grinned sardonically, then let loose an ear-piercing battle cry:

"*Hyyyyyyyyyyyyyyyyaaaaaaa!*"

That's when all hell broke loose.

To the best of my recollection, the full-scale brawl broke out as the husband prepared to defend himself against the hat man. When hubby cocked his arm to throw another punch, his elbow inadvertently whacked the head of a seated passenger. Infuriated by this unprovoked assault, the man jumped to his feet and pushed the husband, who then fell atop a fourth man who proceeded to push the husband upon a fifth. Like the climactic scene in a Jackie Chan movie, fists were suddenly flying everywhere. Stranger battled against stranger in an aircraft skirmish fueled purely by angst and testosterone.

Not to be outdone by the guys, some of the tougher-looking female passengers joined in. I ducked beneath a misguided punch thrown by a thirty-year-old woman in a tank top. I glared at her, thought briefly about delivering a jab to the ribs or maybe an uppercut to the chin. But then I remembered I was at work and in uniform. Besides, she looked like the type who might whup my ass and live to laugh about it. Instead of throwing punches, I threw a look and retreated to the rear of the aircraft.

Unfortunately, my escape was blocked by a massive presence in the aisle. It was the tipsy traveler. The big guy. The one who asked for *un vaso con hielo.* He stood there, wobbling, a sudden sense of purpose gleaming in his bloodshot eyes. Until that moment, I hadn't appreciated the mammoth proportions of the man. He stood well over six feet and weighed in at no less than three hundred pounds. Amid the shouts and screams of the escalating brawl, the big guy gathered his considerable voice and yelled something in Spanish. Something cruel and daunting and suicidal. He charged up the aisle, slamming into the fray with a fearlessness instilled by the makers of Barcardi. Had I not slid into a row of seats, he would have bowled me over like a cricket wicket.

The captain's voice soon came over the P.A. system, demanding that everyone be seated, but the escalating clamor made his command difficult to hear. Cheering sections had formed on the opposite side of the airplane. When a favorite brawler connected a punch, one group would yell "Whoooaaaaa" while the other group sighed "Ooooooh." From a protected position near the aft bulkhead, I watched an entire family—mother, father and three kids—applauding and throwing phantom punches, like spectators at a Tyson fight. I'm certain that in some hidden corner of the aircraft, someone was placing five-to-one odds on the big guy.

As law enforcement officers stormed the airplane, as punches froze in mid-arc and pugilists suddenly became pacifists, the big guy moved to the back of the airplane and looked me dead in the eye.

"Psssssst, pssssst . . ." he said, his eyes like wet tomatoes. *"Yo necesito un vaso con hielo.* Ahhhh, ha, ha, ha, ha . . ."

8 Preventing the "Delinquent-Flier" Upgrade

Moments before the departure of our two-hour flight from New York to Atlanta, I scanned the first-class cabin, wondering if this would be a good day or a bad one. The gentleman seated in 5-D seemed most likely to pose a problem. Scowling, demonstrative, irritable as an old coot who'd forgotten his medication, he'd stormed the aircraft demanding a double bourbon on the rocks. "Now!" he said, before allowing me a chance to respond.

When I asked him to wait until the boarding process slowed, and the aisle was clear of passengers, he flung a hand in the air and mumbled something about lousy airlines and flight attendants who hoard the goddamn liquor.

I had my answer: It was going to be a bad day.

As with most Boeing 727s, our first-class configuration accommodates twelve passengers. On this particular day there were only six passengers aboard: three double-breasted business types on the left of the cabin; three on the right. All of them—as is so often the case—were men.

The gate agent shut the door, the aircraft pushed back from the gate, and I began to feel as though something wasn't quite right. It was more than the constant piercing stare from Mr. Bourbon, who had demanded—and had yet to receive—his second drink. The feeling was more intuitive. It was as if something or someone had suddenly moved out of place.

I made the routine departure announcement, walked through the cabin to pick up pre-departure glasses and returned to the galley. Instinctively, I poked my head in the aisle to take a quick passenger count. Had I been the type of flight attendant who enjoys putting passengers in their place, I would have trembled with glee after finishing my count. Instead, I just shook my head and sighed. Though six passengers were listed and accounted for, seven people were sitting in the first-class cabin. While my back had been turned, someone from coach had given himself a "delinquent-flyer" upgrade.

Throughout my career, I've run into these stealthy passengers many, many times. Here is their standard M.O.:

Convinced that the onboard caste system can be easily thwarted, they wait for just the right moment. Moving quickly and quietly—like high-altitude ninjas—they abandon the crowded coach cabin for an unoccupied seat in first class. Sooner or later, of course, the crew becomes aware of the infraction. We always catch them, but it often seems like not a week goes by without a delinquent-flier conflict.

As is the case with many flight attendants, I've had to challenge men, women—even cute doe-eyed children who plopped their rear end where it didn't belong. I've been forced to eject business travelers who cursed beneath their breath before gathering a laptop and briefcase and slinking back to a sea of mocking faces in steerage class. I've tossed out healthy passengers who cite a mysterious disability that requires the comfort and girth only a big leather seat can provide. I've deposed doctors, college professors, sweet little old ladies, even a member of the clergy who looked up at me and swore that he had misread his seat assignment. (How in God's name can 28-F be confused with 3-A?)

The excuses are as wide-ranging as the personalities on any given airplane: "Oh . . . I'm sorry," a bookish female passenger once said after being asked to vacate the premises. "I'm going to be in a hurry to make my connection. I didn't think you'd mind if I sat up front." Another good one: "I'm a fearful flyer, I'm scared to sit in coach." Slightly more direct, but equally ineffective is the always popular, "Hey, *they* told me I could sit in any empty seat!" The most outlandish response came from a meticulously groomed interloper who was wearing what appeared to be a custom-tailored suit. He'd just requested a glass of champagne when I asked to see his boarding stub. He somehow managed to look down at me, even though I was standing above him. In a voice that could have come straight out of *The Great Gatsby*, he said: "Do I look as if I should be sitting back there with the plebeians?"

Plebian-hating snobs notwithstanding, most flight attendants could care less about who sits where on an airplane. If it were up to us, there would be no first-class compartment or seat assignments. Seats would be occupied on a first-come-first-serve basis, like at Southwest Airlines. The advantages are obvious: no seat duplications, no families complaining that they're not seated together. And no inferiority or superiority complexes related to the size and location of one's throne. It's communism at thirty thousand feet. But hey, whatever works.

Most airlines do not share this user-friendly vision of the skies. Instead, they train flight attendants like police dogs—we're supposed to sniff out perpetrators and put them back where they belong.

Why all the fuss? A first-class seat is a virtual gold mine for airlines—especially on international routes. On one of our recent flights from New York to Paris, the luxury section was filled with full-fare passengers. There was not a single upgrade in the bunch. For the privilege of caviar, fine wine, scrumptious food and comfortable seats, each passenger paid a whopping $9,000. The total first-class revenue came to $117,000. Not bad for only thirteen seats.

Free trips and first-class upgrades are the carrots dangling before frequent-flying faces. Although upgrades normally make up a large portion of the premium population, those who actually pay for a seat can fork up more than ten times as much as their economy-class brethren. This does wonders for an airline's bottom line. Which explains why airline executives bow down to the big seats. Unsanctioned use of these money-makers sends the wrong message and undermines profits in the long run.

Hoping to ferret out the delinquent flier on my flight to Atlanta, I stepped into the galley and studied the Passenger Information List. The PIL is stocked with enough airline intelligence to give a CIA agent multiple orgasms. It lists the names and seat assignments of disabled passengers, grieving passengers, V.I.P. passengers, airline-employee passengers, passengers who ordered a vegetarian meal, passengers who should not be served alcohol, passengers who've pestered other passengers, and passengers enrolled in the airline's frequent-flier program. Occasionally, the PIL contains spicy little tidbits about the guy in 14-C who went ballistic on the agent after the airline botched his reservations. (His seatmates can only wonder why he's being plied with free drinks.) But for my immediate purposes, the PIL provided the first and last names and seat assignments for each and every first-class passenger—along with an "UPGD" designator, that lets us know who paid full fare and who was given an upgrade.

After taking the list, checking it twice, determined to find out who'd been naughty or nice, I walked over to the gentleman seated in 4-B. Gray hair trimmed with military precision, a silk tie loosened round the collar of his slightly wrinkled shirt, he chatted quietly with the man sitting next to him. According to my paperwork, all occupied seats were matched with a name. All, that is, except 4-B.

"Excuse me, sir," I said, in the most humble voice I could muster. "May I please have a look at your boarding stub?"

Raising his eyebrows, he threw at me a look that was both daunting and dismayed. *How dare you question my right to sit here,* it said. *How dare you interrupt my conversation with a fellow first-class passenger.* But rather than vocalizing his displeasure, as I expected him to do at any moment, he let that cold hard stare continue to do all the talking. Because I'd seen that cold hard stare many times before—because I'd felt the same I'm-gonna-intimidate-you-into-caving-in hostility during similar confrontations—I didn't blink.

"Your boarding pass, sir," I repeated. "I need to have a look at it."

"Okay, okay," he said, begrudgingly. "I'm not supposed to be sitting here. My seat is in coach, but I came up to discuss an important matter with my colleague." He then gestured to the man sitting beside him in 4-A. The man nodded in compliance. "Do you mind if we finish our discussion?"

"Sir, I don't mind. But my employer does. I'm afraid you'll have to return to coach."

After another volley of stares, I said that if I allowed him to sit here, I'd have to do the same for everybody else. Still, he pleaded his case. Just then the captain issued his takeoff announcement. We'd be in the air in maybe sixty seconds. Not enough time for me to reason with the man. I needed to strap into my jump seat. "Alright, sir," I said. "Feel free to continue your discussion here until after takeoff. But once I start the food and beverage service, you'll have to return to your seat. Okay?" He sort of rolled his eyes, acquiescing in the most obstinate way.

I had made a big mistake. A mistake that would teach me to never again bend the rules for anyone.

After the aircraft reached cruising altitude, and time came for the beverage service to begin, I walked through the cabin taking drink orders. When I reached row 4 I stopped and smiled at the man in 4-B. This time, he threw a look that was downright hostile.

"Sir," I said. "I'm going to have to ask you to leave the cabin now." I turned and walked to the galley. He got up from his seat and followed.

"What is your name?" he demanded, pushing his face into the galley. "What?"

"You heard me. I want your name."

"Why do you want my name, sir?"

"Because I don't like the way I've been treated."

My last shreds of professionalism were evaporating by the second. The guy was an obstinate prick. If I couldn't get him to leave soon, I feared I might say or do something that would cause a drastic reduction in my income. There are plenty of air-rage reports that tell of passengers attacking flight attendants. But this could very well be the first documented case in which a crazed male attendant unleashed an attack upon a passenger.

A little voice whispered inside my head. "Careful," it said. "Careful . . ."

I took a deep breath.

"You don't like the way I've been treating you?" I said, finally. "You don't like the way that *I've* been treating *you*?" I felt my voice begin to rise, but did not have the fortitude to contain it. "To be perfectly honest, sir. I shouldn't be treating you at all because *you shouldn't be up here in the first place!!*"

Heads turned. The moment froze. It seemed as though I was choking on the echo of my own ill-advised outburst. I heard the familiar rush of air, the distant roar of engines magnified by the sudden cabin silence. Embarrassed, I looked into the eyes of my oppressor. Though his face had begun to swell like an overexcited blowfish, though he cursed and snarled and vowed to "never fly this airline again," he retreated in a flurry of angry footsteps and disappeared behind the curtain.

I was left to attend to five sniggering first-class passengers, and one who started screaming for a bourbon on the rocks.

9 Conduct Unbecoming an Investment Banker

A few years ago, on a flight from Buenos Aires, Argentina, to New York, an investment banker—the president of a multimillion-dollar company, no less—made worldwide headlines by committing one of the most revolting acts ever witnessed on a commercial aircraft. After becoming intoxicated during the flight, he demanded more alcohol from the flight attendants. When they refused to serve him, he began helping himself to the liquor supply. After being cut off a second time, he became visibly angry and told a male attendant that he would "bust his ass" (federal offense No. 1, threatening a crew member) if he didn't get a drink.

While this was going on, a passenger had fallen ill. A flight attendant rushed to the front of the plane to get a first-aid kit, but on his way back the investment banker harassed him, delaying the attendant in his attempt to assist the sick passenger (federal offense No. 2, interfering with the duties of a crew member). The investment banker shoved a female flight attendant in the chest, (federal offense No. 3, assaulting a crew member), causing her to fall into a passenger seat, then he walked up to the first-class cabin, dropped his pants and underwear, and defecated on a service cart (federal offense No. 4, lewd and lascivious behavior) in plain view of the passengers and crew.

But the out-of-control drunk wasn't finished yet.

To add insult to lunacy, he wiped his butt with first-class linen napkins and proceeded to rub his hands on service counters and various utensils used by cabin crew. In one final disgusting gesture, the man stepped in his own feces and tracked it through the main cabin (possible federal offenses Nos. 5, 6 and 7).

The culprit was arrested upon landing in New York. He subsequently pled guilty to assault and was sentenced to two years probation. In addition, he was given three hundred hours of community service, a five-thousand-dollar fine and was ordered to pay more than fifty thousand dollars in restitution to the airline and its passengers.

Not surprisingly, the guilty man's lawyer said his client was "ill" while committing the now infamous in-flight atrocity.

What makes people lose control in such a manner? Three things: alcohol, liquor and booze. In most high-profile cases of passenger misconduct, drunkenness lies at the root of the problem. So why not eliminate booze on all commercial flights? For one thing, the vast majority of passengers have a drink or two or three, and behave in a perfectly respectable manner. Besides, eliminating alcohol from the cabin would create a whole new category of misbehaving passengers: fearful flyers who rely on a vodka tonic to prevent them from screaming bloody murder during turbulence.

But even when passengers are as sober as corpses, many are guilty of conduct unbecoming:

- While a female flight attendant was serving food from the meal cart, a female passenger thrust a small bundle of trash toward her. "Take this," the passenger demanded. Realizing that the trash was actually a used baby diaper, the attendant instructed the passenger to take it to the lavatory herself and dispose of it. "No," the passenger replied. "You take it!" The attendant explained that she couldn't dispose of the dirty diaper because she was serving food—handling the diaper would be unsanitary. But that wasn't a good enough answer for the passenger. Angered by her refusal, the passenger hurled the diaper at the flight attendant. It struck her square in the head, depositing chunks of baby dung that clung like peanut butter to her hair. The two women ended up wrestling on the floor. They had to be separated by passengers.

- Passengers on a flight from Miami to San Juan, Puerto Rico, were stunned by the actions of one deranged passenger. He walked to the rear of the plane, then charged up the aisle, slapping passengers' heads along the way. Next, he kicked a pregnant flight attendant, who immediately fell to the ground. As if that weren't enough, he bit a young boy on the arm. At this point the man was restrained and handcuffed by crew members. He was arrested upon arrival.

- When bad weather closed the Dallas/Fort Worth airport for several hours, departing planes were stuck on the ground for the duration. One frustrated passenger, a young woman, walked up to a female flight attendant and said, "I'm sorry, but I have to do this." The passenger then punched the flight attendant in the face, breaking her nose in the process.

- A flight attendant returning to work after a double-mastectomy and a struggle with multiple sclerosis had a run-in with a disgruntled passenger. One of the last to board the plane, the passenger became enraged when there was no room in the overhead bin above his seat. He snatched the bags from the compartment, threw them to the floor and put his own bag in the space he had created. After hearing angry cries from passengers, the flight attendant appeared from the galley to see what the fuss was all about. When the passengers explained what happened, she turned to the offending passenger. "Sir, you can't do that," she said. The passenger stood up, cocked his arm and broke her jaw with one punch.

- For some inexplicable reason, a passenger began throwing peanuts at a man across the aisle. The man was sitting with his wife, minding his own business. When the first peanut hit him in the face, he ignored it. After the second peanut struck him, he looked up to see who had thrown it. He threw a harsh glance at the perpetrator, expecting him to cease immediately. When a third peanut hit him in the eye, he'd had enough. "Do that again," he warned, "and I'll punch your lights out." But the peanut-tossing passenger couldn't

resist. He tossed a salted Planter's one last time. The victim
got out of his seat and triple-punched the peanut-tosser so
hard that witnesses heard his jaw break. The plane was
diverted to the closest airport and the peanut-tosser was
kicked off.

- During a full flight between New York and London, a
  passenger noticed that the sleeping man in the window seat
  looked a bit pale. Sensing that something was wrong yet not
  wanting to wake him, the concerned passenger alerted flight
  attendants who soon determined that the sleeping man was
  dead. Apparently, he had died a few hours earlier because his
  body was already cold. Horrified by the prospect of sitting
  next to a dead man, the passenger demanded another seat.
  But the flight was completely full; every seat was occupied.
  Finally, one flight attendant had an inspiration. She
  approached a uniformed military officer who agreed to sit
  next to the dead man for the duration of the flight.

Now that's what you call exemplary conduct. Conduct becoming an
officer, indeed.

10 The Passenger from Hell

Suddenly weak-kneed and worried, I cowered behind the front door in my apartment, wondering why a cop had buzzed the doorbell. Like the sugarplums in Clement Clark Moore's *The Night Before Christmas*, a hundred possibilities danced inside my head. Had I broken the law? Had one of my friends or family members been injured or assaulted? Had that drunken indiscretion with a Japanese exchange student come back to bite me in the butt?

Unable to come up with an answer, and a little freaked out by the possibilities, I challenged the voice that had just crackled through my intercom. Turns out he wasn't *really* a cop. He was an ex-cop—a private investigator to be exact. And he was here, at my apartment, because of an incident on the airplane.

I knew immediately what he was referring to: After landing at Dallas/Fort Worth International a couple of months beforehand, one of my passengers was taken into custody by local police officers. I remember watching as he was dragged away by a battalion of cops—fear and confusion supplanting the malice that had once glinted in his eyes. For two months I wondered what had happened to him. Now was my chance to find out.

Through the peephole I eyed a tall, gray-haired gentleman dressed in casual clothes and carrying a briefcase. When I opened the door, he flashed the practiced smile of a door-to-door salesman. I welcomed him in anyway, pointed to a chair and, without offering small talk or liquid refreshment, sat on the other side of the room and waited to hear his spiel.

"My, my, my," he said, admiring the living room furniture, "nice apartment you have here." He didn't sound like an ex-cop. He spoke in a soft, authoritative Southern lilt, like a wealthy plantation owner from nineteenth-century Georgia. His "private investigator" credentials made me think of Barnaby Jones with an upscale pedigree. "My, my, my . . ."

I could almost hear the presumptions churning in his mind: *Antique furniture. Sponged walls. Tidy apartment. And he's a flight attendant? This guy has got to be gay.* I crossed a leg and let my foot dangle, hoping to make him uncomfortable.

"Well . . . ahhh," he said, "I'll get straight to the point. I'm workin' for the lawyer who's representin' a certain Adam Ratliff. He was a passenger who had a little problem on your flight from Guatemala two months ago. You remember, don't you?"

"Yep."

"Well, being that you are the flight attendant who signed the complaint, we'd kinda like to hear your account of the events that took place that day on the airplane."

"Your client lost the plot."

"What?"

"He lost the plot. Went berserk. Lost his frigging mind."

"Oh, okay, I get it. Wait a sec," he said. Barnaby reached into his briefcase and removed a tiny recording device. "Do you mind if I get this all on tape?"

"Go right ahead," I said. The soft-spoken P.I. flicked on the recorder and placed it on the cocktail table.

"Okay. Would you mind starting at the very beginning?"

I took a deep breath, tapped into the memory banks and told him the whole sordid story . . .

About an hour after takeoff from Guatemala City, we began the dinner service—drinks, followed by the ever-present chicken or beef entrées. Halfway through the service, a loud, somewhat primordial scream ripped through the cabin.

"ARRRRGGGH . . . ARRRRGGGH!!"

It sounded as if a large, carnivorous animal had escaped from the cargo hold and was terrorizing passengers at the rear of the airplane. When I swung around, I realized I was only half right. A wild-eyed male passenger was terrorizing passengers at the rear of the airplane. His arms flailed, his head jerked spasmodically—he looked like the deranged criminal in a low-budget biker flick.

"ARRRRGGGH . . . ARRRRGGGH!!"

His screams were directed at a woman who was sitting in a window seat, across the aisle from him. The terrified woman leaned away, far away, so that her back was planted firmly against the window. It seemed, for one absurd moment, that the sheer force of his howling had blown her flat against the fuselage.

"ARRRRGGGH . . . ARRRRGGGH!!"

Walking tentatively, I approached the irate passenger. Every step was measured by the nervous eyes of sixty coach-class passengers who might have gladly bailed out if parachutes, rather than peanuts, had been provided on the flight. The problem passenger was in a row by himself, sitting in the middle seat. I stopped, stared at him and smiled. Dressed in blue jeans and a tattered blue-jean jacket, hair sweeping past his shoulders like frozen fur, he looked up at me, eyes dancing, lips pulled back in a grimace.

"Can I get you something to eat? Sir."

His eyes crawled from my shoes to the crown of my freshly shaven head, looking for a reason to launch an attack. "Nawww," he said. "But I'll have another Jack Daniel's and a beer." On his tray table there were three empty Jack Daniel's minis and a crumpled can of Budweiser.

"I don't think that's a very good idea," I said. "How about a Coke?"

He glared at me with I'm-gonna-kick-your-ass eyes, eyes that meant business, eyes that aren't mentioned in our flight attendant manual. He was going to jump me, I was sure of it. I could see the intent as it blossomed in his eyes. In the split second before he leapt, I planned a three-step defense. I'd read about it in a newspaper article on how to protect yourself against attackers: 1) step sideways as the assailant lunges; 2) grab him by the jacket; 3) use the assailant's own momentum to send him flying.

It seemed perfectly logical in theory. But two problems immediately came to mind. First, the frightened woman remained plastered against the wall where momentum was supposed to send the assailant. Second, all the passengers were watching. If I happened to hurt the guy, even after sixty witnesses watched him attack *me*, I might have problems when we landed in Dallas. Lawsuit. Suspension. Possible termination. (I know a male attendant who was suspended for punching a passenger who had viciously attacked him. The passenger sued the airline and the flight attendant. When the flight attendant spoke to the airline about help with his defense, they told him he was on his own.)

Luckily, for both of us, this guy didn't lunge. I stood my ground in the aisle, ready to do the three-step lambada. He sat on coiled haunches, poised to spring but not quite willing to make the full commitment. He gave me one final, I'm-gonna-kill-you look, then turned to the window—perhaps to study the intricacies of a passing cloud formation.

As soon as I rejoined my serving partner, the irate passenger screamed at a volume that, I would learn later, was heard all the way to the cockpit.

"YOU'RE AN ASSHOLE!"

Now everybody was scared. A few passengers seated at ground zero departed for safer seats. The screaming passenger's eyes rattled in his sockets. His face grew red. Judging by his agitated state, he seemed capable of just about anything. Herein lies the problem of potentially violent airline passengers. At thirty thousand feet you can't call a cop. Nor can you throw a guy out the door like we did on a nightly basis when I worked as a bartender at Nell's (all I had to say was, "Yo, Rico! Eighty-six this mother . . . !" The problem customer would suddenly find himself lying face up on the sidewalk, howling obscenities at an uncaring moon). But there is no beefy backup on an airplane. And most of us aren't up for the physical challenge. Why should we be? We're flight attendants, not Steven Segal wanna-bes.

I returned to the back of the plane and, using a calm, noncombatant voice, I confronted the passenger again. "Sir, please try to calm down," I said. "There's no need to get upset and there's certainly no reason to use profanity."

"GET LOST GAY BOY."

"Sir, I'm straight."

"I DON'T GIVE A DAMN. ARRRRGGGH!!"

At this point, I resorted to passenger misconduct solution #657. "If a male passenger exhibits hostile tendencies toward a male flight attendant, a female flight attendant may be able to intervene and diffuse the anger." I turned to Donna, my diminutive blond colleague. She stepped up to the plate, dug her cleats into the batter's box, and with a bravado that would make Sammy Sosa proud, she took her best shot.

"Sir, please . . ." she said, settling her warm, feminine gaze upon him. "Can you just lower your voice a bit?"

"SCREW YOU!"

He lashed her with insults, most of which are too degrading to repeat. But when Donna had finally had enough, she reached for the interphone and called the cockpit.

"Yeah," she said. Her voice was as flat and expressionless as a veteran cop calling in her third burglary of the day. "We got a problem passenger . . . Coach . . . Twenty-five-F . . . Yeah. Okay."

A few moments later, the flight engineer came lumbering out of the cockpit. He was a little on the chubby side, and as he moved down the aisle he tucked his shirt into his trousers and hitched up his pants more than once. Though flight engineers don't actually sit in a pilot seat, they are nevertheless certified to fly. Engineers are mainly responsible for the mechanical performance of the aircraft, a demanding job in itself, but they don't normally fly the plane. In three-person cockpits, therefore, flight engineers are the expendable ones. The sacrificial lamb sent into the cabin when punches are ready to fly.

As the flight engineer approached, he did not need us to point out the problem passenger. The guy was flailing and gesticulating like a madman.

"Sir, what seems to be the problem?" the engineer said.

"DON'T TALK TO ME FAT BOY."

"Sir, you're interfering with the duties of—"

"SHUT THE HELL UP!" he said, cutting off the engineer in midthreat. "YOU CAN'T TELL ME WHAT TO DO. I KNOW MY RIGHTS!"

"Okay, buddy. If you don't calm down right now we're going to have you arrested in Dallas."

With great emphasis, the passenger raised his middle finger and shook it in the engineer's face.

The engineer gave me a look, then lumbered back to the cockpit.

It was at this juncture that I noticed the woman sitting behind the problem passenger. She was clutching her chest with one hand; her other hand trembled uncontrollably.

"Excuse me, Miss." I said this in a soft voice so she wouldn't jump out of her skin. "Let me move you to another seat. I think there's room up front." She nodded her head like a shell-shocked refugee, allowing me to move her to safer territory. Along the way, she mentioned that the passenger had been reaching in his pocket periodically and sniffing something.

"He do it four, five times," she said in a sweet Guatemalan accent.

Drugs. Amyl nitrate, maybe. Perhaps it was Special K (a liquid animal tranquilizer). No wonder he was acting so weird.

I escorted the Guatemalan woman to a seat in the front section of coach. Next, I informed the lead flight attendant about the escalating problem in the back, obtained the troublemaker's name from the Passenger Information List, then went into the cockpit to relay information about possible drug use.

The captain—a supremely competent woman with whom I've flown on several occasions—twisted around in the cramped left-hand seat and listened to my report.

"That does it," she said sternly. "Well have the police meet the flight in Dallas. Just keep an eye on him. If he gets out of hand we'll . . . just keep an eye on him."

"Captain," I said. "He's already out of hand." The captain nodded. Looks were exchanged. "Just keep an eye on him."

I walked to the back of the airplane which was all but deserted, save for my colleague Donna and one Mr. Adam Ratliff—a.k.a. the problem passenger. He sat there talking to himself. Every few minutes he'd scream.

"ARRRRGGGH . . . ARRRRGGGH!!"

Less than an hour later, and without further incident, we landed in

Dallas/Fort Worth. As our plane taxied toward the gate, the captain spoke over the public address system. "Ladies and gentlemen," she said. "We apologize for the troublesome flight. Authorities will be meeting the aircraft to remove the passenger who caused the disruption."

As soon as the "fasten seat belt" sign blinked off, all the passengers stood up—including Ratliff, who immediately disappeared into the lavatory. A moment later, I heard a mechanized hum, a rush of water. Ratliff was probably dumping his drugs.

Sure enough, police officers were waiting on the jet bridge. They converged upon Ratliff as soon as he stepped through the exit door. They searched his carry-on bag. I filled out a complaint. Then they hauled him away.

Still, I had an issue with the captain. Her announcement had alerted Ratliff to the possibility of a drug search and he'd almost certainly taken advantage of the opportunity. When the captain emerged from the cockpit, I couldn't contain my bewilderment. "Excuse me captain, but why did you make that announcement?" I said. "You knew he probably had drugs. As soon as you announced that the plane was being met by cops, he went into the lavatory and dumped his stash."

The captain just looked at me. "Oh!" That was all she said. Then she walked off the aircraft with the first officer and flight engineer.

"Well," I said to the private investigator. "That's what happened."

He switched off the tape recorder and sighed. "That must have been some flight," he said. He nodded his head as if answering his own question, then gathered his belongings and rose from his seat. "Thanks for your help," he said. "You really opened my eyes to a few things."

Barnaby closed his briefcase and walked toward my front door. That's when I asked a question—a question I should have asked at the onset of my deposition. "When is his trial?"

"Excuse me?"

"His trial? When is he being prosecuted in court?"

"Trial?"

"Yeah, he's being prosecuted for his actions on the airplane, right?"

"Oh hell no," he said. "Mr. Ratliff is suing your airline. We believe he was intoxicated before boarding and should never have been allowed on that airplane. Your airline is at fault."

When the door shut behind him, I heard myself scream.

"ARRRRGGGH!!"

Incidents: Men and women

SINGAPORE, Oct. 20 (Singapore Straits Times) – Ho Ka Wei and Krist Boo – One man pulled a stewardess onto his lap and threatened to throw her off the plane if he did not get a drink. A 19-year-old woman exposed herself, made lewd comments and punched a crew member. Women as well as men were involved in the spate of air rage incidents over the last two years, which arose from arguments about no-smoking rules, seating and more commonly, booze.

In August this year, a 38-year-old American was jailed for six months and fined $1,000 for assaulting the crew and threatening to open an exit door on board a Singapore Airlines flight from Los Angeles to Tokyo.

In January, a Scot on a London-bound Continental Airlines flight from New Jersey tried to wrench open a rear door after injuring a crew member and three passengers.

That month, a Briton, en route from London to Bangkok on a British Airways jet, ripped the headphones off a passenger, bit it into half and tried to break a window, but broke only the inner plastic protective pane.

Air rage also strikes the rich and famous. In March 1998, British pop group Oasis made lewd remarks, ignored the smoking ban and threatened the pilot on a Cathay Pacific flight from Hong Kong to Australia. Cathay Pacific has banned the group from its flights.

In 1997, an enraged Cambodian tycoon shot out the tyre of a Royal Air carrier on arriving in Phnom Penh from Hong Kong, after learning his luggage had been misplaced.

In August, a Pakistani minister and his friends harassed female passengers on a flight home from London before falling into a drunken stupor upon arrival at the airport.

Last December, a 34-year-old Finn who got drunk and assaulted the crew on a Hungarian Malev Airline flight died after he was given a tranquilliser on board by a doctor to calm him down.

Reprinted with permission of Singapore Press Holdings Limited, Singapore, 1999.

Air hostess stages own take-off after losing bet

LONDON, May 4 (Reuters) – British Airways said on Wednesday it was investigating reports that a stewardess staged her own take-off by stripping to parade half-naked at an Italian airport after losing a bet.

Newspapers said the stewardess had bet the pilot on a flight from London to Genoa that she would strip down to her underwear if the plane landed early in Italy.

When the plane landed before schedule, the stewardess waited until most of the passengers had disembarked and then kept her side of the bet, the newspapers said.

The Daily Telegraph quoted staff at Genoa airport as saying passengers and baggage handlers were amazed to see the stewardess walking down the aircraft steps dressed only in panties, shoes, a loose-hanging safety waistcoat and a pilot's hat.

"She then allegedly ran round the plane before skipping back up the stairway," the Telegraph said.

It quoted a spokesman for the airport as saying: "I did not see it. But there were a lot of baggage handlers and customs people here who did, and they are still talking about it . . . I wish I had seen it."

A British Airways spokeswoman told Reuters: "We are looking closely at reports of some alleged pranks involving crew during the turnaround in one of our flights in Italy."

11 Fly Boys and Girls

Somehow, I found myself trapped in a bar at the Mexico City airport, dressed in jeans and a T-shirt, pouring a Corona from bottle to glass, while arguing about gun control with three good ole boy pilots.

Forty-five minutes earlier, our seven-member crew had stepped off the aircraft behind a long procession of passengers. Like a converging river, we spilled into the concourse, joining the flow of travelers who collided like flotsam from half a dozen ships and drifted downstream in buoyant clusters.

Outside the customs checkpoint a huge welcoming crowd had amassed. Passengers reclaimed their bags from the prying hands of officials and leapt into the arms of waiting loved ones. A few weaved through the thickening crowd, sprinting off toward connecting flights to Acapulco or Mazatlán. Others piled into taxis or buses, to be whisked away to hotels and resorts.

My crew didn't leave the premises that night, however. Our schedule required that we check into the airport hotel—a wonderful place to stay if you're a regular guest, a dark isolated experience if you happen to be airline crew.

As always, we bypassed the elevators at the bottom of a nine-story atrium, where twenty-foot tangles of philodendron hung from each balcony, suggesting, but not quite creating the desired effect of a verdant mountain terrace. This is where the real guests stayed. The peasant quarters were a couple of minutes away.

One after another we turned right, walked down a ramp, tramped like nomads across a sterile lounge area that led to an older section of the hotel. There, we took a tiny elevator to our designated floor. When the elevator doors opened, we were greeted by a damp, mossy smell—a familiar odor that has lived in these dim hallways for as long as I can remember. Thankfully, the smell does not invade the guest rooms, which have problems of a different sort. The small size and isolated location make me feel as if I'm sleeping in a coffin.

Wanting to spend as little time as possible in these hermetically sealed body pods, most of the crew—the pilots, myself, and two of three flight attendants—agreed to meet for a nightcap in the atrium bar.

Whenever pilots join the table, the conversation turns to topics that flight attendants aren't necessarily thrilled to discuss. The talk is of airplanes, retirement, military transport, boating, golf, the Republican party, and depending on the amount of beer consumed, we might be treated to a tale or two about the ex-wife who left for no apparent reason. When issues creep into the conversation—education, poverty, abortion, race—the battle lines are drawn. The pilots are always right, the flight attendants always wrong.

A few days prior to the trip, President Clinton's bill banning the sale of nineteen assault weapons had been overwhelmingly approved by the House of Representatives. The "crime bill" was now subject to approval by the Senate. Amazingly enough, the three pilots from my crew—ex-military yahoos from some rural outpost in southern North Carolina, backwoods Goobers who might be living on rations and practicing militia camp maneuvers had they not been busy flying jets—were not happy about Big Bill's bill. The weren't happy one bit.

The captain leaned across the table, jaw set, lips quivering, hard eyes bearing down on me like bowling balls heading for the gutter. "The government has no right to prevent the legal sale of those firearms," he said. "No right!" He pounded his fist against the table to emphasize his point. He took a gulp from his glass, looked first to the flight engineer who slumped in the seat to his left, then he looked to his right, where the first officer sat rigid as a sentry on red alert. All three nodded simultaneously.

As is the case with military flights, the captain of a commercial

aircraft has complete authority over its passengers and crew. His influence, even his personality, can carry over once the crew leaves the
airplane. If the captain is a pleasant, thoughtful, easygoing individual—
and there are legions within the airline industry—the first officer and
flight engineer will tend to show their best side. If the captain is an
overbearing asshole—and there are legions within the airline industry—the first officer and flight engineer can end up stressed out and
intimidated. If the captain happens to be an Uzi-toting fundamentalist
redneck—and there are probably more out there than you'd care to
know—idealistic flight attendants can end up like me, floundering at
the wrong end of an argument.

"But captain," I pleaded. "Why do Americans need the right to bear
Uzis?" I paused to let the question marinate in the juice of logic and reason. "I won't argue with your right to own a pistol or a shotgun, but why
does anyone need a weapon that fires one hundred rounds a minute?"

"The right to bear arms is an inalienable right granted by the Constitution," he replied.

"The Constitution does not grant the right to bear assault weapons
that can wipe out whole neighborhoods."

The captain fell back in his seat. Perhaps the weight of my argument
had stifled him. More likely he was catching his breath.

"Look," said the first officer, jumping into the ring like the second
half of a wrestling tag team. "The bottom line is this: Criminals are
gonna get their hands on assault weapons regardless as to whether
they're legal or not."

"Does that mean it should be legal for noncriminals to buy an assault
weapon?" I said. "Don't you guys read the papers? Noncriminals are
the ones committing the majority of random shootings."

The captain looked to the first officer. They shook their heads in
unison, as if my sensibilities were warped instead of theirs.

"What's wrong, Captain?" I said, mockingly. "Do you need an AK-47 to
hunt deer?"

It was intended as a joke. An attempt to breathe levity into a conversation gone sour. But the captain had no sense of humor—at least
not on the topic of firearms. He locked his gaze on me and for the

first time I felt real hostility. The five remaining strands of hair, which had been neatly raked across his skull at the onset of our debate, were now sticking up haphazardly like strands of dying wheat. There was movement in his body—a barely perceptible trembling that escalated and then abruptly stopped.

At this juncture it might be interesting to note that my two female colleagues were not present. They left without bothering to finish their drinks. Having participated in the introductory stages of this conversation, they were smart enough to retreat before things got out of hand. "You're wasting your time trying to argue with them," one of them whispered before saying good-bye. "You're banging your head against a brick wall . . . pilots *always* think they're right."

Maybe. I *was* banging my head against a wall. But this wall had weaknesses. Big gaping holes in fact. I felt it was my duty to point this out to the pilots, to shine a spotlight on their warped beliefs. And now, I was angry. The first officer and flight engineer were angry. The captain was about to loose control. Had we been in Billy Ray's Horned Toad Lounge in some backwoods borough, instead of at an airport bar in Mexico City, things may have gotten ugly.

As it turned out, things got ugly anyway.

The captain cleared his throat, dispensing renegade politics in a harsh bucolic voice that sliced through every neuron in my brain. "Americans warrant the right to purchase assault weapons . . ." he took a deep breath, looking straight into my eyes, ". . . because we need to protect ourselves in case the government declares martial law."

The silence that followed was palpable. It hung between us like a solid thing—huge, fat, pregnant with absurdity.

I stared at the captain.

The captain stared at me.

The first officer and flight engineer shifted in their seats.

"What?" I said, finally. "You can't be serious, Captain. Tell me you're not serious."

"Of course I'm serious, goddammit." The truth of his conviction glittered between the slits of his eyes. "You think it can't happen?"

I felt my own eyeballs go loose in their sockets.

"Okay, okay, okay," I said, thrusting both hands outward, hoping to gain a better perspective on this hypothetical siege. "Say it does happen, Captain. Say the United States government declares martial law upon the land. When tanks come rolling toward your farm in North Carolina—and believe me, your place will probably be one of the first stops on the list—do you really think assault weapons are going to protect you?"

"It'll give 'em something to think about before they come knocking on my door."

"So this is it?" I said, throwing up both hands in defeat. "This is why the American public needs an assault weapon?"

My three fellow crew members—comrades, coworkers, members of the same airline family—looked at me defiantly, nodding their heads in antigovernment accord.

"You guys are living on another planet." I said this under my breath, so as not to spark further confrontation.

I drained my glass, shook my head and left the bar.

That night I lay in my airport-hotel coffin, dreaming of wild-eyed hillbilly pilots—their jaws set, fingers twitching, an arsenal of assault weapons pointed at me.

Simply put, pilots are the backbone of the airline industry. Strip away air traffic controllers, dispatch operators, gate agents, baggage handlers, flight attendants, employees from other flight-related departments— take away all these employees and passengers could theoretically board a flight and end up at the proper destination. Luggage will never arrive. The threat of a midair collision will increase exponentially. Fistfights will break out over who gets to sit in a first-class seat. There will be no one to yell at when the coffee is cold, or the food is lousy (vending machines don't give a damn), or when the disembodied voice from the P.A. system says, "Due to thunderstorms in the area, we're diverting to Topeka."

Take away the pilots, however, and the airline industry grinds to a halt.

Like surgeons and criminal defense attorneys, airline pilots are highly trained, relentlessly monitored and well paid for their efforts. They guide multimillion-dollar jets through turbulent weather and can land on an emergency strip no wider than a suburban driveway. Without question, they are the most important individuals on every flight. Though most do not entertain the assault weapon fantasies of Jethro, Clyde and Bubba, pilots, by nature of the job, live in a world of their own.

Think about it. Year after year they operate sophisticated controls while sitting in the cockpit—a cramped, claustrophobic chamber that resembles the inside of a computerized egg. Other than periodic visits from flight attendants who deliver coffee, food and much-needed conversation, they have almost no face-to-face contact with humans other than themselves. The bulk of communication occurs via radio transmissions to company dispatch or air traffic control. Instead of actually speaking with passengers, most conversations are one-way information updates dispensed over the intercom: *We'll be taking off to the north, looping around to the south, turning west and ahhh . . . climbing to an altitude of twenty-eight thousand feet. Those on the left side of the airplane can see the town of Little Rock. Feel free to walk around the cabin. Return to your seat. Fasten your seat belt. Sorry for the bumpy ride. We've started our descent. We'll be touching down in Jacksonville in approximately ahhhhh . . . twenty minutes.*

While hard at work, pilots rarely get feedback from passengers; there's simply no opportunity for normal social discourse. After all, pilots are responsible for the safety of everyone aboard the aircraft. They can't afford the distraction of idle chitchat. Dedicated, fearless, brimming with confidence that can foster self-aggrandized comparisons to God, pilots run the show.

Flight attendants, on the other hand, spend an entire career running up and down an aisle in a crowded cabin. Day in and day out, for better or for worse, we work with people. Our job is to communicate with them. Though we don't always live up to standards, though some of us are occasionally cranky or curt, we are, for the most part, friendly, personable and compassionate—traits that have absolutely no bearing on a pilot's ability to perform his or her job.

Because of the innate differences in our jobs and personalities, flight attendants and pilots look at life from different perspectives.

Take money, for example. Despite lofty salaries and retirement packages that allow some pilots to fly into the sunset with up to a million dollars tucked beneath their graying wings, there's a large contingent known for being . . . well, cheap. Sure, there are still a few old-school captains who are quick to buy a round of drinks or spring for an occasional crew dinner. These men and women are to be commended, even revered. But like an old DC-10 aircraft ready to retire after many good years of service, old-school pilots are fading into extinction.

Latter-day pilots are a different breed. Like the new Boeing 777s they operate, the emphasis is on economic efficiency. Ask any flight attendant. Even those who are married to pilots. *Especially* those who are married to pilots. Perhaps it's the strict military background that makes many of them so tight with their cash. Perhaps pressures of the job put a deadbolt on their wallets. Or maybe it's the financial fallout from writing all those alimony checks. Whatever the reason, I've noticed that money issues regularly crop up when pilots go out during layovers.

Case in point: During a layover in Barbados, the entire crew—three pilots and six or seven flight attendants—decided to go out to a nightclub. We met for a drink in the hotel lobby, then set off for a well-known hot spot. At the door, the bouncer told us that airline crew are admitted free of charge, as long as we provided proper identification. Otherwise, the cover would be $5. Only two of us were without airline ID—myself and the first officer. Eager to party, I reached in my wallet and produced a $5 bill. The first officer refused to pay, however. He argued with the bouncer, saying that it was obvious he was a pilot, that he shouldn't have to pay. I paid my $5, followed three flight attendants who flashed their IDs and went to the bar for a drink. When we turned around, the first officer was still arguing. The captain and flight engineer grabbed him by the arm and the trio returned to the hotel.

One afternoon, while on a layover in Santo Domingo, Dominican Republic, I happened upon a small, but elegant restaurant a few blocks from the hotel. Wedged between two slouching buildings, the tiny café sat behind a small parking lot. I walked inside, took a look at the menu and told the manager, in broken Spanish, I'd be back with my crew later that night. We had already agreed to dine together, our crew of four flight attendants, that is. The pilots we'd flown in with had been scheduled to fly elsewhere. A different cockpit crew would arrive later that afternoon. They would fly us home the following morning.

When I returned to the hotel, I telephoned each flight attendant. Everybody agreed to meet in the lobby at 8:00 P.M. At the appointed hour, I stepped out of the elevator and spotted them immediately. But three men were hovering around them. Pilots. I could tell by the way they were dressed: crisp Bermuda shorts, polo shirts, penny loafers, socks. The purser glanced at me, shrugged her shoulders and grinned. (Later she told me that the captain had knocked on her door, and invited himself to dinner. She couldn't say no.)

We exchanged introductions and walked the three blocks to the restaurant.

When flight attendants get together for dinner during a layover, more often than not we bring an atmosphere of leisure. We talk candidly about ourselves and our loved ones. We gossip, laugh easily, and allow ourselves to be swept away by music or scenery or whatever entertainment lay before us. But when certain pilots join the table there is often (not always, but often) a subtle change in atmosphere. The brisk air of authority blows in: a rigidity that sets conversational boundaries, a method of interaction driven by either cockiness or restraint—unless, of course, enough drinks are involved.

After being seated, the waiter came to take our orders. I asked for separate checks. Had it been only the four flight attendants as originally planned, I would not have insisted upon this. The pilots threw sidelong glances but I really didn't care. Neither did the flight attendants. We'd all been burned at the dinner table during one layover or another. Someone would order a $6.50 appetizer, a $14.95 main course, two glasses of wine, dessert and cappuccino. Someone else might order a burger and a Coke, yet somehow the decision is made to divide the check evenly among seven or eight diners. If we decide to split the bill fairly, according to what each has ordered, an entirely different scenario unfolds. Each person (supposedly) calculates the price of his or her meal, plus tax and tip. On many occasions, however, I've turned in the appropriate amount of pounds, pesos or bolivars, only to sit back to watch as someone forgets to add tax and tip to their portion of the bill. Not surprisingly, there's not enough money on the table. My tax and tip have been mysteriously absorbed. Everyone stares at everyone else, fuming, until someone begrudgingly adds a few dollars to the bill. It's a frustrating experience that has taught me to dine in small groups. Which was exactly what we had planned to do before the pilots showed up.

Much of the evening was dominated by two topics: old DC-8 aircraft and the rising cost of diesel fuel for the captain's boat. Whenever the conversation threatened to shift toward a subject of interest to flight attendants, the pilots managed to redirect the flow, their voices growing louder with each glass of wine. At some point, they grew tired of their own rhetoric. "So, how long have you been flying with the company?" the captain asked one of the ladies. "How do you like flying? Have you always been based in New York? Are you married? Do you commute to base?"

I felt like we were eating at a flight attendant interview.

Once the interrogation was complete, the waiter put separate checks in front of us. Seven piles of money materialized on the table. Seven chairs pushed back. We stood up, and one by one walked out the door. I lingered to thank the waiter who had been very pleasant and accommodating. But when he approached there was tension in his face.

"There is problem," he said in broken English. "There is not money enough."

He produced a bill and the money that accompanied it. Sure enough, it was several pesos short. I looked at what had been ordered: steak, salad, wine, coffee, chocolate cake. The captain. This was the captain's bill.

Shaking my head in bewilderment, I walked out to the street where the crew was waiting. Hoping to make this as embarrassing as possible, I walked up to the culprit, and in a loud voice said, "Captain, you didn't leave enough money for your bill."

He looked at me, shock registering on his hound-dog face. The one person who could most afford to pay for a meal at any restaurant, a twenty-year captain who earned more than $100,000 a year, gave a lame excuse.

"Oh, I must have made a mistake on the cash conversion," he said.

The flight attendants looked at each other, knowing full well that airline pilots possess an uncanny aptitude for mathematics. Lift, drag, thrust—the rudiments of airplane physics are based on the conversion of numbers. Pilots can convert U.S. dollars into Dominican pesos in the snap of a finger or the blink of an eye. Not only did our fearless leader attempt to deprive a poor Dominican waiter of a much-deserved tip, he tried to pull a fast one on the restaurant.

He stood in the parking lot, the yolk of a thousand eggs dripping from his face. We walked away, leaving him to wallow in shame.

During another trip, an Airbus captain bragged about how much money he saved every year by collecting toiletries from layover hotels. We were in the crew bus, on the way to the layover hotel in Philadelphia when he decided to let us in on his secret.

"Damn right!" he proclaimed, when one of the flight attendants asked if he snatched the toilet paper from his hotel rooms. "I even take the backup roll." He went on to say that by confiscating hundreds of bottles of shampoo, conditioner, body lotion—and an international collection of tiny soaps—his family saves approximately $1,200 a year.

Every now and then, when a silver-haired fly boy steps out of the cockpit, hitches up his pants and prepares to mix with us, a measure of humor comes right along with him.

During a cross-country all-nighter, a particular DC-10 captain (we'll call him Capt. Spaz) stepped out of the cockpit to relieve himself in the first-class lavatory. But when he opened the door and stepped inside, a woman let loose a scream that woke the dead and nearly killed a few passengers. Apparently, the lavatory light was inoperative. Sitting on the toilet, in the dark, with her pants around her ankles, the woman had evidently forgotten to lock the lavatory door.

Capt. Spaz—startled by a succession of screams that brought flight attendants scurrying from their posts—immediately backed out of the lavatory. At least he tried to. In the process of stepping in, he had somehow managed to hook his foot through one leg hole of the poor woman's panties.

While backing away from the lavatory, Capt. Spaz inadvertently yanked the woman's legs forward. She screamed again. He tried wiggling his foot out of her panties. She screamed once more. He pulled harder. She screamed louder. He fell on the floor, in full view of the first-class passengers, jiggling his foot like a . . . like a man with his foot caught in the leg hole of a strange woman's panties. By the time he extricated himself, by the time her panties had snapped back into place and the door had been mercifully shut and locked, Capt. Spaz had lost most of his self-esteem and one of his uniform shoes. He retreated into the cockpit and was incommunicado for the entire layover.

In the middle of the night, during a South American layover, another captain (we'll call him Capt. Sleepy) woke in his hotel room. Buck naked and barely awake, he opened the door and stumbled into what he thought was the bathroom. "It was really bright in there," he said to me while recounting the story. "Deep down inside I knew I hadn't turned on the bathroom light yet. But I guess I was too sleepy for that to register."

When the door shut behind Capt. Sleepy, he opened his tired eyes. There was no commode, no shower or sink. But there was another door directly in front of him. The door had numbers on it. He looked down and noticed the carpet below his feet. He looked left, then right, half-seeing the row of lights that stretched out in either direction. Then it hit him. He was standing in a brightly lit corridor. In other words, he was standing stark naked in the brightly lit corridor of the twenty-first floor of a four-star hotel. The door had closed and locked behind him.

Suddenly wide awake, Capt. Sleepy ran to the stairway, descended twenty-one flights, poked his head through the lobby door and begged the traumatized night clerk for a spare key and a robe.

Early one morning in Madrid, as a 767 crew left the layover hotel and boarded the crew bus for the airport, an angry woman approached. From what the purser told me, the woman was pissed off at the captain (we'll call him Capt. Horny). She confronted the hotel doorman and demanded an audience with Capt. Horny.

After calming her down, the doorman climbed into the bus and relayed a message to the purser. The purser threw a look at the captain. "The doorman says you need to clear up a room charge with the front desk," he said. Unable to appreciate the purser's diplomacy, Capt. Horny claimed he had no outstanding charges. "You need to pay your bill," the purser insisted, jamming his thumb toward the woman. The pilot refused once more. Frustrated, the purser said in a loud voice, "The prostitute you spent the night with says you didn't pay her."

The two copilots, all the flight attendants, even the bus driver, turned to look at the captain. A sheepish grin spread across his face. Capt. Horny climbed off the bus, smiled nervously at the woman and coughed up the required pesetas.

12 The Flight Attendant from Hell

Pilots have been known to tremble when she comes plodding onto the airplane with a chip on her shoulder and a snarl on her face. Fellow flight attendants cringe when she commandeers the first-class galley, casting an evil eye on those who dare invade her "private" work space. They say she's been chastised by airline management for a list of infractions longer than any single attendant could incur in a lifetime: cussing out first-class passengers, refusing to serve hungry pilots, making unauthorized P.A. announcements that urge the disgruntled to grab their belongings and kindly step outside. She's a frequent-flyer's worst nightmare. The poster girl for curtness and disdain.

She came to be known as Bertha, but we call her "Big" Bertha—not simply because her ass is as wide as the tail section of a jumbo jet (thirty years of feasting on airplane lasagna can wreak havoc on a flight attendant's posterior), not simply because her voice clacks throughout the cabin as if amplified through a megaphone. We call her Big Bertha because she's crass, mean, larger than life—truly the flight attendant from hell.

Like Big Foot and the Loch Ness monster, Big Bertha was thought to exist in the realm of legend and imagination. In more than a decade of flying, I had never actually seen her. But rumors of her existence were widespread, instilling fear in those who had yet to fly with her, inspiring woeful tales from those who had.

During one unforgettable flight, Big Bertha allegedly stormed into the cockpit when the captain demanded to be fed *before* the first-class passengers. Angered by his insolence, she raised her dress, peeled the super-queen pantyhose from her sumo wrestler hips, pointed to a private place which hadn't seen action since the days before airline deregulation, and said: "Dinner is served, Captain! But hurry up, I ain't got all day."

Needless to say, the captain lost his appetite. Some say the poor guy never ate another airplane meal.

Another Big Bertha classic was said to have occurred on a flight to the Caribbean. According to the story, a West Indian dignitary had been complaining about shoddy service. He settled into his first-class seat, demanding champagne and attention. Without giving cabin crew adequate time to respond, he pressed the flight attendant call button. Within seconds he pressed it again. Big Bertha approached him with her arms folded.

Realizing she had brought neither champagne nor an appropriate measure of humility, the V.I.P. passenger went ballistic. "Where is my champagne?" he shouted. "Do you know who I am? Do you know who I am?"

Bertha abruptly turned her back on the inconsolable V.I.P. She strolled into the galley, cleared her throat, picked up the microphone, and in the cool mellifluous parlance of a radio talk-show host, she made an announcement that forever echoes through the corridors of the P.A. hall of fame (many have made this snide remark, but none have said it better).

"Ladies and gentlemen," she said. "May I have your attention. May I have your attention please."

The cabin grew quiet. Three pilots, four flight attendants and more than 130 passengers bent their ears and waited.

"We have a passenger in first class who does not know who he is," she said. "If anyone knows who he is, if anyone has a clue to his identity, would you please come up and let us know immediately."

The airplane erupted in laughter. Not surprisingly, the dignitary found no humor in this personal attack. He had been mocked, raked over the coals of rudeness and embarrassment. When Big Bertha finally delivered a glass of champagne, he gave her a look that could have melted a glacier, and she gave him a look that could have frozen the melt.

Although the dignitary remained silent for the duration of the flight, he complained to agents upon arrival and wrote a scathing letter to company officials. Big Bertha was summoned to the office and unceremoniously suspended—one of many suspensions in a career that seemed defined by a desire to antagonize.

As the years went by, Big Bertha's legend grew to new heights of absurdity. Someone claimed she lived with twenty-six cats in a crumbling ranch house in New England. Someone else said she had been arrested by Swiss police for causing a disturbance in a chocolate shop. Others said she belonged to a cult, slapped an offensive pilot and strapped cans of Purina to her roll-aboard luggage so she could feed stray cats during overseas layovers.

During one of a long line of memorable Big Bertha flights, a passenger rang his call button to complain about the chicken entrée. "This chicken is bad," he told Bertha, in a tone as nasty as the meal he refused to eat. She snatched the gnarl of poultry from his meal tray, raised it high in the air, then smacked the chicken with her open hand. "Bad chicken, bad!" she shouted. She then dropped the bird on his tray, stomped her hooves like a rhino and disappeared into the galley.

If these stories were true, Big Bertha was not someone to screw around with. I considered myself lucky to have avoided her all these years.

But as luck would have it, it seemed that my time to confront her had come.

An hour before departure, I burst through the flight operations door and rushed toward a kiosk of some twenty company computers. Each was occupied by a flight attendant who was signing in for a trip. When a terminal finally opened up, I moved into the slot and hurriedly punched in my password.

After reading twenty pages of e-mail that told of an increase in beer provisioning on flights to Japan, the introduction of an Egg McMuffin-like sandwich for breakfast service on flights from South America, new milk containers on domestic flights, Styrofoam cup shortages and a system-wide crackdown on flight attendants suspected of stealing liquor money, I entered a code that called up the names of my crew.

I tore the sheet from the dot matrix printer and began to read the sequence printout. Rick, Jake and Bob would be our pilots. I wondered why so many pilots take on monosyllabic names: Chuck, Ron, Rich, Dan, Dick, Don, Skip, Pat, Bud . . . the list is as long as a layover in Odessa, Texas. Walk behind a trio of pilots, call out one of the afore-mentioned names, and the chances are pretty good that at least one of them will turn around and say, "Huh?"

Following the pilots were names of the cabin crew: Daniel, Saman-tha, myself, Bertha. Bertha? Big Bertha? No, it couldn't be. The word was she never flew three-day trips on narrow-body aircraft. Not enough room in the galleys. No place to hide from the passengers. No, it couldn't be Big Bertha. But after reading the name again, I noticed the adjacent seniority number. Whoever it was had been flying for a very long time.

I broke out in a cold sweat.

Most flight attendants—young or old, black or white, male or fe-male, straight or gay—are good-natured people. We have to be. The job demands it. But every so often, a malcontent creeps into the ranks. It's difficult enough to deal with the demands of passengers, but when you're working a three-day trip and a member of the crew creates problems, the job becomes twice as difficult, the days last twice as long.

As I tramped toward the departure gate, the prospect of clashing with Bertha weighed heavy on my mind. Could this be the Big Bertha I had heard so much about? Would her uniform be matted with cat hair? Would her breath smell like trout gone bad in the refrigerator? I fought the urge to call in sick, to hop into my Civic and drive home.

I approached the gate, waved absently to the agent, walked through the sliding door and stepped onto the jet bridge. Like the majority of flight attendants, I've had occasional altercations with other crew mem-bers, but the bad memories are foggy. Still, as I moved closer to the aircraft door, a slew of images came at me in Technicolor clarity: the lazy galley guy we caught reading *Cosmopolitan* when he should have been serving drinks; the smoke-a-holic who crawled into an empty meal cart to puff on a Marlboro every thirty minutes; the sky princess who slept in a row of seats during every leg of a three-day trip; the kleptomaniac who stole from the duty-free cart, casting suspicion on the entire crew; the neurotic who sprayed insecticide in the pilot's sleeping bunk because they denied her request to cop a few z's; the tight-wad who refused to give passengers an entire can of soda, even though the galley was overstocked with Coke; the hypochondriac who caused a health scare when she insisted upon wearing surgical gloves during the meal service. And then there was Patrick, the pint-size purser who barked orders like a Yorkshire terrier.

The few times I've been forced to work with difficult souls such as these, words were exchanged, sides taken, feelings hurt.

And now it seemed I was about to meet up with Big Bertha, the most difficult flight attendant in the skies.

Daniel and Samantha were lounging in first class when I walked onto the airplane. We exchanged introductions and the typical pre-departure small talk. How long have you been based here? Are you flying this trip for the remainder of the month? Do you live in town, or do you commute to another city? Do you know if the flight is full?

Suddenly, Samantha leaned forward and whispered, "I hope you guys know Big Bertha is working this trip." Daniel's eyes grew to the size of silver dollars. Apparently, he hadn't checked the crew list.

"Have you flown with her?" I said to Samantha. "Does she really exist?"

"Yeah," she claimed. "*Believe* me."

"What happened?" asked Daniel.

Then from our seats, we heard the thud of heavy feet. It was Bertha. We scattered like thieves.

I rushed to the back of the plane, while Daniel disappeared into the forward galley. Samantha just froze. She was alone to face the legendary beast.

I peeked out of the galley to watch the confrontation. To my surprise, Bertha actually shook hands with Samantha. Daniel popped out of the forward galley and Bertha shook hands with him as well. They stood in the aisle chatting for a moment, but I was too far away to hear anything.

Bertha then walked to the back of the plane and extended her hand.

This Bertha was a large woman, but not nearly the Jabba the Hut that Big Bertha had been made out to be. "I'm Bertha," she said. "Would you like me to help you set up the liquor cart?"

Her smile opened like a desert flower. Corpulent cheeks bore the rosy tint of a department store Santa Claus. Her brunette bob swayed as she tilted her head, waiting for me to answer.

"No, that's okay," I said. "But thanks anyway."

"You sure, sweetheart?" she said. "There's always too much work for the galley flight attendant. I'm happy to lend a hand."

I was magically transported to Sunday mornings in my mother's kitchen, where goodness oozed like the warmed Alaga syrup she poured on homemade pancakes. This Bertha wasn't the flight attendant from hell, she was kind-hearted, considerate, the flight attendant from heaven.

"Ahhh . . . well, maybe I could use some tea and Equal from first class," I said.

"Be right back," she said.

Maybe the horror stories were all lies—flight attendant folklore aimed to break up the boredom of a trans-Atlantic trip. Bertha was no monster. No airborne Antichrist. This was a woman of good intentions, a sweetheart by all rights.

By the time our plane reached cruising altitude, Bertha and I were best buddies. Having been squished together (literally) on the aft jump seat, I learned that she owned one dog, not twenty-six cats. She lived on the West Coast, not the East, and that she was definitely not the type who would pull down her pantyhose to freak out hungry pilots.

Moments later, in an action that proved her dedication to the job, Bertha almost leapt out of her jump seat when a passenger rang his call button.

But a moment after that, I poked my head out the galley to find Bertha locked in a heated debate. Judging by the way she jabbed her finger at the passenger's face, Bertha had fallen off the happy wagon. When she finished giving a piece of her mind, she straightened her skirt and stomped down the aisle which suddenly seemed too narrow to accommodate her swinging hips. Bertha turned into the galley where I had retreated. She hunkered over me, allowing no means of escape. Gone was the sweet woman who reminded me of Momma. Like Bruce

Banner after a precipitous rise in blood pressure, Bertha had meta-morphosed into the Incredible Hulk.

Maybe there was something to the legend of Big Bertha after all. Maybe Loch Ness and Big Foot do exist. Bertha looked down at me, her face twisting into a scowl that vaulted her eyebrows as she spoke.

"Asshole passengers bring out the worst in me."

13 Tests, Drugs and Swollen Bladders

Like a worn inner tube filled with too much compressed air, my bladder felt as if it were about to burst. I was the Hoover Dam after an apocalyptic rain, the A-bomb descending upon Hiroshima. Still, I held the explosion in check as our inbound aircraft eased toward the arrival gate and a jet bridge rolled forward to greet us.

A passenger in this state of urinary trepidation would have already sprinted to the lavatory. He would have ignored pleas from flight attendants asking that he remain seated until the airplane came to a complete stop and the seat belt sign flicked off. FAA rules be damned, he'd burst into the lavatory to answer Mother Nature's urgent call. But I wasn't a passenger, of course. I was on the job, sitting in a flight attendant jump seat—lips pursed, thighs crossed, trying to stem a mounting urge to purge. And though I longed for the friendly confines of an airplane lavatory—to hear the rush of digested Coca-Cola ricocheting off the metal splash plate, the reassuring whoosh of a mechanized flush, and the sigh of my own blessed relief—I refused to evacuate the contents of my bladder until the threat of a drug test had abated.

Flight attendants are subject to random drug tests at the completion of every trip sequence. Mandated by the Department of Transportation and implemented by every U.S. airline, such tests are designed to protect the flying public from druggie cabin crew members who, under the influence of narcotics, might mistakenly deliver a chicken entrée when the passenger asked for beef. That's fair enough. But when an arriving crew member is asked to provide a urine sample and the well happens to have run dry, the employee is forced to sit in an airport medical facility—ingesting liquids, dreaming about mountain streams and waterfalls—until the well is replenished and an appropriate amount of urine can be extracted for analysis.

As the passengers filed through the aircraft door on this particular day, I listened for, but did not hear the "flight attendants all clear" P.A. This unauthorized announcement is occasionally delivered by a benevolent purser. Once the airplane door has opened and the purser realizes that the pee collector is not waiting to nab a crew member, the "all clear" announcement is made—hardly raising the eyebrows of deplaning passengers.

Immediately after hearing this signal, flight attendants disappear into lavatories like audience volunteers in a magic act. But this time, there was no such announcement. As I crept toward the exit door, bladder on fire, my Travelpro crew bag jouncing behind me like an obedient pet, I noticed a grim-faced supervisor with a clipboard in hand. She stood on the lip of the jet bridge, trading whispers with the purser.

As I wheeled around the corner they both turned to look at me.

"Sorry," said the purser, wearing a look that said *I'm glad it's you and not me.* "It's your turn for a drug test."

I followed the supervisor down the jet bridge, up an escalator, into a concourse, along a moving walkway, through the immigration check point, down an escalator, past a gauntlet of customs officials, through a set of automatic doors, up another escalator, into another concourse, through an unmarked door, down one of those dingy airport corridors that passengers never see, and then stepped into the company medical facility. There, greeted by the unsmiling face of a health care professional, I was given a plastic cup and told to get down to business.

In the bored stentorian voice of a prison guard addressing a new inmate, the health care professional (we'll call her Nurse Nancy) told me that a proper level of urine was necessary in order to achieve adequate test results. If I failed to fill the cup to a mark approximately two-thirds up, the sample would be negated and I would be banished to a chair, watched like a pedophile in a grade-school playground, and told to drink, drink, drink until my bladder swelled and a more appropriate level of urine could be extracted. (I've heard horror stories about employees forced to wait for hours because their internal plumbing failed to produce.)

Providing an adequate sample was not going to be a problem for me. Hell, I almost peed in my uniform pants while trekking from the airplane to the medical facility. In my condition, I could have filled three or four plastic cups and then watered the office plants for good measure. Just give me the goddamn plastic cup, I thought to myself, and tell me where to deliver the flood.

The bathroom was not a functional one; it was a sanitized, pee-in-the-cup-only type of bathroom. The tiny cell was lit by a bright fluorescent light that bounced off the white walls like sunlight off mirrors. There was no running water in the sink. The toilet bowl held a small portion of blue liquid—a deterrent for unscrupulous employees who attempt to dilute their urine with water. (Mixed with the right amount of H_2O, a urine sample can be rendered useless. Cocaine, marijuana, Ecstasy—and a long list of drugs we might have been tempted to ingest before putting on our uniform—can be easily masked.) In one of those paranoid moments that we are prepared for by too many *X-Files* episodes and not enough common sense, I felt like I was being watched. I unzipped my pants anyway, heckled by the ghosts of those who'd aimed and missed before me.

Once the cup was filled, I fought the urge to yell for Nurse Nancy. *Quick, I need six or seven more containers.* The joke would have fallen upon humorless ears; Nurse Nancy was a no-nonsense kind of gal. Instead, I snapped the plastic lid onto the plastic container and carried it from the bathroom in one outstretched hand as if it were a vial of nitroglycerine. Nurse Nancy threw a disdainful look. She double-sealed the container, placed it inside one half of a Styrofoam mold, covered that half with the other half, wrapped both halves together using a mummylike application of "caution" tape, put the taped mold in a box, and put the box in a file cabinet filled with other samples that would be picked up by a Federal Express courier later that night.

The following day, a different Fed Ex courier would deliver dozens of Styrofoam containers (a collection of samples from airline crew bases across the country) to a secret pee pee processing lab somewhere in

Montana or South Dakota or some equally underpopulated state where a toxic urine spill would cause the least number of wrinkled noses. Once inside the lab, gallons of liquid would be analyzed and reanalyzed, the medical technicians testing each sample as if they were forensic pathologists at the onset of a murder trial. My stuff tested negative, thank God. But many days later, one of my colleagues wasn't so lucky.

With a level of efficiency almost unheard of when addressing customer complaints or employee labor issues, the airline's antidrug machinery sprang into action. A base manager was informed of tainted piss. The information was relayed to a supervisor. An employee file was opened and meticulously reviewed. The suspect—a five-foot, three-inch, ninety-pound flight attendant without so much as a fart on her record—had not tested positive, however. She was accused of providing a "diluted" urine sample, the result, she claimed, of drinking prodigious amounts of bottled water on her inbound flight.

I watched the television screen as this diminutive flight attendant told her story to a news anchor. "I come from a very strict family," she said in a fractured voice. "I've never even seen drugs." She went on to tell about her habit of drinking water, lots of water, whenever she flies. It keeps her from being dehydrated during long hauls to and from Asia. She talked about how the airline terminated her because her urine was "tainted" with water, about how the company refused to grant another test, even refused to accept the findings of an independent drug test she took the next day. Her own supervisor—aware of the employee's seven-year perfect attendance record, and all the passenger commendation letters—burst into tears after being forced to dispense the horrific news.

Looking at her tiny ninety-pound body on the television screen, it was easy to see how even a small amount of water could dilute her urine sample. What I could not see, however, was how a major airline failed to admit that it had probably made a mistake.

Evian abuse. Apparently it's nothing to piss at.

Two Israeli pilots trick stewardess by hiding during flight

JERUSALEM, July 15 (Agence France-Presse) – Two Israeli pilots who hid from a stewardess during a flight from Eilat to Tel Aviv lost their licenses but continue to fly with the Israel-Air company, the Haaretz newspaper reported Tuesday.

One of the pilots ordered a drink from the stewardess during the flight but when she arrived with it, she found the cockpit empty.

The two pilots had left the plane on automatic pilot while they went and hid in an adjoining compartment in order to "trick" her.

When the plane landed, the incident was reported to the civil aviation authority, which revoked the pilots' licenses.

Reprinted with permission of Agence France-Presse, 1997.

FOUR "Huh?" Traveling in the State of Confusion ✈

Pig flies first class across U.S.

PHILADELPHIA, Oct. 27 (Associated Press) – Yes, a pig really flew – first class. It flew US Airways, and the company, embarrassed, says it's never going to let it happen again.

On Oct. 17, the six-hour flight from Philadelphia to Seattle carried 201 passengers—200 people and one hog, which sat on the floor in the first row of first class.

"We can confirm that the pig traveled, and we can confirm that it will never happen again," US Airways spokesman David Castelveter said. "Let me stress that. It will never happen again."

Sources familiar with the incident told the *Philadelphia Daily News* in Friday's editions that the hog's owners convinced the airline that the animal was a "therapeutic companion pet," like a guide dog for the blind.

The pig was traveling with two unidentified women who claimed they had a doctor's note that allowed them to fly with the animal, according to an internal airline report. US Airways and Federal Aviation Administration rules allow passengers to fly with service animals.

The animal became unruly as the plane taxied toward the Seattle terminal, the report said, running through the jet, squealing and trying to get into the cockpit.

"Many people on board the aircraft were quite upset that there was a large uncontrollable pig on board, especially those in the first-class cabin," the incident report stated.

The pig made it off the plane but continued squealing inside the Seattle airport.

FAA officials in Seattle said they were unfamiliar with the incident but promised to investigate.

Reprinted with permission of The Associated Press, 2000

14 I Thought This Plane Was Heading to Antigua

Though I had not uttered a word, though I had yet to toss a disparaging glance her way, the woman yelled at me as if I had just pissed on her azaleas or stolen her grandmother's purse. "This is pathetic!" she said, lurching toward me with real menace in her eyes. For one nerve-rattling moment it seemed as though she might actually snatch my head with her massive paws and squeeze until it burst like a grape. Instead, the woman made a nonviolent, albeit equally intimidating gesture. Lips pursed, nostrils flaring, she brought her face to within a few inches of my own and thrust her hands upon hips that jiggled like Jell-O in an earthquake. Then she sort of growled. That's the best way to describe it. She took one deep breath after another and growled.

I was assaulted by harsh breath that shot from her nostrils as if from a high-pressure air hose. The nose blasts hit me right between the eyes, on and off, on and off, in tune to the rhythm of her animosity. Despite a nervous twitching in my upper lip, I stood in front of the boarding gate like a true airline professional: a phony smile pasted across my face, fingers locked behind my back, shoulders back, chin up, chest thrust forward like an army recruit in the face of a maniacal drill instructor. I was dauntless. Unflappable. Quite capable of handling the situation. But as the hulking passenger loomed before me, growing angrier with each blink of her eyes, I felt the first pangs of vulnerability.

She was a big woman. A very big woman. Maybe 220, 230 pounds—an inch or two taller than me and forty or fifty pounds heavier. With the exception of her hips, the rest of her body was as sturdy as an offensive lineman's. The only barrier between us was the flimsy podium which I had been standing behind while plucking tickets from some two hundred passengers who were now safely aboard the aircraft and ready to fly to Barbados.

Professionalism be damned, I clutched the top of the plucking podium and felt myself take a tiny step backward. In my mind's eye, I saw the irate passenger turn the podium into kindling with one sledgehammer blow of her fist. But she wouldn't do something like that, would she? It was 9 A.M. We were standing in front of a departure gate at John F. Kennedy Airport. She wasn't going to go psycho on me. But when I looked into her eyes and saw storm clouds gathering there, I though it best to brace for the worst.

"How can you charge so much for extra baggage?" the woman demanded. "How can you!" When I opened my mouth to answer she waved one hand, compelling me to silence. The barrage of questions continued as if I was the subject of an FBI interrogation. "Why did you change the checked baggage rates? Huh? Why are you making it so difficult for me to carry my belongings on your airplane? Do you have any idea how expensive this is? Huh? Do you? Why are you so inflexible? Why?"

She paused, gathering her hostility in one great exhalation. "You people are so . . . so . . . ughhh!"

Am I the one responsible for charging passengers for extra baggage? Am I the one to blame for a change in rates? Is my goal in life to make it difficult for passengers to carry belongings onto *my* airplane?

Because flight attendants spend more time with passengers than do other employee groups, we're often hit by the crap passengers want to throw at less reachable targets: baggage handlers, catering chefs, aircraft cabin designers, and airline CEOs with $10 million salaries and golden parachutes that make them twice as rich upon retirement—even if the airline goes belly up in the interim.

We aren't the ones who design tiny overhead bins that can scarcely accommodate a tote bag, yet we get yelled at when there's not enough room for a carry-on bag the size of an Amana fridge. We don't establish short connection times, though we bear the brunt of passenger rage when they come stumbling onto an aircraft, clutching at their chests due to the thirty-minute sprint from gate Z-29. We don't determine seat pitch, the boarding hierarchy or whether passengers should be served peanuts or lobster thermidor on a three-hour flight. And we most certainly don't create the pricing structure for additional checked baggage. All this is left up to some bonus-motivated number cruncher sitting at a computer in an ergonomic airline office (far away from seething, fist-clenching, flight attendant–hating passengers) creating policies that give shareholders a more profitable bottom line.

As for the female passenger who ached to put me in a headlock, she never gave me a chance to say what I'd been trained to say: *We're sorry for any inconvenience the change in rates may have caused, ma'am. The increases were necessary because of bla, bla, bla in the bla, bla, bla due to bla-bla.* She went on and on, refusing to let me speak, while lashing my ears with her ceaseless rant about unfair baggage rates.

Rather than bite the bullet and hand over her ticket as a couple of hundred passengers had done before her, the woman shook the ticket in my face. "This is ridiculous," she continued, spraying me with spittle as she spoke. "You should be ashamed."

"Please, ma'am," I said, wiping my face with a sweep of one uniformed arm. I pushed both hands forward in a gesture intended to make her step backward and settle down. "I don't know anything about a change in baggage rates. I don't impose company policy. If you have a question about rates you need to return to the boarding desk and speak to the agent. I am a flight attendant, ma'am. I am not here to argue with you. I am not here to be spat upon either. I am here to take your ticket voucher, return your boarding stub, welcome you aboard the goddamn . . . welcome you aboard the airplane and point you in the direction of your seat. That's it. That's all. I'm sorry!"

Apparently, my sermon fell upon deaf ears. The angry passenger proceeded to light into me with an I'll-never-fly-your-airline-again tirade that ranked among the best I've ever heard. "You people are the worst. The very worst!" she screamed. "I never have this problem when I fly other airlines."

I looked straight into her eyes, unable to quell the anger that had been bubbling inside. "When *you* fly other airlines, ma'am," I said, "I never have this problem either."

With that she was speechless.

Out of the corner of one eye I noticed both gate agents rushing toward me. I looked at my watch. It was about a minute before departure. The agents were anxious to close out the flight on time. From about twenty yards away, one of them made a throat-slashing motion. This was a signal for me to pluck the passenger's ticket and hurry aboard. Reluctantly, I turned to face my tormentor. Eyes wide, mouth open, face scowling like an NBA coach after another bad call by the referee, she began to shout, showering me with spittle and unmerciful morning breath. As if to make an exclamation point, she tapped the ticket against my nose.

Two seconds later she repeated the infraction.

Repressing a primordial urge to punch the woman in her face, I snatched the ticket, removed the voucher and the large portion of the boarding pass, gave the woman the boarding stub and told her to either board the aircraft or be left behind. She responded with one final insult: "Only stupid people work for stupid airlines," or something of that nature. She then grabbed a duffel bag that seemed more like a body bag, and lumbered onto the jet bridge. I followed, making sure to stay at least ten feet behind.

Once inside the airplane, I asked the agent about the new baggage premium. The way she explained it, the airline had imposed a temporary increase due to heavy summer traffic. It was charging fifty dollars for every additional bag to the Caribbean. Nobody was happy about it. Least of all the passenger who was presently plodding down the aisle.

After the woman found her seat, our twin-aisle DC-10 aircraft pushed back from the gate and began rolling down the taxiway. I'm not sure exactly how far we had gotten when the trouble began. It all happened after the purser announced our flying time from New York to Barbados. One minute I was gulping down some o.j. and sharing layover plans with a member of my crew. The next minute a horrible scream ripped through the airplane. The sheer volume of the outburst could have made Alfred Hitchcock roll over in his grave. My guess was that a carry-on bag had fallen from the overhead bin and slammed into a passenger's head. Or maybe one of the more melodramatic female attendants had broken a polished fingernail. Perhaps someone had spotted a mouse in the cabin. More likely, the scream had come from an outraged passenger who found out her seatmate paid a couple hundred dollars less for the flight. (The range and complexities of airfares can make some people mad enough to scream.)

As cabin crew converged upon the coach-cabin screamer, instinct told me not to join them. I waited in the service center—the galley area between first class and coach—running one finger across the edge of my empty cup while the drama unfolded. Somehow, I knew who the screamer was. And though I refused to acknowledge this consciously, deep down inside I had an idea why she was screaming.

After attending to the passenger along with half the crew, flight attendant Maybelle Montrose crept up the aisle, shaking her head in the slow jittery manner of a woman who should have retired long, long ago. Maybelle was a senior mamma. A dinosaur. When asked about retirement she once said, "They're gonna have to carry me off the airplane in a body bag." Though age and mileage had diminished her physical abilities (it took her about twenty minutes to prepare and serve a first-class gin and tonic), her tongue was as sharp as a Ginzo knife. "We got chicken, we got beef, we got drinks," she would say to startled first-class passengers. "Speak up if you want something. They tell me I'm deaf in one ear."

Maybelle saw me standing in the service center and fixed her good eye upon me.

"Did you pluck that passenger's ticket?" she asked.

"Ahhhh . . . yeah."

"Did you bother to read her boarding pass?"

"Ahhhh . . ."

"I didn't think so," she said, rolling her eyes. Maybelle put a frail hand on my shoulder. "That passenger isn't supposed to be on this airplane."

"What do you mean?"

"That scream you heard."

"Yeah."

"It came from her. She let loose when she heard this plane was headed to Barbados."

"She's not going to Barbados?"

"She is now."

I stared at the floor, the grim realization of my ineptitude creeping up like a mugger wearing Nikes. "According to her ticket," Maybelle continued. "She's supposed to be flying to Antigua."

"Damn!"

"Damn is right," she said. "Where on Earth did you learn to read?"

Today, this incident would have never occurred. Major airlines have spent millions of dollars on Enhanced Gate Readers, those ATM-like machines that stand before the boarding gate, swallowing and then spitting out boarding passes fed by flight attendants like me. Inside the belly of this electronic beast, boarding passes are scanned to check passenger name, date, and flight number. A video display shows which seats are taken. Seat duplications are supposedly a thing of the past. Above all else, the machine is designed to prevent mistakes exactly like the one I had made. Had I been privy to an EGR while boarding the Barbados flight, the woman's ticket would have been spat out like a rotten apple. The words "Invalid Flight" would have blinked across the screen, urging me to send her to the proper gate.

But because EGR machines had yet to be invented, because I was rushed by agents, attacked by the passenger and driven by demons that still haunt me to this day, I failed to take a good look at her boarding pass. In frustration, I had snatched it and forced her to go on board. It was my fault, I admit it. I really screwed up this time. An Antigua-bound woman was stuck on a Barbados-bound airplane, and there wasn't a damned thing I could do about it.

A few seconds after Maybelle and the purser entered the cockpit, the aircraft came to a sudden halt. I knew exactly what had transpired. The two women had no doubt informed the captain of our dilemma. In the process, they named me as the culprit. After firing off a couple of expletives, the captain probably radioed dispatch for consultation. We were in the middle of the morning rush hour at JFK. Planes were lined up nose to tail, moving down the taxiway in a stop-and-go procession that crawled toward the runway. Ultimately, the captain would make the final decision as to whether or not the aircraft would return to the gate and allow the passenger to deplane. He was probably chewing on his options at this very moment, and wondering if I actually had a brain.

While this was happening, a couple of flight attendants continued to console the misboarded passenger. Her screams had diminished, tapering down to gut-wrenching sobs that permeated the cabin like audio from an in-flight movie. From my hideout in the service center, I could hear her. I hunkered down in front of the elevator, worried about retribution, plotting an escape, afraid to show my face in the cabin for fear of being spotted by 220 pounds of pissed off passenger.

"That woman is really upset." Having heard a new voice, I turned to find a colleague standing next to me. Her name was Brenda or Glenda, I think. Maybe it was Melinda. We had been introduced during the pre-flight briefing. As is often the case with new faces (with the exception of rare characters like Maybelle Montrose) I had already forgotten my colleague's name.

"She's looking for you, you know," Brenda or Glenda or Melinda said.

"What?"

"That woman. The one whose ticket you plucked by mistake. She's looking for you."

"You're kidding me."

"Nope. She said you're the one who took her ticket. You're the one who made her board the wrong flight. She wants your name. She wants to report you to the company. Judging by the way she keeps clenching her fists, I'd say she wants even more." Brenda or Glenda or Melinda raised an eyebrow. "She's demanding to speak with you."

I just looked at her.

"Well?"

"I'm not going back there."

B.G.M. chuckled. "I can't say I blame you," she said. She is a rather large woman and she's really ticked off."

Just then Maybelle and the purser emerged from the cockpit. Walking briskly through the first-class cabin, the purser wore a grim look on her face. Maybelle hobbled along, trying her best to keep up. When she reached the service center she threw a disgusted glance at me and sucked at her dentures. Worse than chalk being dragged across a blackboard, the sucking sound drove spikes into my ears.

I threw a look at Maybelle. Maybelle threw a look at me. The sucking sound intensified.

Despite the high-pitched shrill of air being drawn through dentures, all eight flight attendants huddled together, waiting for the purser to speak. "The captain says he's not going to return to the gate," she said. "There are apparently several aircraft waiting in line behind us. We're number five or six in line for takeoff. It'll take forever to get back to the gate. By the time we offload the passenger, get another departure slot and creep through traffic, the flight will be more than an hour late."

"So what about the misboarded passenger?" Brenda or Glenda or Melinda said.

The purser let out a sigh. "The captain said she's going to have to fly with us to Barbados and fly back later tonight on the return flight. There are no flights from Barbados to Antigua. Dispatch says the company will provide hotel accommodations at JFK for the night. Tomorrow she'll have to show up at the airport for her flight."

Maybelle and the purser broke the huddle and walked down the aisle to deliver the bad news. The shouts that ensued were even louder than before. There were harsh words. Threats. The half-hearted promise of a lawsuit. Murmurs washed through the cabin as concerned passengers learned of the injustice. Above it all there was Maybelle's creaky voice, explaining, in no uncertain terms, that nothing could be done.

Unable to contain her anger, the woman rose from her seat. She was coming for me. All 220 pounds of her. From my position in the service center, I could hear heavy footsteps falling against the cabin floor. *Thump, thump. Thump, thump. Thump, thump.* What should I do? Where could I go? Should I hide in the cockpit? *Thump, thump. Thump, thump. Thump, thump.* Sneak down the right side of the aircraft as she marched up the left? *Thump, thump. Thump, thump. Thump, thump.* Dial 911? *Thump, thump. Thump, thump. Thump, thump.* The footsteps were getting closer. No time for deliberation. In a true act of cowardice, I opened the elevator door, pushed the down button and descended to the lower-lobe galley. There, in the belly of the aircraft, I was haunted by the sound of footsteps from above. *Thump, thump. Thump, thump. Thump, thump.*

Suddenly, there were shouts from the elevator shaft. Then the frantic pitter patter of flight attendant feet. There was a moment of silence, followed by muffled sobs and a heavy-footed retreat. *Thump, thump, thump, thump . . .*

Soon afterward, the elevator engaged. As it descended, I looked through the elevator window and saw Maybelle Montrose's scrawny ankles, then her kneecaps and the loose-fitting shape of her uniform dress, which was way too short for a woman of her age. When the elevator completed its journey, I finally saw Maybelle's face. A face crisscrossed with wrinkles and drawn into a permanent grimace. A face that could curdle milk. A face beaten, but not bowed, from decades of confrontations with passengers and crew.

She was smirking.

The elevator door swung open. Maybelle stepped out. She folded her arms and looked at me. Moments like these are what she lived for. There was a twinkle in her eyes that had not been there before my ticket-plucking fiasco. For an instant she was a spry young stewardess, anxious to see the world and all the wonders held within it. But when she opened her mouth, the façade crumbled.

"You caused quite a commotion upstairs," she said, her voice like a screen door on squeaky hinges. "But you can relax now. The passenger you screwed over is finally in her seat."

"Please," I said. "You've gotta do me a favor, Maybelle."

Her smirk blossomed into a full-grown smile. It grew wider, brighter. Her false teeth seemed to clatter with anticipatory glee. She knew what I was about to ask, and I knew what her answer would be. I asked anyway.

"Will you switch positions with me?" I said. Maybelle's jump seat was located in the first-class cabin, while mine was in coach—perilously close to the enemy. "Please? I don't want to deal with that woman again. I don't think I can handle it."

Maybelle looked at me, twin beams of triumph gleaming from her ancient eyes. Without saying a word, she pointed a long, crooked finger toward the elevator. I stepped in, closed the door and felt myself rising, slowly, inescapably, toward the fate I deserved.

15 Anatomy of a Carry-On Bag

There was a time when carry-on bags were actually *carried* onto the airplane. A time when travelers faced a physical challenge, when only the strong managed to hoist their luggage from curbside, through maddening airport concourses, across wobbling jet bridges and into airplane cabins where the totes would then be loaded into a spacious overhead bin.

During this postderegulation epoch, most flight attendants—and a select group of passengers—strapped their carry-on bags onto collapsible metal dollies using bungee cords with metal hooks protruding from each end. Pity the poor traveler who lost his or her grip after stretching the elastic cord to its full extent and wrapping it around a piece of stubborn luggage. Many a bungee cord has unraveled with lightning quick speed, bull-whipping the victim on the arm, chest, even in the face.

Though I have no recollection of bungee cord incidents in which passengers or crew suffered serious injury, I have seen quite a few people get whacked. It ain't pretty, let me tell you. And from what I've heard, a bungee strike hurts like hell. I bet there are more than a few passengers flying the friendly skies with a black patch over one eye.

This is not necessarily why I chose to eschew the practice of strapping my carry-on onto a collapsible metal dolly. During my rookie year as a flight attendant, I carried bags in my own two hands—not because I feared a bungee attack, not because I was too cheap to invest in a collapsible metal dolly, but because I worried about being laughed at.

I figured that any man who worked in this traditionally female profession needed a tactic that would make him look macho.

Biceps aching, shoulders on fire, I'd show up at the airplane dripping in sweat. Coworkers often shook their heads or shrugged their shoulders, but they never heard me complain about my bags being too heavy. I bit the bullet. I sucked it up. Still, every trip down the concourse was an unwelcome workout.

Almost anyone can carry a ten-pound bag for twenty or thirty yards. But carry the same bag from the airport parking lot to gate Z-27 and your body will start screaming obscenities before you make it to the security checkpoint. Millions of passengers suffered the same fate. It was not unusual to see men and women pulled over to the side of a busy concourse like overheated cars in the breakdown lane, sweating profusely, clutching at their chests, staring down at a fallen tote as if it were a pet that had turned on its master.

Though many passengers continue to head toward the boarding gate with hand-held bags, more and more of today's frequent fliers utilize carry-on luggage with built-in wheels. Travelpro USA, one of the leading makers of crew luggage, markets several lines of "Pilot Designed, Flight Crew Tested" roll-aboards. (Although I was not chosen to be part of the crew test group, I'm the proud owner of a trusty Flight Pro model that has more mileage on it than my five-year-old Honda Civic.) Other manufacturers refer to these airline-approved chariots as wheelies or rollies. Whatever the moniker, roll-aboard luggage allows people to cruise through airports effortlessly, one hand guiding the precious cargo, the other punching the keypad of a cellular phone. But now that everyone's rolling, there's no room left in the overhead bin.

Anyone can roll a bag, regardless of its weight, across miles and miles of airport real estate. Elderly people, six-year-olds, the undernourished, the overfed—all have enough strength to do the deed. Some companies manufacture entire lines of kiddie luggage. Ironically, the kids who use these bags rarely pack much inside; often they're as light as a bag of feathers. I should know, I've lifted enough of them. In their desire to be "big" boys and "big" girls, the kids have probably pestered their parents into buying these little bags. I bet some parents purchase kiddie roll-aboards as "accessories" that make their kids look cute while traveling.

The invention of wheeled luggage has spawned a new carry-on mentality. Now, more than ever, passengers are rolling bags that are impossible to lift into the overhead bin. A single carry-on is often stuffed to the seams with enough weight to break a grown man's back. Often the bags are packed with a bizarre array of items: canned food, power tools, rock samples—I've seen them all. While helping one passenger stow an unbelievably heavy bag, I wiped my brow and asked what was inside. "Auto parts," he said.

And you wonder why flight attendants roll their eyes when you come onto the plane with a monster bag.

Even worse is a bag packed with fragile items.

During the Christmas holidays, on a flight from New York to Caracas, a disgruntled flyer threatened to file a lawsuit against me, my airline and a flight attendant colleague. The reason for his threat? Because the closets and overhead bins were crammed with enough coats, suitcases and Christmas packages to sink a new and improved *Titanic*, we were unable to accommodate his bulging carry-on bag.

According to the litigious passenger, his roll-aboard bag was filled with twelve bottles of expensive wine which he had successfully carried aboard a twin-aisle 767 from Paris to New York. Our 767s have endless space for carry-on bags. In addition to overhead bins that run along each side of the airplane cabin, a procession of larger, deeper bins swing down from both sides of the center ceiling section.

Unfortunately, his connecting flight from New York to Caracas was aboard a single-aisle 757, a nightmare for carry-on stowage. This long, narrow tube is configured with 166 coach seats—three more than a 767, yet with less than half the cabin stowage space. The overhead bins are smaller. There are no bins that swing down from the center ceiling section. There is no overhead space for the six passengers sitting in the last row of coach (these bins are loaded with emergency equipment and a video player). And above the four people sitting in the first row of coach, in bulkhead seats 9-A, B, D and E, there is no overhead bin at all. If bins had been installed here, they would block the emergency exit.

As a result, the front-row coach passengers, like their bin-less comrades in the last row, are forced to stow their bags elsewhere.

Peeved at this lack of overhead bin space, the passenger in 9-A plopped down in his seat after throwing his briefcase and carry-on bag to the floor. "You put me in a lousy seat," he screamed. "This is ridiculous! Why do I have to sit in such a lousy seat?"

Although the plane was completely full, I found space for his luggage. "This is ridiculous!" he repeated, as I prepared to walk up to the front and help the purser deal with our wine-toting passenger. "Why do I have to sit in a lousy seat?"

I looked down at the fuming passenger in 9-A. I looked back at 166 faces crammed together like rows of matches ready to ignite. I looked back at the guy in 9-A. "This is not ridiculous," I said. "Look behind you, sir. There are 166 seats and 166 passengers. Somebody has to sit here. Is there any particular reason why it shouldn't be you? Besides, you've got more leg room than anybody else on this aircraft."

He ignored my comments, of course.

Before I could make it to the front, a first-class passenger asked for assistance. Apparently, someone had jammed a roll-aboard atop a layer of bags in the coat closet. In the process, the inconsiderate passenger had wedged the bag against a row of hanging suit jackets. The jackets were now wadded up against the wall, wrinkling like forgotten laundry.

I grabbed the bag, straightened out the row of jackets and rolled the bag to the front of the airplane. But before I could state the problem, a passenger who happened to be arguing with the purser, turned and began shouting. "That's my bag!" he said. "What are you doing with my bag?"

That's when the purser stepped in. "Sir," she said, "I told you there was no room on the aircraft for your bag. I'm sorry. We're going to have to check it."

"I've got twelve bottles of wine in that bag," he said. "If you check it, they're going to break." The purser shrugged her shoulders and apologized. "This is ridiculous," he continued. "I'm a frequent flyer. I'm supposed to be in first class, but they put me in coach. The bottles are going to break if you check my bag. This is ridiculous!"

"But there's no room, sir," the purser retorted. "I'm sorry."

"Don't I get some consideration?"

"Yes, sir. You do," said the purser. "We made an announcement inviting high-ranking members of our frequent flyer program to board early. Why didn't you take advantage of our offer?"

"I . . . I . . ."

Standing there, listening to his argument, I actually felt sorry for the guy. Sure, he was entitled to space for his carry-on bag. But there simply wasn't any space on the aircraft.

"Let me check the overhead bins one last time," I said. The gate agent, who had been standing impatiently at the door, looked at her watch and gave me a look that said hurry the hell up.

I personally double-checked every last overhead bin on the aircraft. With the help of other crew members, I asked several passengers for permission to move their bag from one bin to another in a futile attempt to make space for the bulging bag of wine.

Following FAA guidelines, we had lined the closet floors with as many bags as could be accommodated. We made repeated announcements, asking passengers to stow smaller items under the seat in front of them. Though many people complied, there still was not enough space in the overhead bins.

Because departure time had come and gone during our attempt to accommodate the bag, the gate agent finally put her foot down. "It's time to go," she said, tapping on her watch.

Gate agents are neurotic about on-time departures, and rightfully so. When a plane departs late, the agent is often brought before a group of supervisors and forced to make a detailed explanation. Too many preventable late departures and the agent becomes roadkill on the airport tarmac.

"Sir, this plane has to leave right now," the agent said sternly. "We're going to have to check your bag. I'm sorry. Your only alternative is the next flight. We can guarantee you a seat in first class, and make sure you're one of the first to board the plane."

"But I want to get on this flight!" the passenger said.

"That's fine," said the agent. "But we're going to have to check your bag. You've got five seconds to make up your mind." At this point we were all threatened with a lawsuit.

Finally, the passenger acquiesced. The bag was checked and along with nearly two hundred overcrowded passengers and crew, the wine-lover flew to Caracas. After the passengers deplaned four hours later, the crew piled into the crew van that would take us to our layover hotel. But the purser was not yet with us. We waited in front of the airport terminal while she made a company-related call to New York.

When she finally boarded the crew van, she apologized for making us wait. There was a reason for her extended delay, we soon found out. As she walked through the customs area, she noticed that the wine-toting passenger had just claimed his bag. When he opened it, nearly every bottle was broken. "His clothes had turned pink," said the purser. They were soaked through and through with expensive Merlot.

Angry beyond comprehension, the man began flinging shards of glass to the floor, oblivious to the people milling around him. Somehow he spotted the purser. According to her, the man started screaming about a lawsuit again. And before she could get away, he demanded her name for the third and final time that day.

Instead she offered packing advice.

16 Good Ole Airplane Sustenance

"What would you like, sir? Chicken or steak?"

I posed this question to the slack-shouldered man in 15-C. Sitting quietly with both arms laying limp upon his lap—palms up, thumbs rubbing absently across the tips of his fingers—he seemed docile as a Buddhist monk. He stared straight ahead, seeming to study the intricacies of the seatback. Were it not for the outburst that followed, I would have sworn he was a pious man, dedicated to a life of peace and contemplation.

"I ORDERED A SPECIAL MEAL!" he yelled, looking up sharply.

The hostility caught me off guard. I jumped back instinctively, ramming my buttock into the face of a passenger across the aisle.

What do you say to a woman you've smacked in the face with your ass? Sorry? Ooops? Please excuse me? Bestowing these apologies and others, I begged for forgiveness in such profusion that the woman couldn't help but smile.

Then I turned to address the man who had "ordered a special meal."

"No need to get upset sir," I said. "If you give me your name, I'll check the special meal list."

"Anderson," he said. "I requested a fruit platter." His voice held within it a measure of contempt that is usually associated with drill sergeants and authoritative parents.

I reached into my back pocket, pulled out the computer-generated list, and looked for his name. There it was, plain as pasta: Anderson, 15-C. Just below the names of three passengers who had also ordered special dietary meals. One low-fat meal, one low-sodium and one ko-sher. Upon closer inspection, I noticed that Anderson's seat number had been crossed out. Written in ink beside it was "7-D."

I conferred with Natalie who worked along with me on the opposite side of the meal cart. Before departure, she had been kind enough to walk through the cabin, matching names and seat assignments with those on the special-meal list. By Natalie's account, a different passen-ger—a young man sitting in 7-D—had identified himself as Mr. An-derson. He specifically said he ordered a fruit platter. Because the customer is always right, she crossed out 15-C, assuming Mr. Anderson had changed seats.

While I served other passengers, Natalie walked up to 7-D to make sure there had been no mistake. There was none. The passenger as-sured her that his name was Anderson and that he had ordered the fruit platter. (Later we found out that the two men were brothers trav-eling together but sitting apart. The brother in 7-D had stolen the fruit platter from his sibling in 15-D. All we knew at the time, however, was that two men—both with the last name of Anderson—claimed to have ordered a special meal. And one had already begun to eat it.)

I turned toward the Anderson in 15-D, delivering the news as po-litely as I knew how. "Sir," I said. "I apologize for the confusion, but—"

"Take your excuse and shove it up your ass!" he said, cutting me off in mid-sentence.

On a scale of one to ten, passenger hostility usually begins at level two or three. As the argument intensifies, the level of anger tends to rise accordingly. But this guy went straight from zero to ten before the battle had even begun.

I stood there, blinking, the numbness in my body giving over to the first harsh waves of resentment. For all intents and purposes, Mr. An-derson had turned my good intentions into an enema. *Take your excuse and shove it up your ass.* The invasiveness of his comment was unnerv-ing; it had a chilling effect on me. In all my years of flying, no passenger had been so rude, so vulgar, so . . . so . . . infuriating.

"What did you say?" The words sprang from my mouth like gym-nasts from a trampoline. Mr. Anderson did not answer. He continued to stare into the seatback.

"What did you say?" I repeated.

A hush had come over the cabin. The passengers looked up from their meals and their magazines, eyes flickering. *Take your excuse and shove it up your ass.* Had this insult come from a passenger who had failed to receive the special meal he'd requested, or was it a chant from a disappointed Denver Broncos fan? *Hey Braddock, take your excuse and shove it up your ass . . . Take your excuse and shove it up your ass . . . Take your excuse and . . .*

I leaned close to Mr. Anderson, close enough to smell stale cigarette smoke on his breath. Close enough to hear the faint wheeze from his nostrils. Close enough to kiss. My index finger shot out as if spring-loaded, coming to within an inch of his eyeball. "Don't you ever speak to me that way again," I said. "Do you understand?"

Mr. Anderson said nothing. He simply stared past my finger, boring a hole into the seatback.

This was just one of many food-related squabbles. But it was one of the worst. Another incident took place a few years earlier. After running out of chicken, I asked a female passenger if she would be dining with us this evening.

"Yes," she said. "Whaddya got?"

"Sliced beef with gravy and mashed potatoes."

"What happened to the chicken?"

"The chicken is all gone, I'm afraid. All we have is beef."

Judging by the woman's reaction, you would have thought I had called her a cow. She blasted me with insults. After accusing me of holding out on chicken (which she alleged I had stashed for some unknown reason) she got personal, calling me names that are too vulgar to repeat.

When she settled down, I leaned close so no one else would hear. Then I whispered a few choice words of my own. I'm not proud of what I said, nor do I choose to repeat it. But suffice it to say, the comments came from the gutter.

Food—or the lack thereof—is as volatile an issue for crew members as it is for airline passengers. Many union contracts require that airlines provide onboard meals for pilots. Flight attendants at some carriers have no such luck. Unless we happen to be working on a long-haul international flight, there's often no food designated for the cabin crew. And during long, multileg flight sequences, when we're on duty for up to fourteen hours, and quick connections require sprints from plane to gate—three, four, sometimes five times a day—there simply isn't time to eat on the ground. Often, there's not enough time to stand in line for a take-away meal at an airport McDonald's. When time is short and hunger opens a crater in our stomach, we rely on the old standby: leftover airplane food.

After the passenger meal service is completed, flight attendants often gather in the first-class galley. We don't just come here to socialize, however. When we crowd into the galley we mean business. Like vultures hovering over the half-eaten corpse of an antelope, we lick our beaks, lusting for an appetizer or a dinner roll and hoping to snare some leftover meat.

If there aren't enough entrées for the entire crew, someone might make a halfhearted offer: "Wanna split this with me?"

"Oh, no, no . . . that's okay," a polite, albeit starving colleague might respond. "I'll see if there's any food left in coach." But catering companies have gotten much better at matching the number of entrees to the number of passengers. After all, the airline ends up paying for extra meals. It's in their best interest to match the number of meals with the exact number of passengers.

If every passenger decides to eat, and the plane has been stocked with the appropriate number of meals, the galley ovens should always end up empty. So too will the stomachs of luckless crew members who fail to bring food from home.

Packing your lunch before setting off for work is no big deal if you're working at an office or a construction site. You can make a sandwich or wrap up the previous evening's pasta and you're in business. But for flight attendants, especially those of us who work three- and four-day trips, it's difficult to pack food for the duration.

Still, I've flown with coworkers who lug their own food through three countries in three days. Inside their insulated food pouches, you'll invariably find a potato, the perfect food for crew members on the go. It's healthy, durable and can be heated up in the galley oven while passenger meals are cooking. Homemade lasagna, sandwiches, bags of fruit, Tupperware containers filled with pasta or tuna salad—these are favorites of the polyester jet set.

Trouble is, the U.S. Customs Service restricts the importation of food into the country. Even if the food is prepared in Texas that morning, once you get on a plane and fly to . . . say, Central America and back, the very same food can be confiscated by customs officials. Many a flight attendant has been forced to smuggle in their own ham and cheese sandwiches.

Don't think for a minute that we aren't sensitive to passengers' concerns about airplane food. Few travelers understand the problem better than we do. We've heard the complaints. We know the portions are too small. We know the chicken is sometimes as bland as broiled tofu. Like you, we question whether that paltry piece of in-flight gristle once belonged to a cow. During short-haul domestic flights, we're embarrassed when we have to say, "I'm sorry, but there's no meal service. All we've got are peanuts and drinks."

It's not fair, dammit! We're the first to admit it. If it were up to us, every main-cabin passenger would dine on lobster, prime rib or the very best vegetarian creations. We want you to be well fed. Well-fed passengers are happy passengers, and happy passengers make our job much easier. Besides, we get to eat your leftover food.

After listening to grumbling stomachs for years, my airline began providing employee "snacks." Delivered in individual plastic bags, the snacks appear on flight sequences that make it difficult, if not impossible, for the crew to grab lunch or dinner. The company calls the bag of goodies a "Snack Attack." Or maybe it's a "Snack Pack" or "Snack in a Sack." Or some cutesy moniker hatched in the brain of an airline executive who wouldn't dream of eating this crap.

Inside the bag there's usually a main course. Sometimes it's a peanut butter and jelly sandwich. Other times we're presented with a carton of "just add hot water" vegetable soup. The broth is drinkable, but the vegetables taste like morsels of soggy cardboard. The main course is accompanied by an apple or orange, and maybe a couple of crackers or cookies. In short: everything your humble servants need to keep their tummies from growling through a fourteen-hour day.

17 Doing the Non-Rev Shuffle

The plane that I hoped would fly me from New York to Los Angeles was crammed with restless passengers. They sat shoulder to shoulder in pre-flight agony, kicking mercilessly against the bags stowed improperly beneath the seats in front of them, battling for sole possession of the armrests, redirecting reading lamps, twisting away at the air vents, tucking books and portable CD players and God knows what else into bulging seatback pockets that pressed against their knees like inflated air bags in a Volkswagen Beetle. I guess you could say the passengers were packed in as tight as proverbial sardines. They were wedged into elfin airplane seats that left them scrunched together, row after identical row, like cigarettes in a pack of Marlboro Lights.

Having been the last person issued a boarding pass by the gate agent, I was hustled onto the aircraft and told to sit in any available main-cabin seat. I slid sideways down the single aisle, scanning the split sea of contorting faces, careful not to whack heads with my shoulder bag, hoping there was an aisle or window seat available, praying, believing—but ultimately stung with a dose of reality when I finally found the last remaining seat in coach. It was a center seat in the very last row. A seat flanked by two beefy business types who rolled their eyes maliciously when I stopped, cleared my throat and shrugged my shoulders in apology.

Because my carry-on was small, finding space for it in an overhead bin was a cinch. I squeezed into my seat, closed my eyes and began to pray. I prayed not for a safe flight, not for the strength to withstand a six-hour squeeze between two fleshy bookends. I prayed instead to hear the agent's departure announcement. To hear the distant clamber of the aircraft door being closed and locked. To feel the head-tingling rush of cabin pressurization and the reassuring voice of the gate agent who claims it was her pleasure to have served us on the ground. I was an airline employee traveling on a company pass, after all. Experience had taught me that it's never too late to get bumped from a flight.

Airline employees traveling on a company pass fall into a category known as "non-revenue" passengers. We're lowest of the low in the onboard pecking order—and justifiably so: beneath ticketed revenue passengers, standby revenue passengers, deadheading crew members, employees traveling on decreasingly important levels of company business, and non-revenue passengers who were smart enough to check in before their last-minute brethren.

Each airline has its own non-revenue service-charge policy. Some allow their employees to travel free of charge. Others charge a flat fee. Many impose a nominal service charge based on the actual number of air miles flown. The cost for my one-way trip from New York to L.A., including taxes? Fifteen dollars and change. From the U.S. to Europe? About fifty dollars each way. Asia? A few dollars more. Adding more sugar to an already sweetened pot, more than one hundred airline companies participate in an interline agreement that allows employees from one airline to travel on another airline at a spectacular discount. Payment is either 10 percent or 25 percent of the highest unrestricted airfare. But there is a catch to all this discount jet setting: We travel on perpetual standby, hoping for an empty airplane seat.

The irony, of course, is that the starting salary for flight attendants (the one airline employee group with a work schedule flexible enough to take full advantage of airline industry travel benefits) is so low, we can't do much at a non-rev destination until after six or seven years on the job. It's true. A few years back, a group of New York–based flight attendants made the front page of the *New York Times* after applying for and receiving food stamps. The carrot dangling in front of an aspiring flight attendant is not wrapped in money. Rather, it is dipped in the elixir of free travel—a perk I was so desperately trying to taste on my ill-fated flight from New York to L.A.

During the final stage of boarding, especially on full flights like the one I had just entered, non-revs huddle around the departure desk, waiting like anxious game-show contestants to hear our name called over the intercom. "Peterson . . . Morrisette . . . Jankovic . . ." Jankovic? We shoot daggers at Jankovic who was just issued a boarding pass, feeling certain that we checked in before her, feeling lied to, cheated. We wonder if she is the agent's cousin. A knot begins to tighten in each and every non-rev's stomach. We begin mumbling to ourselves, cursing our own poor judgment. *Why didn't I check in an hour earlier? Why didn't I take the six* A.M. *flight that departed before most non-revs staggered out of bed?*

One more name is called. Then another. The shrinking crowd presses against the podium. The gate agent covers the microphone with one hand and whispers something to her colleague. We try lip reading, but this simply adds to the anxiety. The agents are extremely busy, under pressure, trying to fill every available seat before departure time. Nevertheless, we fear that when time expires they'll close out the flight and the plane will depart with empty seats.

Most of the time this is not the case. Most of the time the process flows smoothly if not fairly. But occasionally things do go wrong. Mistakes are made. And who are we to complain? It's not like an employee can puff up his or her chest and threaten to take the business elsewhere.

While attempting to board a flight to Chicago, I was left standing at the gate by an overworked agent who later apologized for forgetting to process my boarding pass. Another time I was told that the plane was completely full, though when I checked the computer I found plenty of available seats. I've been bumped from flights at the last minute, been given a seat assignment only to have it taken away a moment later, and believe it or not, though I was dressed well enough to enter churches, synagogues, mosques, and fine dining establishments across America and the rest of the free world, I was once prohibited from boarding an aircraft because the agent decided my appearance didn't live up to company dress-code standards.

I've been stuck for days on end in foreign countries. I've been asked to switch seats with a full-fare passenger who was overwhelmed by the "foul stench" of her seatmate. Most recently, on a full flight from New York to Miami, I rode a flight attendant jump seat (the "ironing-board" collapsible that folds out and into the aisle of a 727), dressed in civilian clothes that drew curious stares from fellow passengers. "Are you traveling on a super-discount fare?" the passenger sitting next to me asked tongue-in-cheek. I simply nodded and smiled at his sagacity. I *was* traveling on a super-discount fare of sorts, a non-revenue fare that required me to hop out of the ironing-board jump seat—thus unblocking the single aisle—as soon as the plane reached cruising altitude, and spend the next two-and-a-half hours standing between the aft lavatories, flipping through a copy of *Field & Stream* while trying to stay out of everybody's way.

It may sound like I'm complaining, but I assure you I am not. The ability to fly for next to nothing is the reason I took this job. It's the reason many airline employees signed their name on the dotted line. Inconvenience is the first law of the non-revenue jungle. We all know the drill. We accept it. We embrace it like a problem child. Uncertainty and inconvenience are a small price to pay for not having to pay, but sometimes, fed up with such wing-and-a-prayer travel arrangements, airline employees choose to purchase full-fare tickets. Not me, though. No sir. I'm a non-revving maniac addicted to travel by whim.

So there I was, sitting in the center seat in the last row aboard the flight to L.A., knowing from experience that it ain't over till the fat lady sings—or at least not until the captain releases the parking brake. The flight attendants had closed all the overhead bins. The passengers were finally settled in their seats. I looked at my wristwatch. It was four minutes before departure. Still enough time left for me to get yanked.

I knew I was in trouble the moment the gate agent lurched into the cabin. Even from where I was sitting I could see her intent: The robotic head pivoting on its axis as if operated by hydraulics; the eyes scanning the cabin with the intensity of twin search beams. Robo Agent. Terminator III.

She marched down the aisle, sweeping the wide expanse of faces, causing cardiac arrest in every non-rev passenger along the way. Her movements were sharp, crisp, efficient. A Chinese army general would have been damn proud. Her head swiveled relentlessly, looking, looking, until the search beams stopped suddenly and decisively upon me.

I was caught. Busted. I shook in my shorts. My seatmates had had me hemmed in with heavy arms and thighs. But now they leaned away, far away, staring at me with scrupulous eyes.

"Grab your belongings and come with me," the agent said. She spoke in harsh Brooklynese, the voice of too many cigarettes or too many kids. I followed orders and threaded my way up the aisle. I was Sean Penn shuffling toward a lethal injection in *Dead Man Walking*. Joan of Arc heading for the burning stake. Everyone on the aircraft was staring, whispering, no doubt wondering how I could have done whatever it was that necessitated my removal from the aircraft. I might as well have been led off the airplane in leg irons.

When we reached the aircraft door and stepped onto the jet bridge, the agent looked into my eyes and shrugged her shoulders. As it turned out, there had been a mix-up. There was, in fact, a non-revenue passenger who had checked in before me and with a higher priority. He was traveling on company business, apparently.

"Sorry," she said apologetically. My replacement scooted past me and disappeared inside the airplane. Though I secretly hoped he would spend the next six hours being squished to death by my old seatmates, though I felt cheated and embarrassed and just a tad bit out of sorts, I smiled at the agent and said, "Thanks anyway," because that's how non-revs are supposed to behave. No argument. No protest. Just the humble acceptance of our frequent-flying fate.

I slunk down the jet bridge and stood in front of the unoccupied departure desk, waiting for the agent to return so she could roll my name onto the next L.A. flight. But wait a minute. There were no more flights to L.A. that day. The next flight departed sometime the following morning. Dejected, I left the terminal and waited outside for the bus that would take me back to Forty-second Street. From there I caught the subway home, where I doused my travel woes with an ice-cold Amstel Light.

"Screw L.A.," I said out loud, after watching the national weather forecast on television later that evening. Southern California was being pounded by torrential rain. There were mud slides. Floods. Talk of voluntary evacuation in low-lying areas.

The next day I flew to Barbados.

Dressed in my poly-wool flight attendant uniform, a set of gold wings glinting from my lapel, I am standing in an airport concourse in front of departure gate B-12. As the final Caribbean-bound vacationers file into the jet bridge, I collect their tickets and welcome them aboard the aircraft. It is precisely 5:52 P.M. The flight is scheduled to depart at six o'clock. Two passengers walk up and present their tickets, but hesitate before handing them over. Judging by their wedding rings, they are married (hopefully to each other) and appear to be in their late thirties. They are well dressed and seemingly intelligent. This is the conversation that transpires between the husband and me:

"What time does the plane leave?" he asks, looking at his watch.

"Six o'clock," I say.

"Do we have time to buy a bagel before departure?"

"Well, sir, the plane is departing in eight minutes."

"Yeah, yeah, yeah," he says, in a voice suddenly strained with irritation. "But do we have time to buy a bagel?"

"As I said, sir . . . the plane—"

"DO WE HAVE TIME TO BUY A BAGEL?"

Now, here's my dilemma: If I say, "No, I don't think you have time to buy a bagel or a newspaper or a souvenir for your kid," as I've said to countless last-minute boarders in the past, he may respond—as some of those last-minute boarders have—as if I have a personal vendetta. "*You*, a lowly flight attendant, are telling *me* that I don't have time to get a bagel?" (This makes me wonder why they bother to ask in the first place.)

If I say, "Yes you have time, but hurry," and the passenger returns to find that the plane has departed without him, he'll want to sue the airline. Or at the very least, he'll demand a first-class upgrade. "So what if it took me forty-five minutes—the flight attendant told me I had time to get a bagel."

It's even more unbelievable when a last-minute boarder asks, "Do I have time to go to the bathroom?" *That depends, sir. Will you be performing a Number one or a Number two? Are you going to have a seat on the toilet and flip through a copy of* Architectural Digest, *or are you planning to get straight down to business?* An airline employee has no idea how quickly a passenger can complete his bodily functions or obtain food from an airport vendor. All we can do is state what time the plane is scheduled for takeoff.

So, in an effort to maintain my sanity and my job, I respond to the bagel-loving husband with politically correct logic. "I'm sorry sir, but I do not know how long it will take you to walk to the bagel counter. I do not know how many people are standing in the bagel line. Nor do I know how quickly the bagel people can prepare, package and ring up your bagel order. As a matter of fact, I don't even know where the bagel shop is located. What I do know is that this plane is departing in exactly (I look at my watch) seven minutes. If *you* think that's enough time to buy a bagel, then by all means, sir, go and buy a bagel."

Both the husband and wife give me a dirty look. They stomp into the jet bridge, twin Travelpro roll-aboards swerving behind them like tiny black automobiles out of control. The husband tosses a last-minute insult over one shoulder. "We're never flying this airline again."

Once our plane reaches cruising altitude, I begin the dinner service with my flight attendant colleagues. The woman in window seat 12-A is staring at the ocean some thirty thousand feet below. The scene is breathtaking: a group of tiny islands—turquoise water encircles their shores like ringlets of fresh paint. Cotton-ball clouds drift above it all, leaving shape-shifting shadows to crawl across the rugged landscape.

When I ask if she'd like dinner, the woman turns and gives me a worried look. She is about forty-five years old. She is well dressed and seemingly intelligent. This is the conversation that transpires between the woman in 12-A and me:

"Why did the airplane stop moving?" she says.

"Excuse me?"

"Why did the airplane stop moving?"

"What?"

"The airplane. It's not moving anymore. Why did it stop?"

"What exactly do you mean, Miss?"

By now, passengers sitting within earshot are beginning to stir in their seats. Eyes widen. Brows wrinkle. In an attempt at suppressing laughter, the flight attendant working the other side of the meal cart bites her bottom lip. She bites so hard, in fact, I am surprised there is no blood.

"I mean the plane isn't moving anymore," the woman in 12-A continues. Her voice has gotten louder. The teenager in 11-A doubles over in a fit of silent sniggering.

"Trust me," I say. I push my open hand toward her in the universal gesture that says: Calm down, everything is fine. "I assure you the plane did not stop moving, Miss. As a matter of fact, it's traveling at almost five hundred miles-per-hour. Look out the window. See those clouds?"

"Uh huh."

"See how they're moving away from us?"

"Oooh yeah," she says after a few seconds.

After the dinner service, we roll a pickup cart through the cabin. As customary, an insert sits on top of the pickup cart. Inside the insert is a pot of coffee—along with Styrofoam cups, milk, nondairy creamer, sugar and Sweet N' Low. An assortment of juices and after-dinner cordials round out the beverage selection.

After removing meal trays and offering drinks to the first six or seven rows of passengers, I approach a man wearing headphones. He is sitting in a window seat. Eyes wide, mouth open, the man is staring at the flickering images on the video monitor. Despite the look on his face, he is well dressed and seemingly intelligent. This is the conversation that transpires between the businessman and me:

"Sir, would you like an after-dinner drink?"

He is engrossed in the video and does not hear me.

"Sir!" I say, raising my voice a couple of octaves.

Still, he does not respond. The two passengers seated beside him begin to laugh.

I wave my hand, interrupting the mesmerized man's line of vision. He gives me a dirty look.

"Would you care for an after-dinner drink?"

He hands me his tray and continues to look at me. The look turns from dirty to puzzled. He opens his hands and shrugs his shoulders.

"Would you care for a drink?"

He shouts back at me: "WHAT?"

Realizing the passenger is talking above the sound of the headphones he is still wearing, I put both hands to my ears and make a pulling motion. His headset finally comes off.

"What would you like to drink?"

"Coffee," he says.

"How would you like it?"

"Black."

I pour the coffee and hand it to the man. I release the parking break with my foot, and begin to roll the cart to the next row.

"Hey!" says the man whom I've just served. "Where's my sugar?"

"You told me you wanted black coffee."

"I always have sugar with my coffee," he says.

"How am I supposed to know that?" I say. I shake my head, hand him three packs of sugar and move to the next row. After I pick up the first tray and shove it into the pickup cart, the coffee man makes another request.

"Can I have some milk for my coffee?" he says.

I look to my colleague at the other end of the cart. The same colleague who a moment earlier had bitten her lip, is now laughing out loud. In fact, everyone within ten feet of the coffee man is laughing. Suddenly, I am laughing too.

But the coffee man is not laughing. "Milk?" he says bitterly.

An hour later, I answer a flight attendant call light. The passenger in seat 20-F is complaining about the man sitting directly behind her. Each time she reclines her seat, the man pushes her seat back to the upright position. I turn to look at him. He is a businessman. He is well dressed and seemingly intelligent. This is the conversation that transpires between the businessman and me:

"Sir, why are you pushing this woman's seat to the upright position?" I say.

"Because I don't have enough room."

"But sir, she has the right to recline her seat."

"And I have the right to the space in front of my face."

"Well sir," I say. "She has the right to recline her seat, and you are entitled to whatever space remains. If you need more space in front of your face you have the option to recline *your* seat."

He stares at me as if I just insulted his mother. "What is your name?" he asks, after giving me a dirty look.

"Excuse me?"

"You heard me. What is your name?"

I give him my name.

"You are not very accommodating," he says. "I am going to write a letter to your supervisor explaining just how helpful you have been." The woman in 20-F, the victim of the businessman's transgression, shakes her head incredulously. She turns around, hurls a profanity-laced insult at him, then offers to write a countermeasure letter to my supervisor.

A few minutes before landing, I make a final pass through the cabin to check for seat belt compliance. The woman seated in 26-C is wearing her seat belt. She is well dressed and seemingly intelligent. Her daughter, a precious four- or five-year-old, is sprawled across a row of seats on the opposite side of the aisle. The sleeping child is not wearing a seat belt. This is the conversation that transpires between the woman in 26-C and me:

"We're landing, Miss. You might want to make sure your child is buckled up."

"Oh, that's okay," she says.

"Excuse me?" I say.

"She's sleeping. I don't want to wake her up."

"You don't want to wake her up?"

"I don't want to wake her up."

"It's not safe for her to land without wearing a seat belt, you know. The FAA requires that all passengers buckle up."

The woman in 26-C glares at me in silence. A moment later she says something under her breath. Something sharp and rude and insulting. Still, she makes no attempt to buckle up her child.

I stare right back at her.

"Look!" she says, realizing that I'm not leaving without a response. "My daughter is sleeping!"

"Let me rephrase this," I tell her. I lean forward and speak in a confidential whisper. "When this plane touches down on the runway it will be traveling at more than one hundred miles-per-hour. Do you understand? If the pilot is forced to hit the brakes abruptly—as pilots have been known to do on occasion—do you have any idea what will happen to your child?"

A wave of comprehension washes over her face. She gets up, fastens the seat belt around the groggy kid, then throws a dirty look at me.

Just before I strap into my jump seat, a passenger steps into the aisle and hurries toward me. "I'm dehydrated," he says, in a flustered voice. "I need a Perrier."

"The plane is landing in a few minutes, sir. You need to return to your seat and buckle up."

Instead of returning to his seat, he stands in the aisle, unyielding.

"I said I'm dehydrated and I need a Perrier."

"I'm afraid we don't have Perrier on the airplane, sir," I say. "But I'd be happy to get you a glass of water if you'll return to your seat."

"You do too have Perrier," he insists. "I fly this route all the time and there's always Perrier on board."

"No, sir, we don't have Perrier."

"Yes you do."

"Sir, perhaps you've been flying on a different airline. I've been working this particular flight on and off for the last eight years. I can assure you that in all that time, this flight has never been catered with Perrier. Not even in first class." I take a deep breath, struggling to keep control of my senses. "If you're suffering from dehydration, plain water should do the trick."

Without waiting for me to supply the hydration he so desperately needed, the thirsty man gives me a dirty look and walks away.

This is the fifth dirty look thrown my way today. The twenty-fifth dirty look of the week. The one hundredth of the month. And in an airline career that has spanned sixteen years, this is dirty look number 19,200.

You'd think I'd be used to it by now.

Four chickens booted from aircraft

LONDON, Feb. 17 (Associated Press) – A flight to Malta was delayed Thursday when the crew discovered four chickens hidden in carry-on luggage.

The birds were discovered when one of the cabin crew moved a piece of hand luggage into an overhead bin, said Jason Nicholls, spokesman for GB Airways.

The chickens and four passengers were booted off the flight, which departed 90 minutes late, Nicholls said. The chickens were taken to a holding area for animals at Gatwick airport and the four passengers were left to make their own travel arrangements, he said.

"We apologized to passengers for the delay caused, but most of them were quite amused when they were served a chicken meal when the plane finally took off," Nicholls said.

Reprinted with permission of The Associated Press, 2000.

19 *Adiós* Hydraulics

Late one night, as our 727 began its descent toward rain-swept Agua-dilla, Puerto Rico, as my three flight attendant colleagues and I stowed and locked the service carts, completed the passenger seat belt check and strapped into our jump seats, as our three-leg, two-country, fourteen-hour work day was about to transform into a thirty-hour lay-over spiked with laughter and cold beer, the captain rang on the crew phone with distressing news. "We've lost both hydraulic systems," he said. "We're diverting to San Juan . . ."

Without hydraulics, our pilots flew the aircraft in a condition known as "manual reversion." It's like driving the world's largest tour bus without power steering. The plane responds sluggishly. Manipulating the steering wheel, or in this case, the yoke, requires a level of physical exertion that can make sweat pour from a pilot's wrinkled brow. But the scariest aspect of our hydraulic-less 727 was that the landing gear refused to deploy automatically. Upon approach to the San Juan airport, where clear skies promised less hazardous landing conditions than in Aguadilla, the captain would attempt to crank down the landing gear by hand.

As the captain announced an abbreviated version of our dilemma over the P.A. system, an eerie silence swept through the cabin. The sixty passengers stirred in their seats, exchanging disconcerted glances. Throughout the two-and-a-half-hour flight, strangers who had yet to acknowledge one another, who had yet to partake in casual conver-sation or trade a simple smile, were suddenly locked in tacit com-munion. The previously unintroduced leaned toward the previously unconcerned, drawn together by a sudden need to share previously unthinkable emotions.

In a potential life or death situation, the most condescending passenger on the airplane no longer regards flight attendants as simple-minded peanut-pushers. Suddenly, we're viewed as professionals who might help to save his life. As I walked toward the front of the aircraft for an emergency briefing with my crew, one woman turned and stared at me as if searching for her soul inside my own. An elderly man smiled nervously while clutching a rosary that dangled from his neck. Another passenger—a gentlemen who had refused to cooperate during the safety check—tightened his seat belt and stared at me intensely, as if ready to play a serious game of Simon Says.

We were at the mercy of a God who seemed to care little about aircraft hydraulics and even less about final destinations. This made me nervous. More nervous than I'd ever been in all my years of flight service. But like a professional athlete matched against a more powerful opponent, I tried to flash my game face to the crowd—hoping to instill in them, and in myself, the belief that our pilots had the situation under control.

The purser, a senior flight attendant who retired shortly after this incident, let his nerves get the best of him, however. When he stepped out of the cockpit to relay critical information from the captain, his eyes seemed to swim out of focus. "Oh my God," he said, after repeating what we already knew about the landing gear. "Oh God." He blinked repeatedly, as if trying to clear a wayward eyelash.

He turned left, then right, then left again. His mouth hung open in a lingering O. Standing in clear view of the passengers, looking like the bumbling professor who could not remember where he'd left his car keys, or his car for that matter, the purser descended into a functionless stupor. The crew agreed that emergency preparations would be best accomplished with him sitting in his jump seat.

A moment later, there were shouts from the main cabin. The man who had been clutching the rosary was now trying to open the emergency window exit. His fingers cupped the exit handholds; he started to pull. "What the hell are you doing?" I said, yanking the man away by the back of his shoulders. Though cabin pressure makes it impossible for anyone to open an emergency exit at high altitude, such an attempt is distressing for everyone on board. The offending passenger babbled a nonsensical excuse. His chin fell to his chest, and he began to whimper like a scolded child.

Next to react were two passengers who sneaked into an aft lavatory together. Judging by the repeated sniffing sounds emanating from the lav (I had put my ear to the door when a passenger said something fishy was going on inside), and the conspicuous way in which both passenger's eyes jittered once they finally emerged, and the fine dusting of white powder on the wash bin, it seemed obvious that their in-flight angst had been numbed by a few snorts of cocaine.

Moments later, in the opposite lavatory, the smoke detector began to chime. One of the flight attendants walked in and found smoke billowing from an abandoned cigarette. Someone had left it burning on the wash bin, inches away from a roll of toilet paper.

Oblivious to our hydraulic crisis, to the outbreak of precarious be-havior that followed in its wake, and to the fact that the aircraft was about to attempt landing in San Juan instead of Aguadilla, an attractive, albeit inebriated, female passenger suggested that she and I get to know each other better. Much better. So much better, she promised, that her attentions would prevent me from leaving my hotel room until it was time to fly back to Miami. Sitting alone in the last row of seats, she'd had one too many vodka tonics, but apparently not enough compan-ionship. I respectfully declined her invitation, though under less stress-ful circumstances I might not have been so noble.

As the aircraft prepared for its final descent, our captain began crank-ing down the landing gear. To insure that it had been successfully deployed, the flight engineer and I were dispatched to the first-class aisle where we proceeded to rip the carpet from its Velcro emplace-ments. Beneath the carpet lay a small manhole cover. While worried passengers peered over our shoulders, we pried open the cover with a flat-head screwdriver. The flight engineer shone a flashlight down into the darkness, hoping to spot the proper indicator that would tell us the gear had been successfully deployed. Apparently, he saw what he was looking for. He gave a thumbs up, then told me to follow him to row 23, where we repeated the procedure with similar results.

With both gears seemingly deployed, the plane was now ready for landing. But as the engineer returned to the cockpit, one unanswered question still haunted me. "The landing gear is down," I said, after the engineer gave me the first thumbs up. "But did it lock in place?" He muttered an answer, something brief and halfhearted. Something I was unable to discern.

The purser, having regained limited use of his facilities, made the routine "prepare for landing" announcement. But shouldn't we have made an emergency "brace position" P.A.? Would the landing gear hold up?

With no time to have my questions answered, I made a final compliance check—as did my other two colleagues—insuring that seat belts were fastened, tray tables were locked, and that emergency exits were completely clear of carry-on bags.

Along the way, I made direct, see-through-to-the-soul eye contact with seemingly every passenger on the airplane. Sixty upturned faces were suddenly framed against the black wall of my consciousness: the whimpering man with the rosary; the apologetic smoker; the jittery-eyed cocaine couple; the lonely woman in the last row of seats; the previously uncooperative gentleman who would probably kill if we instructed him to do so. Some sat quietly, others prayed out loud.

I squeezed hands, patted shoulders, gave verbal encouragement to those who seemed to need it most. After strapping into my jump seat, I exchanged a look with the female flight attendant seated beside me. What was her name again? Where did she grow up? How many children did she say she had? We had flown together for the last fourteen hours, yet most of her conversation had prattled into one ear and faded, like so much elevator music, in some forgotten recess of my mind. I wanted to ask—no, I *needed* to ask a hundred questions about her life.

But as her hand closed around mine, as we skimmed the tops of San Juan's high-rise apartment buildings, as the airplane wheels kissed the runway and my heart tried to leap from my throat, I realized that by simply holding my hand, my colleague had answered the most important questions. Yes, I am as scared as you. Yes, we're here for each other when it really counts. And hell yes . . . that was a close one.

20 Pass the Defibrillator Please

Like a knife wielded by a covert assailant, a long pointed finger lunged from between two rows of seats and sank into the soft flesh of my thigh. The stabs came in triplicate—*stab, stab, stab*—sharp, penetrating, decisive. Swift as the jab of a welterweight, hard as a slap in the face.

A moment earlier I had been treading down the airplane aisle, eyes forward, head bobbing, humming the theme song to *Bonanza*. The next thing I knew, my haunch was under attack. I looked down, half-expecting to see the gush of my own blood and the satisfied grin of a loon. My eyes were met instead by those of a pleading passenger. He needed something. He needed something *now!*

Whatever happened to, "Excuse me sir, may I please have a pillow?" or "Can you get me a cup of coffee when you get a chance?" or even "Yo! Where's my goddamn drink?" In the bars and restaurants scattered around the planet we had just blasted off from, millions of impatient customers were, at that very minute, employing acceptable methods of speech to gain the attention of service employees such as myself.

Excusez-moi. Entschuldigen Sie mich. Excúseme. Pardon me. Desculpe-me.

Put some of these same customers on an airplane, however, and their attention-getting techniques revert to gruff, Neanderthaloid gestures that would make Darwin turn over and grunt in his grave: an elbow in a flight attendant's flank, an index finger to the kidneys, a knuckle tapped gratuitously against the buttocks.

Jab! "When are we going to eat?"

Poke! "What time are we going to land?"

Tap, tap, tap on the butt! "Hey, what's the name of that island we just flew over?"

I'm surprised more crew members aren't indicted for assault.

Our plane had departed Miami International Airport exactly fourteen minutes earlier. During the boarding process we had sustained only one major uproar. My cabin crew seemed hard-working and friendly— at least initially. Yet that one painful jab in the thigh managed to kill my good mood. That one intrusion of personal space, that one stab of passenger impropriety sent a flood of anger rushing through my veins.

As always . . . well, almost always, I composed myself. I took a deep breath. I chilled. Then I turned to look at my tormentor and saw in his eyes a look of pure panic.

"Please, we need to go back to Miami," he said. "We need to go back *now!*"

This was no ordinary request from someone who suddenly realized he'd left his passport in a bathroom stall at MIA. This was an urgent plea for help. "My friend is sick," he said, pointing to a man in the widow seat who at that very moment began clutching at his chest with both hands. "I think . . . I think he's having a heart attack!"

When the man's head flopped in my direction, I could see that the whites of his eyes were no more. Through two rheumy slits of crimson, his unfocused eyeballs swam up in an attempt to meet my own. This guy *was* sick. Really sick. It seemed as though one foot had already stumbled into the grave and the other would be following posthaste. I hit the call light three or four times, alternating waves of guilt, fear and adrenaline crashing through my body in tidal proportions.

My three coach-cabin colleagues arrived on the scene in seconds. Melissa rushed to get an oxygen generator. Joanne grabbed the microphone and made a P.A. requesting the services of a doctor. With help from Ron, the remaining main-cabin attendant, I moved the passengers who had been sitting in the preceding row and folded the now-empty seats forward to make more room for our patient. After laying him lengthwise along the row of seats, we propped up his head against an avalanche of pillows. Then, after he seemed comfortable, after tiny buds of cognizance began to blossom in his eyes, the passenger promptly passed out.

That's when I rushed to get the onboard defibrillator.

The automatic external defibrillator, or AED (some crew members refer to it as the automatic electrocution device, or the Zapper), is a marvel of medical technology. Essentially, it delivers a pulse of electricity that can restart the heart after sudden cardiac arrest. It's a much smaller version of the hospital defibrillator featured in every TV medical drama from *Marcus Welby, M.D.* to *E.R.* The difference here, of course, is that the AED is just a tad larger than the Spider-Man lunch box I used to carry as a kid—perfect for life-saving heroics on the ground and in the air.

When I returned with the AED, having informed our purser of the pending emergency, we quickly scrutinized the patient, checking for three conditions that justify use of the unit: unconsciousness, lack of breathing and no pulse. During my brief absence the patient had regained consciousness. His breathing came in fits and starts, like an economy car engine that wouldn't catch.

When a doctor materialized, we all breathed a sigh of relief. I asked to see the doctor's medical identification (an awkward, company-mandated question designed to prevent traveling quacks from taking a shot at in-flight heart bypass surgery) and offered our assistance.

The doctor, a potbellied Canadian who had waddled down the aisle like a woman about to give birth, breathed heavily through hairy nostrils and asked us to unbutton the victim's shirt and attach the defibrillation pads. The doctor planned to use the AED, not for the chore of delivering a few thousand volts, not as the Zapper, but as a dedicated heart monitor—a task for which it was equally capable of performing.

While Melissa and Joanne attached the defibrillation pads to the man's bare chest and plugged in the connector, our captain made an announcement. "Ladies and gentlemen," he said. "Because of a medical emergency, we are returning to Miami immediately."

A man seated across the aisle let out a miserable, "I can't frigging believe this" kind of sigh. Our flight schedule had been interrupted; the world had come to a sudden, apocalyptic end. According to the captain, we'd be arriving in Miami in about fifteen minutes. There, we would be met by paramedics, pumped with fuel, given a new departure slot, and in less than an hour-and-a-half after our initial departure, we'd take off again with our passenger load reduced by at least one.

The man across the aisle wasn't happy about this change of plan. An angry slap against his thigh and subsequent jerks of his head made everyone in the area aware of his feelings. He knew that a passenger was in the midst of a medical crisis, knew that he might even be close to death. But he didn't seem to care. I shot him a nasty look, the same look used on a hurried businessman who once tried to push past a teenage girl limping down the jet bridge on a prosthetic leg. The same look used on jerks and assholes and at least one intoxicated passenger who was only a sip away from spending his vacation in the slammer.

This latest bastion of humanity—the sighing, thigh-slapping, head-jerking saint who seemed oblivious to pain and human suffering—caught my sidelong glance, caught the collective stare from our entire crew in fact. He then dropped his head, having developed a sudden interest in his seat belt buckle. A thin, metallic, slapping noise echoed through the cabin. *Clack . . . clack . . . clack . . . clack . . .*

Despite this one unspoken objection, the aircraft banked left, descending as it turned, the accelerated thrust of three engines roaring through the cabin like a beast late for supper. As always, when the cabin began to depressurize my ears popped. With one hand I pinched my nose and blew to equalize. With the other, I held the patient's hand. He lay helplessly across the row of seats, shirt open, eyes closed, two twelve-inch defibrillation pads glued to his heaving chest like Band-Aids from a Frankensteinian nightmare.

There was a slight, almost imperceptible shift of the patient's head. His eyes opened partially, revealing razor slits the color of blood. The five of us huddled around him, hands on our hips, eyes wide, faces peering downward like the starting squad of the L.A. Lakers during a fourth-quarter time-out. The doctor stared beyond his own massive belly, watching and waiting while the AED took a deep electronic breath and passed down the verdict on another airborne heart.

Forty-five minutes earlier, toward the end of the boarding process, I was standing in the galley of the 727, counting meals, loading them into the ovens, cracking ice, inserting packs of coffee into the coffee makers, and stacking milk and o.j. and bags of peanuts into a wobbly liquor cart while giving directions to the lavatory every two or three minutes.

Most of the departing passengers were already on board, the riot of twisting torsos and hoisted bags no longer clogging the aisle. There was an eruption of good-natured laughter. The faint cry of an infant. Then I heard *the voice*. It was loud, accusing, imperious. A voice to end all voices.

I poked my head out of the galley and was shocked to learn that this was not the voice of a disgruntled passenger. Not the voice of someone who had rushed to the airport at the very last minute, stood impatiently in line at the ticket counter, repeated the trauma at the security checkpoint and again at the departure gate, someone who struggled onto the aircraft with a carry-on that had to be wrestled into an overhead like a wild animal, someone who had gone through all this, only to be confronted by a sprawling woman who was trying to nurse a shrieking child in the seat adjacent to his own. No, this was not the voice of a frequent flyer on the verge of a nervous breakdown. This was, instead, the voice of a pissed-off flight attendant.

His name was Ron. The same coworker who would later help me clear passengers from the row of seats and attend to our patient. We had introduced ourselves, as crew members usually do, in the first-class cabin, about ten minutes before boarding commenced. Ron seemed unobtrusive then, barely looking me in the eye when we first shook hands, hardly raising his voice loud enough to say hello. But the anger that now sent blots of blood to his cheeks, showed an entirely different side of his personality.

"I'm gonna have you thrown off this aircraft!" he shouted. "We don't have to put up with threats from people like you." Ron was gesticulating wildly, his wrinkled uniform shirt billowing in his own tumultuous wind. From my position in the galley, I stared at him, wondering what the ruckus was all about.

"Uh huh . . . that's right . . ." he continued, looking down at a passenger whom I could not see. "Just you wait and see."

Ron hitched up his pants and moved down the aisle in one of those cocky, I-guess-I-told-him struts that conjured up images of John Wayne and Gary Cooper. He was chewing gum. Juicy Fruit, by the smell of it. The gum fell between his chomping teeth like a wad of laundry tumbling in a dryer.

"What's the problem, Ron?" I said, as he stormed past the galley. He made an abrupt U-turn, and then ducked into the galley after realizing there was no place left to strut.

"That guy threatened to kill me," he said.

"What?"

"He threatened to kill me!" he repeated, doubling the volume of his voice as if I'd asked him to speak up. He paused for a few seconds, the wad of Juicy Fruit spinning at warp speed. "The guy threatened to kill me. I saw him—"

"Hey man, lower your voice," I said, cutting him off. "The passengers are starting to freak out." Ron turned around and scanned the bevy of upturned faces, their eyebrows arched in question marks, their mouths open like caves.

He lowered his voice.

"I saw him putting his carry-on bag in the overhead bin above row eleven," he said. "His boarding pass read twenty-three-F. That's where he should put his bag. Not above row eleven. Above row twenty-three. Right? When I insisted he remove the bag he got belligerent."

I just looked at Ron, amazed at how it's always the seemingly unimportant issues that spark the most serious problems in the cabin. Ron was wrong. Plain and simple. Sure, we can suggest that people seated in the back of coach not place their bags in the bins up front. It's more convenient for everyone concerned. But main-cabin overhead bin space is shared space, ripe for any coach passenger to pluck as he or she pleases.

In a perfect world, all passengers would stow their carry-on bags in an overhead bin above their seat, and all seats would have ample bin space above. But we don't live in a perfect world. We live in a world of flight delays and lost baggage and overhead bins designed by people who never fly. We live in a world where a gum-chomping flight attendant has nothing better to do than snatch a perfectly happy bag from its location (I found out later that Ron had done this), thrust it toward a protesting passenger and insist that he park it above row 23.

Forcing someone to move his bag, especially when there's plenty of room for everyone, is tantamount to kicking an ant hill when you could just as easily have stepped aside.

"He said, 'I am going to have you keeled when we get to my country,' " Ron continued.

"Keeled?" I said.

"Yeah, that's what he said. Anyway, the captain is in the process of having the guy removed from the aircraft."

But the passenger was never removed. Ron strutted back to the point of infraction where apologies were soon offered. Apparently, the combative passenger was part of a soccer team entourage. A couple of players (I'm not sure if they belonged to the national team or a non-professional facsimile) and a team coach begged the captain for leniency. The passenger withdrew his murderous threat. He promised not to keel Ron at our destination. No keeling now, no keeling ever.

With the threat of homicide averted, we took off on schedule and that, I thought, was that.

Paramedics were ready and waiting once we landed in Miami with our ailing passenger. An announcement was made, asking all passengers to remain seated so that the team would have unrestricted access to the patient. Dressed in baggy dove-blue jumpsuits with an EMS patch stitched onto one side of the chest, three paramedics strolled down the aisle and descended upon the patient with all the eagerness of automobile mechanics who had been forced to work overtime.

"Alright, what's the problem," one of them blurted. While the paramedics checked the patient's blood pressure and pulse, one of the flight attendants, I think it was Melissa, told the whole sordid story. Our benevolent, potbellied doctor offered information about the victim's heart. According to the defibrillator, he said, "everything was fine. His heartbeat is normal. Has been all along." The problem lay else-where, apparently.

There was something in the way the paramedics spoke to the patient that raised questions about the validity of our medical emergency. Their questions seemed a bit too nonchalant, their probe into the problem too matter-of-fact. In a voice filled with doubt and suspicion, one of them finally asked, "Have you been drinking?" When the patient re-sponded with a sidelong glance and a halfhearted shake of the head, two paramedics exchanged a look.

Then I remembered.

When the drama had first begun, I bent over to adjust the pillows behind the passenger's lolling head and noticed the faintest whiff of liquor. Johnnie Walker Black, maybe? Absolut perhaps? Had our ailing passenger engaged in a bit of pre-departure quaffing at an airport bar? Was his medical condition triggered by alcohol consumption, or was alcohol consumption the sum of his condition? At the time, I failed to let the question register in my consciousness. But now it burned in my stomach like acid indigestion.

The paramedics strapped the passenger into a gurney, packed up their gear and began to wheel the gurney off the aircraft. "Hey!" I said, recalling a dictate from an AED training class: *Always remember: When paramedics remove the passenger, be sure to maintain possession of the AED unit.* "This high-tech equipment cost the airline a lot of money," the instructor had said to a classroom of chuckling employees. "Paramedics would love to get their hands on one."

I grabbed the AED, which was sitting on the patient's abdomen, and unplugged the connector from the defibrillation pads. "I think we need that," I said. One of the paramedics threw a look at me. He was smirk-ing. He was definitely smirking.

We took off an hour later, landing in Central America, nearly three hours after that. The trip had been uneventful, unless you count the hand shaking and declarations of gratitude heaped upon the cabin crew by the passengers. I have to admit, it felt good. Even though the victim was probably suffering from food- and alcohol-related heartburn, it nevertheless felt good to have assisted in the emergency medical process. After all, this is what we're paid for. Like bank security guards who stack deposit forms and empty trash cans between robbery attempts, we serve chicken and beef between infrequent episodes of childbirth, air rage and mouth-to-mouth resuscitation. Yeah, I felt pretty good about being a flight attendant that day. I felt damn good as a matter of fact. The rest of the crew felt the same way. We took a little extra time with the meal service. We struck up conversations, passed out extra liquor and heaped attention onto passengers at the slightest hint of need.

But after we landed, our feel-good movie dissolved into a Shakespearean tragedy.

After the passengers disembarked, Joanne and I were the first crew members to leave the airplane. The others, we figured, were either making use of the lavatories or raiding the liquor cart—a practice that had all but ceased after the company sent out an e-mail about a flight attendant who was terminated for having a cache of liquor minis in her flight bag.

Tired and hungry, we shuffled down the jet bridge and into the terminal where we were processed by immigration, cleared by customs and carried by our own inertia through a door that led outside.

It was unusually crowded outside the airport that night. Throngs of smiling people crowded the exits holding "Welcome Home" signs high in the air. Children darted through the forest of legs, moving to the front where they could better assess the arrivals. Whoever they were waiting for was important enough to attract a television news crew. A reporter and cameraman stood at the ready; both of them had frowned when Joanne and I walked through the door.

We walked past the crowd and stood at the curb where the hotel bus would soon be arriving. "They're probably expecting a big celebrity," I said to Joanne.

She smiled and shrugged her shoulders.

I drew in a breath of crisp evening air. Joanne lit a cigarette. I took a few evasive steps, moving upwind to get away from the first billowing Camel emissions.

"You know Ron is a bit aggressive," I said.

"Yeah, I know. I've flown with him before. He got into a fist fight with another attendant."

"You're kidding me?"

"No, it's true. I saw the whole thing. They were arguing about one thing or another. Ron called the guy a goddamn liar. The guy called Ron a goddamn prick. Next thing I knew they were rolling around on the galley floor. The emergency door was wide open. They could have rolled out the door and fallen to the tarmac."

"How did it end up?"

"Well," Joanne said, taking a long drag from her cigarette. She leaned her head way back, releasing a seemingly endless coil of smoke from between her lips. "After the cockpit guys broke up the fight, Ron got yanked from the remainder of our sequence."

"What happened to the other guy?"

"I heard he got fired."

"Man, that's lousy," I said.

"Yeah," Joanne said, grinding her half-finished cigarette into the pavement, while reaching into her purse for another.

We stood there, watching the crowd and trading rumors about pugnacious flight attendants. Five minutes passed. Ten. Where the hell was our crew? Finally a man approached us. When he smiled, I recognized him. He was a passenger from our flight. He had shaken my hand on the airplane and commended the crew on a job well done.

"You better go back to immigration," he said. Joanne and I looked at each other. "They're not letting one of your crew members into the country."

"What?" Joanne said.

"The immigration officers are refusing to allow one of your coworkers into the country."

"You're kidding me," I said.

"I wouldn't kid about something like that." He shook his head in apology, shrugged and then walked away. I asked Joanne to watch my bag, then rushed through customs and back to the immigration area where Ron was busy arguing with an official. His uniform shirt had taken on a few more wrinkles, as he once again demonstrated the art of passionate gesticulation. Both his hands thrust forward suddenly, rising to the heavens with an evangelical quiver. The red blots in his cheeks seemed to glow from the heat of his anger. Melissa and our purser, Esperanza, as well as three queues of arriving passengers stood and watched. Members from the soccer delegation wagged their fingers and hissed behind Ron's back.

"I've never seen anything like this before. They're actually not going to let him in." Melissa told me this in the hushed voice of a TV golf commentator. When I asked why they weren't going to let him in, she proceeded to deliver a thirty-second recap that could have earned an audition at ESPN. Here's what happened:

When Ron first approached the immigration counter, he was confronted by a group of passengers from our flight. They were members of the soccer team—players, coaches, officials—traveling home from a match in the U.S. The team was angry, Melissa said. Angry at Ron for causing one of their own to have a heart attack.

The news hit me like a Lennox Lewis uppercut. I must have stood there blinking for ten seconds, images from our in-flight emergency coming at me in quick-edit flashbacks: the patient's crimson eyes; the panting, potbellied doctor; the clot of petrified passengers; the red, digital readout of the AED; the cynical paramedics dressed in dove-blue overalls. As it turned out, our airborne patient was the same guy who had threatened to keel Ron. The same guy Ron threatened to have thrown off the airplane. The same guy whose plight sparked the fiasco in which we were now all embroiled.

Ron ignored the angry footballers, according to Melissa. They wanted his name, she told me. Wanted to report his actions to the airline, to the immigration officials, to the television news crew that waited for them outside. "They started shouting at him, yelling at the officers to do something," she said. "But Ron just kinda blew past the inspector without saying anything."

This is not a good thing to do to an airport immigration officer. During that seemingly trivial moment when a traveler is on the threshold of entering a country, an immigration officer is the king of the world. Master of your universe. A nasty look from a passenger, a jutting chin, an impatient flick of the hand, a disparaging remark—any of these actions can put the traveler on the bad side of the law. Most officers are bored and easy to deal with, especially when processing flight crews. But every immigration staff has at least one individual who twists his mustache behind the glass, waiting for that rare opportunity to puff up his chest and put a smart-mouth traveler in his proper place.

Ron was dealing with such a man. When Ron had rushed past the immigration booth in an attempt to avoid the angry soccer entourage, he committed a sin that would make Moses shake his head and sigh.

At this point, I went up to Ron, hoping to calm him down before his problems escalated, before we spent half the layover at the airport. He was still arguing with the immigration officer when I reached for his shoulder. "Calm down, Ron," I said.

"This is bullcrap, man!" He jerked away from my outstretched hand as if it were charged with electricity. He was Dennis Rodman whistled for a flagrant foul. I was Michael Jordan trying to get him under control. *Hey Dennis. Dennis! You got five fouls, man. One more and you're done for. Stay cool, man. Compose yourself. You're a professional, remember? Forget about the referee, he's a jerk. All referees are jerks. You gotta play to win, baby, play to win.*

"This is bullcrap!" he repeated.

"It's not bullcrap, Ron," I whispered. "This is serious crap. And if you don't calm down right now you're going to be up to your crotch in it."

I looked down the row of immigration booths. An officer sat motionless inside each hut, an immigration stamp in one hand, passport in the other, lips paused halfway between "Welcome" and "Have a nice stay." Their narrowed eyes were trained on us like spotlights at a prison break.

"Ron, you better relax *right* now!" I said. "These guys aren't screwing around." But Ron wasn't listening. His chest heaved in the manner of a hyperventilating mental patient. Eyes wild, fists clenching and unclenching, he then made a statement that I will carry to the grave: "I can take two of these pricks."

"What! Are you crazy, man?" I spat the words between clenched teeth. "These are immigration officers, Ron. They have guns." In some dim corner of my mind I heard the faint clink of handcuffs, the clank of rusted prison bars, saw huge lustful shapes rising from the back of a cell that suddenly seemed a bit crowded. Right then and there, I gave up. I just backed away before the twisted mustache assumed I was part of the problem.

Let John Wayne fend for himself.

When the cockpit crew showed up, we all huddled in a corner of the immigration area, trying to figure out a way to get Ron past the checkpoint. He had managed to calm down quite a bit. Mumbling quietly to himself, he now paced alongside the information booth like an expectant father worn down by the wait. The officer whom he had disrespected was pissed off beyond belief. Anger can do strange things to language. The officer lit into Ron using hard, thrashing, guttural sentences that seemed to gather momentum, rushing toward their target like sticks swinging at a *piñata*.

All Ron could do now was mumble to himself.

Our captain went over to speak with one of the immigration officials. He returned to the huddle in less than half a minute, shaking his head all the way. Ron was not allowed into the country. Period. But when a benevolent airline agent came to help us, our spirits lifted a bit. He would talk to the officer, he said. The two were friends. They played cards together. But even if they granted Ron entry, we would still have another hurdle to clear. Word of the heart attack–causing flight attendant had leaked to the welcoming party outside. According to the agent, a militant faction had reinstated the threat to keel Ron. They were waiting outside for us, he said.

Joanne!

Her chain-smoking face suddenly popped into my mind. She'd been outside all this time, alone, dressed in the uniform of the enemy.

While the airline agent began schmoozing with his immigration officer buddy, I went outside to check on Jo.

The crowd had swollen. Television lights played over the faces of soccer players and soccer fans alike. It was like a scene from a movie. I walked tentatively through the crowd, feeling a bit like Rod Taylor in the final scene of Alfred Hitchcock's *The Birds*.

Taylor inched his way through a yard crawling with demonic birds that had pecked to death half the island's population. The getaway car was only thirty or forty feet away, but there must have been a thousand birds in his path. Tippi Hedren—traumatized, scared, yet not a hair out of place—was cradled in his arms. There was a look of measured confidence in his eyes, a splattering of bird crap on his shoes. Step on one pigeon claw, rustle the wrong group of feathers, and the whole bloodthirsty flock would launch a deadly beak-by-beak attack.

I walked slowly, peeling my way through the mass of bodies, looking for Joanne, wondering why I hadn't changed into civilian clothes, wishing I had never pinned on a set of gold wings, when suddenly, I felt a hand on my left shoulder. I spun around. And there, in front of me, was one of the passengers from the flight. He swallowed me in a bear hug.

"Thank you for helping out our sick friend," he said, stepping away from our embrace so he could shake my hand properly. "You did a good job. A very good job. But that other one . . ." he craned his neck, looking for Ron. "That other one, I want to keel him."

A moment later, I found Joanne sitting in the crew van, plugged into her Walkman. I knocked on the window. She opened her eyes, then the window. "What's taking you guys so long?" she said.

"You wouldn't believe it if I told you. Sit tight, I'll be back in a minute."

By the time I returned to the scene of the crime, an agreement had been worked out. Ron was required to approach each immigration officer, shake his hand and apologize profusely. He did so, wearing a sheepish grin that would fit nicely on a box of humble pie.

The agent, worried that Ron would be attacked by the soccer fans, said he would tell our driver to pull around to a remote area of the airport, where we could get in and away without inciting a riot. As it turned out, such evasive measures were unnecessary. By the time Ron was allowed to clear immigration, most of the crowd had dispersed. We piled into the crew bus, unmolested.

Our chariot lurched away from the airport, the crew jammed shoulder to shoulder as always. Ron reached into his flight bag. There was the rustle of plastic, the faint clink of twelve-ounce cans. His voice was a whisper. The same shy unobtrusive voice I'd heard earlier that evening when he scarcely raised it to say hello.

"Anybody want a beer?" he said. We all stared at him and rode to the layover hotel in silence.

21 Sorry, Captain, I Broke the Airplane

Bill Clinton dropped his pants in the Oval Office. Bill Buckner let a routine ground ball roll beneath his careless glove—an error that ultimately cost the Boston Red Sox the 1986 World Series. A few years ago at a Florida hospital, a medical professional (his name was probably Bill) pulled the plug on the wrong life-support system. At some point in life, each and every one of us has pulled a "Bill." Anyone who claims otherwise is lying, living in denial or suffering through the first cruel phase of Alzheimer's. The rest of us 'fess up to imperfection. We pray that when the big inevitable blunder descends upon us, our ass doesn't end up in a big proverbial sling.

At 7:00 A.M. one bright and cheerless morning, my ass was in such a sling. But when airline management came to castigate me, when the cold iron hand of guilt reached out and snatched me by the neck, I protested my innocence with the skill of an indicted politician: "I am not aware of, nor have I ever been aware of any wrongdoing on my part."

It happened before takeoff, on a Boeing 757 destined for Mexico City. The plane was packed with the usual cast of characters: bilingual businessmen wearing dark suits and darker dispositions; unwitting vacationers headed for a week of Montezuma's revenge; a group of snobs who were beside themselves, literally, after being denied a first-class upgrade; and a Salma Hayek wanna-be with sculpted nostrils, collagen-injected lips and surgically enhanced breasts that protruded from her torso like Tomahawk cruise missiles set to launch.

Shortly after the agent closed the aircraft door and passengers began to nod off in their seats, our purser made the "prepare for departure" announcement over the intercom. This announcement does to flight attendants what Pavlov's bell did to dogs. But instead of salivating with the expectation of food, we stop whatever it is we're doing and move, as if under hypnosis, toward the emergency doors. There, beneath the conspicuous gaze of passengers, the designated attendant engages a door "arming" mechanism.

When an armed door is opened (ideally, this should happen only in the event of an emergency evacuation), a canister of compressed air is punctured and the emergency slide/chute rapidly unfurls. The slide stiffens within seconds, like a huge incredibly excited penis, then angles toward the ground, providing a life-saving escape route for passengers and crew.

Door arming is of paramount importance among crew members. Failure to do so could jeopardize the safety of everyone on board. We might forget to deliver that drink you asked for a half-hour earlier. We might give you chicken instead of the beef you desire. Hell, we might even forget the names of crew members we've been working with for the entire month. The arming of emergency doors, however, is one of two things flight attendants never forget. The other is disarming the doors upon arrival.

Imagine what would happen if a crew member failed in this regard. After positioning the jet bridge and opening the door to welcome passengers, the unsuspecting agent would be greeted by the inflating emergency slide/chute and sent ricocheting down the jet bridge like a pinball. A multimillion-dollar aircraft would be temporarily out of service while mechanics worked feverishly to repack the slide. Hundreds of passengers would be inconvenienced. Anarchy would ensue.

The flight attendant responsible for this fiasco—a blabbering simpleton reduced to tears by the magnitude of such an unforgivable blunder—would be snatched from the trip, dragged before a tribunal of growling supervisors and berated, mocked, sent home to bathe in the sweat of irresponsibility and maybe, just maybe, if a history of screwups clutter his or her personnel file, the guilty flight attendant would have his wings clipped.

None of this entered my mind until seconds before departure to Mexico City.

My door-arming responsibilities were 4-Left and 4-Right. These two doors, located off the aircraft's aft galley, are hidden from passengers by bulkheads behind the last row of seats on both sides of the aircraft.

Having heard the "prepare for departure" announcement, my Pavlovian conditioning kicked in. I ripped my eyes away from Salma Hayek's chest and found myself standing in the aft galley, in front of the 4-Right emergency door. I lifted the clear plastic cover, pushed the metal lever to the "armed" position—all the while wondering how such a tiny body managed to support such enormous breasts. The woman was less than five feet tall. The sheer weight of her accessories should send her toppling to the ground.

A cavalcade of questions began marching through my brain. Do newly implanted C cups affect a petite woman's posture? Might the added weight cause lower-back trouble later in life? Do plastic surgeons prescribe special exercises to the artificially endowed?

Preoccupied with mammary thoughts, I moved across the galley to the 4-Left door. But when I tried to push the lever to the armed position, it only moved a couple of inches, about one-fourth the required distance. At first I thought I had done something wrong. I tried again. Still, the lever barely budged. Perhaps something was stuck in the door. A stray strap. A forgotten blanket. An uncooked steak dropped by a careless caterer. I stepped back, surveyed the door seal, and found myself locked in an inner debate about real breasts vs. fake breasts, silicone vs. saline, size vs. quality.

I called the captain on the interphone.

"Hey Captain . . ." I said, realizing I had failed to introduce myself to either of the two pilots. (Occasionally, I'll fly across the Atlantic without seeing a pilot's face until after the aircraft lands and we find ourselves seated together in the van on the way to the layover hotel.)

After a quick introduction, I told the captain about the problem with 4-Left.

"I can't arm the door."

"Ahhhhhh . . ." he said, in the all-too familiar jargon known as pilot-talk. "Ahhhhhh . . ." He was apparently checking the instrument panel. "Ahhhhhh . . . yeah. Four-Left is definitely disarmed."

"Want me to open the door and see if something's stuck inside?" I said.

"Ahhhhhh . . . yeah, why don't you do that."

Strictly speaking, flight attendants aren't supposed to open doors except in an emergency. I knew this. The captain knew this as well. But the clock was ticking, it was a few seconds after departure time. It would be easier for me to open the door and remove the obstruction than to have the captain leave the flight deck and trek to the rear of the plane. Besides, I've opened doors many times before. Not just during annual emergency training drills, but while the plane was parked at the gate and the air conditioning system was inoperative. Or when galley straps were caught inside the door. Or when catering needed to re-enter for one reason or another. We never open doors without first informing the captain, and most of the time it's not a problem.

But this time it was.

After first making sure the arming lever was pushed to the "disarmed" mode, I grabbed the long silver door handle, rotated it clockwise.

In the split-second in which the galley filled with sunlight, I entered a Salvador Dali–like world of incongruity. There was an improbable ripping noise, and the gnashing of iron teeth upon metal. My heart beat a wicked conga rhythm against my chest—something by Gloria Estephan and the old Miami Sound Machine. Then I heard a hard, flat thud from far away.

Suddenly, there were voices from below. I looked down and saw a half-dozen ramp workers standing in a circle. In the middle of the circle was an object. A large, square, heavy-looking object. An object that looked somewhat out of place, lying still and bleak, smack dab in the middle of the airport tarmac. In my gut I knew what had happened, even before it registered in my brain. It was the slide pack. The big canvas sack containing the emergency slide/chute. Somehow it had ripped from the door and fallen twenty feet to the tarmac.

My ass was most definitely in a sling.

As I peered down from the open doorway, the stiff morning breeze was like a slap on my cheek. I felt my mouth opening, my eyes bulging in their sockets, a freight train of stupidity bearing down on me. Had someone been standing beneath the door when the slide pack ejected, had some unsuspecting baggage handler been driving past in a tug, he or she might have been severely injured or maybe even killed. This fact was not lost on the crowd of eight or nine rampers who stared up angrily at me.

"What the hell!" someone shouted.

Perhaps, while distracted by thoughts of saline and silicone, I had forgotten to make sure the lever was in the "disarmed" position. Maybe I'd left the handle partially engaged. Maybe a couple of inches was not enough to engage the slide, but enough to yank the slide pack from its hinges. Or maybe the door had simply malfunctioned.

Within minutes the galley filled with airline personnel: the captain, the flight attendants, a couple of gate agents, numerous supervisors, a customer service agent—even a wheelchair operator who was wedged in one corner, watching the circus with a smirk on her face.

"You the one who blew the slide?"

I turned to answer, focusing on a gray-haired supervisor and wondering what former president Bill Clinton would say in this predicament.

"No, I did not blow a slide," I said, pointing to the slide pack on the ground. "Do you see an inflated side? No, you see a slide *pack*. The door was stuck. I tried to open it so I could remove the obstruction. The captain gave me the okay. Somehow the door malfunctioned and the slide pack was ripped off its hinges. There is no *blown* slide. What you see is a slide pack that has fallen from the door."

He rolled his eyes and grunted.

Unbeknown to me at the time, arrangements were being made for my removal from the flight. A standby flight attendant was preparing to take my place. This was standard company procedure.

In the six-month period preceding this incident, flight attendants at one major airline were responsible for twenty "inadvertent slide deployments." These are embarrassing, dangerous and extremely expensive screwups. It can cost more than $28,000 to install a new slide on a 757 aircraft. A 767 slide goes for as much as $60,000.

But in breaking the plane, I had broken new territory. This particular slide/chute was detached, not inflated. And technically speaking, I did not open the door in the armed mode. After analyzing the facts, supervisors allowed me to remain on the trip. Mechanics took about thirty minutes to reattach the fallen slide pack. The plane then took off for Mexico City.

On board was the usual cast of characters: bilingual businessmen, unwitting vacationers, and a Salma Hayek wanna-be who glared every time I looked her way.

22 The Thing About Turbulence...

Imagine you are floating.

Released from the grip of gravity, you soar through recirculated airplane cabin air, high above those who were wise enough to heed the captain's P.A. announcement. You are still clutching a plastic cup in one hand, but the beverage is now dripping from your seatmate's face. The other hand has released the periodical you'd been reading, bringing a whole new meaning to the term "in-flight" magazine. You see these images, and more, in the slow-motion, frame-by-frame vision of one who has been forcibly ejected from his seat.

From this new and unusual vantage point, you look around and catch glimpses of insanity: a walking cane, minus its owner, hurtling through the cabin; a laptop crashing against a bulkhead; an explosion of peanuts; a sea of twisting heads; overhead bins opening like a chorus line of jaws—ejecting hats, coats and a whole slew of carry-on bags. No longer do you have to imagine how it would feel to fly. You *are* flying. You are a virtual Peter Pan—an airborne tourist, caught in the seismic upheaval of midair turbulence.

This is what can happen when you fail to buckle your seat belt.

And don't forget that the seat belt sign blinked on several minutes earlier. The flight attendants had roamed down the aisle, reminding everyone to buckle up, and the captain had warned of bumpy skies ahead. He told you to stay in your seat, to strap in tight, to be ready for a good jolt or two. However, as with most airplane announcements (except for those warning about delays or flight diversions), you regarded the captain's remarks as gibberish. Besides, you don't like wearing your seat belt. It's too restrictive. You were annoyed when a flight attendant interrupted your conversation to tell you to buckle up. In fact, you rolled your eyes and frowned at her.

So, just to piss her off, you think about getting up to go to the bathroom—even though the plane is trembling as if hit by an earthquake. You'll just walk right on over to the lavatory, stumbling if you have to, ignoring the attendant who will probably be strapped in her jump seat, pleading for you to sit down. You decide to do this, but you never get the chance. While you're still in your seat—with your unfastened seat belt dangling from the cushion—the airplane suddenly drops a couple hundred feet.

Now look at you. Folded like a pretzel between rows 27 and 28, five rows from where you once sat.

In-flight turbulence is nothing to kid about. Our Emergency Procedures & Training report claims that each year, an average of fifty-eight passengers are injured in the U.S. while not wearing their seat belts during turbulence. This is the leading cause of injury to passengers and crew in nonfatal accidents.

In the ten-month period between October 1999 and August 2000, some seventy-two passengers were injured in four separate incidents involving Chinese, Japanese, U.S. and British airliners. Perhaps the most serious incident occurred when a China Southern Airlines flight—en route from Kunming in southwestern China to Hong Kong—plunged two thousand feet, injuring forty-five passengers in the process. Though several of the injured were treated at a hospital and discharged, twenty-one had longer hospital stays. Seven remained in serious condition.

Chances are, none of the injured was wearing a seat belt.

This brings to mind a video that is part of the New York Department of Motor Vehicle license application process. After finishing the driver's test, applicants are required to attend a few hours of class, which includes a video showing in glaring detail a series of gruesome accident scenes. A state trooper then appears on-screen to address the group. When the other driver wanna-bes and I watched the video, we began to have second thoughts about driving the streets of New York. In a strong, authoritative, "I've seen it all so you better listen" voice, Trooper Johnson left us with one parting thought about driver safety. "In all my years on the force," he said. "I've never had to pull a dead person from behind a buckled seat belt."

Trooper Johnson had a good point.

Since that day, I have never failed to wear a seat belt while riding in a car. And because the trooper's advice can be easily applied to airplane passengers faced with in-flight turbulence, I always wear my seat belt when traveling as a passenger. While on duty, however, I'm forced to throw caution to the wind. The nature of the job demands that flight attendants check for compliance when the seat belt sign winks on during turbulence. It's no surprise, then, that we're usually the first to get injured.

During one particular flight to the Caribbean, I stood before the toilet in an airplane lavatory, eyes closed, pants gathered around my ankles, answering the primal call of nature. When you stop and think about it, relieving oneself is one of life's most tranquil experiences: a moment of reflection, an escape from the rigors of the work day, a blessed accomplishment that ends with a sigh of relief. But before my bladder could be purged, I found myself mashed against the ceiling with my feet dangling precariously above the toilet.

Over the years, colleagues have told me they've been slammed against the cabin ceiling or thrown into the laps of startled passengers. I've heard about the busted backs, fractured limbs and bloodied faces that resulted when passengers didn't buckle up, even after the seat belt sign flashed on, even after the crew had completed a mandatory safety check and P.A. announcements warned of dangerous bumps ahead.

One fellow flight attendant was slammed against the ceiling so violently that his uniform shirt ended up covered with blood. Luckily, he sustained no permanent injuries. But when the plane landed, and the more severely injured passengers were removed, an airline supervisor walked up and asked him to change his shirt.

Can't have bloodied flight attendants limping through the airport terminal, now can we?

Like most flight attendants, I've been forced to scramble to my jump seat during moments of rough turbulence. When chaos strikes, and the plane starts bucking like a mechanical bull gone berserk, we slam and lock galley doors, strap into our jump seats, then look at each other with disbelieving eyes. If ever I was to be launched toward the ceiling, I always imagined it would happen out in the aisle or in the galley, surrounded by shrieking humanity. I never thought that turbulence would strike when I was alone, in the lavatory, with my underwear at half mast.

Without warning, I seemed to float toward the ceiling. I was an astronaut in the middle of a weightlessness experiment. A mortal sent airborne against his will. In a split second I had gone from the sublime to the ridiculous. With my back pressed high against the lavatory wall, neck bent against the ceiling at an angle that only a contortionist could appreciate, I was at the mercy of God and aircraft dynamics.

That's when I peed all over the toilet and the walls. I even let loose on my own shoes. This embarrassing act was not the result of fear. There wasn't enough time to be scared. It happened because turbulence hit before I could finish my business.

The experience brought back childhood memories of an amusement park ride. Twenty or thirty people entered a large round room devoid of straps or any safety apparatus. The door shut behind us. A disembodied voice then instructed us to lean back against the wall. The room spun slowly at first, then picked up speed, with the centrifugal force pinning us against the spinning wall. Then the floor dropped, and we spun around and around, stuck to the wall like wet clothes in the final wash cycle.

Everybody loved it. I did too.

But I did not love my experience in the airplane lavatory.

In the next split second, I watched in horror as a couple of gallons of d-germ came splashing up and out of the toilet. (D-germ is the pungent blue chemical that swishes around the toilet bowl after every flush. It's designed to break down waste and mask unpleasant odors by creating an unpleasant odor of its own.) It was a true comic moment. A Monty Python sketch come to life. My trousers became soaked with d-germ. My only consolation was that there were no chunks.

The airplane suddenly regained its composure. Gravity reestablished its grip. Wobbly as an Olympic gymnast who'd been drinking martinis the night before a crucial vault, my feet hit the floor and I came sprawling through the open lavatory door.

Nobody on the plane was hurt. Everyone, including my fellow crew members, had been wearing seat belts. Startled and only slightly bruised, I strapped myself into the jump seat, smelling of urine and d-germ.

Sex aid gives flight a shaky start

LONDON, April 20 (London Evening Standard) – A pilot made an emergency landing when a suspect device was detected on a jet packed with British holidaymakers—but the threat turned out to be a sex-aid vibrator.

The A-300 Monarch Airbus was two hours into a flight from Goa when the crew became suspicious about a piece of hand luggage. The pilot, Captain Dave Johnson, radioed a bomb alert and was ordered to divert to Bombay.

The plane, carrying British-based passengers and crew, was taken to an isolated handling bay where 369 people were evacuated.

Bomb disposal experts boarded the plane and examined the suspect baggage and identified the device as a battery-powered sex vibrator.

A Monarch Air spokeswoman applauded Capt. Johnson's actions. "We are looking into the incident to find out how it got on board," she said.

The passengers later continued to Gatwick.

Reprinted with permission of Atlantic Syndication Partners, London, 1999.

SIX Layovers in Purgatory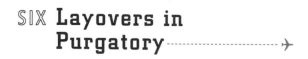

BA sacks airgirls in "2 for 1" sex romp

LONDON, March 5 (London Mail On Sunday) – Christopher Leake – Two British Airways stewardesses have been sacked after a drunken party which ended with them having three-in-a-bed sex with a male colleague and damaging a hotel bedroom.

The women, both in their 30s, even asked a waiter to join in the romp when he took late-night drinks to their room.

He declined as he handed a tray of beers to the fully-dressed crewman who answered the door. The women were lying in bed together naked.

The lurid behaviour took place at the four-star Arora International Hotel at Heathrow, which is used exclusively by BA air crew and is not open to the public. Friends of the three say the male steward, who was on a day off, joined the two women, a blonde and a brunette, in the bar for drinks while they were spending the night at the hotel before flying from London to New York the next day.

A cabin crew source said: "This is the talk of the airline.

"The three of them had been having a wild party in the hotel bar, which went on until the early hours.

"The two girls are pretty wild types and were clearly having a good time.

"Then, much later, it got out of hand and the guy went upstairs with the girls to the room they were sharing." According to hotel insiders, the three phoned down for beers to be brought to the room at about 1 a.m.

A source said: "When the room-service waiter got to the room, the guy answered the door and he could see the two girls in bed with their clothes off.

"They tried to involve the waiter in the party as well. But he fled immediately after putting the drinks down." The three left the next morning, but failed to report a cigarette burn in the carpet and damaged furniture.

The hotel complained to BA, which agreed to pay several hundred pounds in compensation for repairs.

When BA managers quizzed the trio, one of the women claimed she had been sexually assaulted by a hotel member of staff. Police investigated, but no proof of the allegation was found.

Initially, BA dismissed all three cabin crew members for causing damage to the hotel room and failing to report it.

The three had made it clear to colleagues after being investigated by BA that they had had sex together in the hotel room.

A cabin crew source said: "The three of them were in there together late at night and spent the night in the room. They have made it clear to others that they had a wild party followed by sex." The male steward has been reinstated following an appeal, after successfully arguing he had been off duty at the time of the incident last month. A final appeal by the stewardesses is being considered, but BA insiders predict they are unlikely to regain their jobs.

A senior cabin crew manager said: "We don't put up with these kind of antics in the air, so why should we accept them on the ground especially when crew are due to go back on duty the next day.

"They are expected to be sober. It is not clear whether these two stewardesses were when they went back on duty, but there are no exceptions."

A BA spokesman confirmed: "Two cabin crew who were dismissed have appealed against the decision.

"It would be inappropriate to comment further on the details of the case."

23 Beer and Loathing in Caracas

With a devilish smile spreading across his ruddy face, and the slightest glint of lust in his eyes, the captain danced on two unsteady feet in the middle of the crowded hotel suite. He was staring, as were we all, at a sultry flight attendant who had taken it upon herself to perform an impromptu striptease.

Like the twelve or thirteen off-duty crew members who watched from wobbly clusters, el capitán had consumed his fair share of booze. He'd had his choice of Tanqueray, Absolut, Bacardi and Johnny Walker Red. There were even a couple of bottles of Campari in the collection. An enterprising flight attendant had taken an entire insert of liquor miniatures from our inbound airplane. Some of it was used to make "crew juice —a dubious concoction of orange juice, cranberry apple juice and various spirits created in the airplane galley and consumed in the crew van on our way to the hotel. The remaining liquor minis were brought inside, to be used with mixers in the crew lounge.

This crew lounge is, in fact, a guest room. It's the designated playpen for members of our airline staff. Among the layover hotels system wide, this one always seemed to have a crew party going. An endless supply of Cokes and Sprites, a cluster of fruit, a television set, refrigerator and boom box were always on hand. We brought the music and the booze—neither of which were in short supply on this particular evening.

In addition to the liquor, we had beer. Lots of it. The captain had managed to knock back three cans of Venezuelan brewski. I knew exactly how many beers he drank. So did everybody else, for that matter. Each time he finished one, he crushed the can in his hand and announced in a loud down-home drawl (conjuring up images of an inebriated Gomer Pyle) that it was "time to water the plant." I don't remember how often the plant was watered that night, but the water supply never ran out. Knowing there would be five flight crews in town (one from New York, three from Miami and one from company headquarters in Omaha, Nebraska) on this Saturday night in Caracas, our crew had pooled its resources and picked up a couple of cases of Polar from a nearby grocery store.

And now our captain was dancing. To be more precise, he was attempting to dance. As the flight attendant-stripper undid the first few buttons on her blouse, the captain's feet moved with a kind of torpid angst that gave the impression of a man running in quicksand.

It wasn't as if he had not seen this particular flight attendant naked before. After all, they were boyfriend and girlfriend. Had been for two or three years. The word was they flew together often and were, as one gossiping coworker put it, "more than a little kinky."

As the captain's girlfriend undid the final buttons on her blouse, he let out a feeble yelp. It was as if a week-old pup had come stumbling into the room, wagging its tail in anticipation of a snack. This striptease was no doubt a kinky routine designed to spice up their sex life. They flirted with each other, right there in front of us—blowing kisses back and forth, making vague sexual gestures, using the crowd to stir their own libidos into a frenzy.

Dancing provocatively on the cocktail table, stripped down to a push-up bra that had both cups filled to capacity, the captain's girlfriend was something to behold. A tight, compact body that seemed sculpted from years in the gym, she was liquored up, loose as a goose and happy to show off her feathers.

Having heard the rumors about the captain and his girlfriend, I suspected she was the type who would walk into a bar, order a drink and dismiss the advances of all those who sat down beside her. At some point, the captain would walk in. (This would be planned in advance, of course.) No one at the bar would know he was her boyfriend. No one could guess they knew each other at all. The two "strangers" would make eyes at each other, talk about their zodiac signs or some equally lame topic, and then start tonguing each other right there at the bar.

Aroused by their own audacity, they'd rush home and screw each other's brains out.

This was the impression I got from the captain and his girlfriend.

But right now she was stripping. And doing a damn good job, I might add. As her hips rotated in the slow slinky grind of a Pink Pussycat professional, both hands slid up and down her body as if feeling the curves for the very first time. She even closed her eyes and tossed back her head, seemingly lost in the rapture of her own magnificence.

I stood in the corner, watching, next to two female flight attendants who seemed to be enjoying the show. Both of them, and pretty much everyone else in the room, moved to the beat of a ten-year-old Madonna tune that bellowed from the boom box in the corner.

Get into the groove, boy you've got to prove your love to me . . .

The captain's girlfriend was certainly in the groove. She turned her back to the drunken spectators, bent over in the most suggestive way and wiggled her ass in his face. The man damn near had a heart attack.

"Yeeeee haaaaaaaa!" he roared, slapping the side of his crisp denim jeans. "Work it darlin', work it."

Darlin' was working it, I had to give her that. But the captain gave her something else. To help whip his girlfriend into a fever that would serve him well when they retired to their room, he reached into his wallet, peeled off a five-dollar bill and tucked it in the waist of her jeans.

That's when things got crazy.

Perhaps in need of a few extra bucks, a second flight attendant—I believe she was from the Omaha base—jumped on an adjacent table and ripped off her blouse. Blam! There was no gradual unbuttoning. No finagling of a zipper or a clasp. One minute she was climbing onto the table and the next minute her shirt was on the floor. Blam! Suddenly, it was a battle of the flight attendant strippers. Both were thoroughly intoxicated. Both seemed eager to see who had the better body.

This was a horny man's dream. Booze pumped like blood through our bodies. Sex crackled in the air as if it were static electricity. Most of the seven or eight women in the room seemed caught up in the moment. They laughed out loud, tossing glances at the dancers and trying to mimic their moves. Two pilots from another crew were standing in one corner, rigid as fence posts, their eyes tracking the ladies the way a hunter tracks deer. One woman—an overbearing, unattractive, garrulous blonde—stumbled around the room, throwing herself at one pilot, then the other. Sooner or later, one of them would be drunk enough to take her to her room and do the dirty deed.

And then there was Junior, a flight attendant from New York. He had systematically hit on every woman in the room. The only one he hadn't tried was the blonde. As he gulped down another Polar, his eyes roving from behind the upturned can, he set his sites on the woman who seemed so unappealing an hour earlier. The *cerveza* had worked its magic.

Suddenly, the music got louder. From the boom box in the corner, Madonna yelled at the top of her lungs. A new energy surged through the room. It was as if the party had reached another level. Struggling to be heard above the music, our voices grew louder. We actually had to scream to be heard. The physical exertion required to do this made communication a more visceral thing.

That's when the captain's girlfriend unzipped her jeans. Her nemesis reacted in kind. The two flight attendants faced each other, not two feet apart, wiggling out of their pants in a tantalizing effort that brought shrieks of disbelief from the women in the audience. None of us thought they would go this far, though all the guys hoped they would.

Now that the music was blaring and everyone in the room seemed to be whooping as loud as they knew how, the noise level was completely out of control. It was so loud, in fact, that I eased over to the boom box and turned down the volume a bit. I'm no prude, mind you. I wanted to have a good time. But it was well after midnight. We could only make so much noise before someone released the hounds. Besides, every person in the room had been on the other side of an out-of-control hotel party. During one layover or another, we'd all been fast asleep, scheduled for van pickup at 6:00 A.M. the following morning. But because the inconsiderate people in the next room—quite often it's another airline crew—made so much noise, we had to call the front desk to complain.

I turned the music down a little.

A moment later someone turned it up. This time, it was even louder.

Sooner or later something bad was going to happen. It always does.

A few months earlier, an Airbus crew had been suspended for getting a bit too crazy in a Caribbean restaurant. There were six or seven of them, I think: the captain, first officer and several flight attendants. Though they were in a secluded dining area, drinking themselves under the table, they made so much noise customers started complaining. The manager had to come in to ask them to be quiet. Apparently, they calmed down for a while. But when liquor gets the best of an airline crew, there's no way to stop the party. Especially when they start drinking "belly" shots.

Urged by the captain and the rest of the crew, one of the female flight attendants laid faceup on the table. She pulled her shirt halfway up her chest, exposing her midriff. Then someone poured liquor (I believe it was tequila) in the concave receptacle of her naval. The captain sucked out the tequila. More tequila was poured into the flight attendant's navel. Again, the tequila was sucked out. As some point, the captain actually stood on the dining table and dropped his pants. He danced a goofy dance in his boxer shorts, directly in front of one of the ladies.

All this was harmless enough. But soon after returning from the trip, the crew had its collective head chewed off. As it turned out, someone had been watching the entire time. Someone who knew a bigwig at the airline. The informant filed a report. Management called in the suspects. The crew was suspended without pay. It took months for the union to get their jobs reinstated. Even then, having been forced to sign a conciliatory agreement, they had to walk on eggshells for the next two years.

On this Saturday night in the Caracas hotel crew lounge, we were one step away from a similar fate. I stepped back and weighed the consequences, surveying the scene with drunken eyes.

It was Sodom and Gomorrah, airline style. The flight attendant strippers were down to their panties. The two rigid pilots had their lips licked, Polar beers held flush against their chests. Junior had latched on to the blonde. Oblivious to the rest of the crew, they were doing a nasty bump and grind in the corner. The rest of the revelers whooped it up, while the captain yanked his shirt from his trousers.

Then the phone rang.

Junior answered it. He put a finger in one ear and tilted his head so that the other ear lay flush against his shoulder. After hanging up the phone, he tried to speak.

"Hey everybody," he said. "That was someone from the Omaha crew with the 5:00 A.M. pickup. They asked if we would keep the noise down."

Nobody listened. Nobody cared.

You never know what the Caracas crew room will be like. On any given night there are the same number of crew members occupying the same hotel rooms. Some nights the crew lounge is a deserted oasis. Other nights there might be two or three flight attendants who are too scared to venture out into the dangerous city, but unwilling to be alone in their room. But this night was different. It was as if the planets had lined up, bringing the airline's wildest crews together for a night of debauchery.

Those who had to fly the early trips were already snuggled in bed, having had a beer or two before retiring to their rooms. But some didn't have to leave until the next afternoon. And a lucky bunch—among them the kinky captain and his near-naked girlfriend—didn't depart until early the third day. They would be here in the crew lounge, drinking, dancing and more, until the wee hours of the morning. Or until management decided to break up the party.

Wishing I could stay until the ladies completed their act, but not wanting to be here when the hatchet fell, I staggered to my room and passed out.

The next morning rumors swarmed through the hotel. According to a clerk, the hotel manager had walked into the crew lounge at around 3 A.M. What he saw apparently made his jaw drop.

Having gotten the thrill necessary to rev up their libidos, the captain and his girlfriend had long departed. But four crew members remained:

Junior, the blonde, the flight attendant stripper from the Omaha base, and one of the pilots. When the hotel manager walked in, both men were crawling around the floor like ponies in heat. The blonde rode drunkenly on Junior's back, the stripper was saddled to the pilot. Neither of the women wore a bra. The only remaining item of clothing were their panties, which, had the manager not come in when he did, might have been lost to the party as well.

No report was filed. Airline management never contacted the suspects. The guilty parties party on in Caracas, Venezuela.

24 Sex and the Thin-Walled Hotel Room

Much like traveling salespeople, concert musicians and professional basketball players, we flight attendants seem to spend half our careers in an unending succession of hotel rooms. And like anyone who sleeps at hotels on a regular basis, we often get rooms cursed with paper-thin walls.

Late at night, while sleeping in one thin-walled room or another, I've been snapped to sudden consciousness by blaring televisions, driven to the brink of insanity by the "clang, clang, hiss" of water pipe concertos and tortured by electronic shrieks from someone's unheeded alarm clock. Once, at a papier-mâché hotel in New York, I woke to the sound of fierce grunting. At first it sounded like the mating call of a hopelessly horny moose. *Gruuugh! Gruuugh! Gruuugh!* But soon I realized it was the guy in the adjacent bathroom—he was suffering through a difficult bowel movement.

Errant bathroom noises are probably a hotel guest's most hated nemesis. Next on the don't-want-to-hear-it list, however, is a somewhat more erotic sound: that of two people engaged in loud, unadulterated sex.

My most vivid memory takes me back to Montego Bay, Jamaica. After a brutal three-leg, fourteen-hour day marred by long delays and disgruntled passengers, I stumbled into the layover hotel with my exhausted flight crew. None of us ate dinner. No one had drinks. We simply retreated to our separate rooms and passed out.

Sometime around 2 A.M., just a few hours before my scheduled wake-up call, my dreamless trance was shattered by a woman's scream.

The ear-splitting sound emanated from the room adjacent to mine, blasting through the adjoining wall as if it were made of facial tissue. Was the woman in the next room being assaulted? Had there been a terrible accident? Was the hotel on fire? I leapt from bed like an animated action hero and promptly tripped over my Travelpro.

As I reached for the telephone in an attempt to summon hotel security, the woman in the next room screamed again. And again. And again and again and again. Slowly, my sleep-deprived brain began to detect a pattern. Each shriek was of the same split-second duration, punctuated by the breathy gasp of a swimmer going under for the third and final time. This woman wasn't in any danger. Quite the opposite, in fact. She was knocking boots. Doing the horizontal mambo. She was, as Will Smith so eloquently put it, "gettin' jiggy wit it."

I knelt there on the floor with the telephone pressed against one ear, frozen by the vocalizations of an unseen woman who was rapidly approaching the apex of her evening. Did she have any idea that I could hear her voice so clearly? Did she have any idea what time it was? Did she care?

Just then I heard a soft, repetitive knocking sound. The sound grew louder, louder still, until my room was soon filled with rhythmic thunder. It was as if a gang of cops were beating their clubs against a suspect's door. As if a hundred-mile-per-hour wind slammed a shutter against the wall. Knowing full well that room service was not whacking on my door at this ungodly hour, the source of the knocking was obvious: my next-door neighbor's headboard was banging against the wall at breakneck speed.

Amusement. Embarrassment. Shock. All three emotions hit me at once. The couple in the next room was whipping up a hurricane of lovemaking, and I was a trailer park caught in its path. The walls shook. The knocking intensified. The screams grew louder and louder. It seemed as if the force of their passion would cause the goddamn ceiling to collapse. But what was I supposed to do? If I stayed there and listened, I'd feel like a voyeur. If I left the room, I'd feel like a victim. If I called the front desk, I'd feel like a jealous anal-retentive moron. So I hung up the phone, sat on the edge of my bed and waited for them to finish.

But they didn't finish.

They went on and on, rocking their world, ruining mine, shrieking and panting and slurping like hyenas in a feeding frenzy. At one point, the woman was kind enough to introduce me to her lover. His name was *"Jonathan, Jonathan, oh . . . my . . . God . . . Jonathan!"* Judging by the number of times his name clamored through that flimsy wall, Jonathan was a young man blessed with extraordinary talent and energy. His name was repeated so loudly and with such escalating abandon that it seemed as though his girlfriend was screaming directly into my ear. *"Oh yes . . . right there Jonathan! Uh huh, Uh huh . . . that's it Jonathan! Harder, harder . . . harder Jonathan! Don't stop, don't stop . . . Jon—a—thaaaaaaaaaaaaaaaaaaaaan!!!"*

It is not unusual to hear sex sounds drifting from the adjacent room. I've heard people going at it in hotels from Aruba to Zurich. More often than not, the sounds of sex are generated by members of my crew. I've listened to the muffled roar of hard-core banging, the panting, the moaning, the cries of pain and pleasure, the shouts to almighty God. I've listened to lewd dialogue and the next day repeated it verbatim over the airplane's P.A. system, just before passenger boarding. "Do me, do me, do me papi . . . I like when you do me like that!" Recognizing the words as her own, an embarrassed colleague locked herself in a lavatory until just before takeoff. The more tactful among us wake up in the morning and slide notes beneath the door of egregious offenders:

I HOPE IT WAS AS GOOD AS IT SOUNDED.
NEXT TIME PLEASE WEAR A MUZZLE.

DO YOU MAKE AS MUCH NOISE
WHEN YOU'RE SLEEPING WITH YOUR HUSBAND?

Sitting on the edge of the bed, I doubted the Montego Bay lovers were members of my crew. None of the pilots were named Jonathan. There hadn't been enough time for any of my female colleagues to pick up some guy at the beach bar (or maybe there had been). Besides, we were all dog-tired.

Be that as it may, *Jonathan, Jonathan, oh . . . my . . . God . . . Jonathan* was putting on an impressive show. It's not easy to drive a lover to such extremes; and Jonathan had my next-door neighbor singing like an opera diva with too much cocaine in her system. Her sex-triggered solo blasted through my hotel room as if from loudspeakers hidden above my bed. Yes, I was impressed. Anyone who appreciated good sex would be. But I was also becoming somewhat . . . well, I guess you could say I was becoming somewhat aroused by her voice. To counter this perfectly natural erection . . . er, reaction, I imagined that the screamer was Janet Reno. The mere thought of former Attorney General Reno—naked, sweaty, locked in an orgasmic twitch—sprang me from the vicarious trap in which I had been temporarily snared.

Still, the walls shook, the screaming continued. I really needed to get some sleep.

But sleep would not come easily. More than the noisy lovers themselves, it was Jonathan's incredible stamina that began to unnerve me. He had this woman screaming for nearly forty-five minutes straight, yet he still had gas in his tank. I flashed back on a lifetime of bed partners and could not remember a single instance when my sexual prowess caused a woman to scream for forty-five minutes straight. Fifteen minutes maybe. Twenty, during those times in my life when I worked out regularly at the gym. But *forty-five* minutes of nonstop in and out–ing? Without a break? I decided that Jonathan and his vocal vixen were really pissing me off. It was past two o'clock in the morning, dammit! I needed to get some sleep. I had a long day of flying ahead. Pickup was at 7 A.M. for crissakes. The two of them were being totally insensitive to the hotel guests. Besides, what if there were children down the hall?

I pressed both hands against my ears (wondering why soundproof walls aren't as common as hotel smoke detectors), while plotting ways to bring this love-fest to a halt. I would telephone the front desk and complain. *No!* I would telephone Jonathan and politely ask him to gear down. *No, no!* I would pound my fist against the wall, shout excerpts from their racy dialogue, and hope that sheer embarrassment would stifle their activity. *Yessss!* But before I summoned the courage to do so, Jonathan's name exploded through the wall.

"JONATHAAAAAAAAN!!!"

His name shook the walls, shook the very Earth itself. And then, like the sound of a faltering outboard motor, Jonathan's name dissolved into unintelligible gibberish.

A blissful silence settled over my hotel room.

Soon after I drifted off to sleep, however, Jonathan and his lover dived crotch first into round two. For the second time that evening, I woke to the sound of a woman screaming. For the second time that evening the headboard banged against the wall. Jonathan's name roared with a ferocity that made my eyes bulge. Who the hell was this guy anyway? A vacationer hauling massive equipment and an unlimited supply of Viagra? And who was this woman who seemed so pleased with his performance? Was she his wife? (Probably not). His girlfriend? A porno star rehearsing new lines?

After their thirst had been quenched for the second time, I heard laughter and muted conversation. A moment later their balcony door slid open on a squeaky runner. Unable to resist the urge to see their faces, I found myself peering through the curtains as the couple stepped outside.

Caught in the soft Caribbean moonlight, cigarette dangling from one corner of his mouth, Mr. *Jonathan, Jonathan, oh . . . my . . . God . . . Jonathan* was staring at a full moon with one arm around his cohort. She turned abruptly and disappeared into the room before I had the chance to see her face, but I got a good look at superstud. A smiling sort with a balding head, an emerging pot belly and the face of a monitor lizard, Jonathan stood about five feet, six inches tall. And if hotel walls could talk, they would bear witness to my honesty: Jonathan appeared to be about sixty-five years old.

25 Just Another Flight to Cali, Colombia

Having completed the dinner service midway through a three-hour flight from Miami to Cali, Colombia, I am sitting in the last row of passenger seats, taking my allotted fifteen-minute break and reading a disturbing article in the *Miami Herald*.

Yesterday, a fifty-five-year-old rural Colombian woman was literally blown to bits when she refused to pay a fifteen-million-peso ($7,500) extortion demanded by leftist guerrillas. The assailants had placed a tube containing explosives around her neck, rigged it to a detonator belt around her waist and demanded that her family pay up. If they refused, the bomb would be set off by remote control. While police and military bomb experts tried to disarm the device, it inadvertently exploded. The woman and one officer were killed, four others were injured.

I shake my head while reading, finding no comfort in the fact that this particular act of violence occurred outside of Bogota, rather than Cali—our destination. As is the case with most large Colombian cities, the government and police claim control of Cali. Venture past the city limits, however, and the roads give way to unimaginable lawlessness. Here you're likely to run into leftist rebel groups like the Revolutionary Armed Forces of Colombia (the group suspected of murdering the fifty-five-year-old woman) or the National Liberation Army. If you manage to slip past them unmolested, there's a good chance you'll be stopped by right-wing militias who've been known to slaughter those who they believe support the leftists.

Then there are bandits, and of course the drug cartels . . .

When a passenger call light blinks on, I place the newspaper on the adjacent seat and get up to answer the call. The last six rows of seats are empty, save for one male passenger from Arizona. He asks for another Budweiser. When I return, I ask what brings him to Colombia. He hesitates. His eyes flicker suspiciously as if he were a stockbroker deciding on whether to cough up insider information. Suddenly, he breaks into a big smile. "I'm going to get married," he says. He whips out a photograph of his fiancée. She lives in Cali and is drop-dead gorgeous. I stare at the photo a couple of seconds longer than I should. Judging by the number of attractive local women on the airplane, however, it seems that beauty is abundant in Colombia's third largest city. The women sitting in 14-C, 16-A, 21-E, 22-B & C, and 25-D, E & F could easily be finalists in the Miss Universe Pageant.

My *Lonely Planet* guide to South America claims that Cali boasts the most beautiful women in Colombia, and Colombia, it is rumored, has the most beautiful women in all of South America. I take another look at the photograph and agree with *LP*'s assessment.

After another sip of beer, Mr. Arizona tells how he and his *señorita* hooked up.

The fiancée, it seems, had registered with an *agencia matrimonial,* or marriage agency. The same agency to which Mr. Arizona belongs. He tells me that Cali is rife with similar organizations. He heard about marriage agencies on the Internet. "You fly down, look through a book of photos, pick the woman [or women] you want to meet and the agency arranges an introduction," he says. "The rest is left up to you."

Mr. Arizona goes on to tell me that some women are looking for a green card, others are looking for excitement. Most are hoping to find true love. He confesses that on a previous trip, he fell head over heels in love with his very first date. But after subsequent meetings she confessed her true feelings. "She told me I was too short."

I wish him luck with his marriage, then walk toward the aft galley and begin a conversation with a passenger from Oklahoma. He is not traveling to Cali to meet women. He is coming for sport. As it turns out, he is a wrestling coach for the U.S. Olympic team. The Pan American Games are being held here in a few days, and several spots remain open on the U.S. freestyle and Greco-Roman wrestling teams.

"The team to beat is Iran," he says, in a soft-spoken Oklahoman twang.

"Iran?"

"Iran. They've got one of the best wrestling programs in the world."

A few minutes before landing, I walk through the cabin to do a seat belt check. The man seated in 10-C does not have his seat belt fastened. I suggest that he do so, but he doesn't respond. I look at his face more closely and notice that his eyes are wet. I ask if he is okay and he shakes his head. No. He is definitely not okay. I drop to one knee and listen to his story. As it turns out, he is traveling to Cali for the funeral of a friend. His friend, a young Colombian man, was driving a Ford Explorer near the better-watch-your-ass zone on the outskirts of the city. He was killed for his automobile by leftist rebels or right-wing militias or members of a drug cartel. Maybe it was an independent carjacker. Nobody knows for sure. The funeral is tomorrow. The murder, he says, will probably go unsolved.

While walking down the aisle toward my jump seat, I remember an incident that occurred on a flight from St. Thomas to Miami. It happened a couple of days after the island had been battered by a killer hurricane. On board was an American woman traveling with her young daughter. Their clothes were dirty, their blond hair greasy and unkempt. But the strangest thing was that they had no carry-on luggage—not even a purse between them. After takeoff, the woman began to sob uncontrollably. I sat in the empty seat beside her and put an arm around her shoulder. She cried nonstop for nearly fifteen minutes, then regained composure long enough to tell her story. As it turns out, her home was destroyed. She had no insurance. Now she had no job. No money. No belongings, save for the clothes on her back. Because water was scarce on the ravaged island, she and her daughter hadn't bathed in three days. She apologized for the smell. I told her not to worry about it. They were flying to Connecticut "to live in my mother's living room," she said.

The memory fades as I strap into my jump seat in the rear of our Boeing 757.

As the aircraft descends into Cali, something goes wrong. Suddenly, the aircraft pulls up. Or so it seems. There is a powerful thrust from the engines, a noticeable trembling of the fuselage. I trade a glance with my colleague who is seated across the galley. "Are we aborting landing?" he asks, in a voice much calmer than one would expect. I peer out the tiny galley window, unable to tell for sure.

"Dunno," I say.

We are both a little nervous, and for the same reason. It was here, on Dec. 20, 1995, that a Boeing 757—just like the one in which we sat—headed down a valley toward the Cali airport and crashed into a mountain. Four people survived; 159 did not. Neither of us mentions this. Working flight attendants rarely discuss airplane disasters. Especially while the plane we're on is vectoring toward a landing strip. I close my eyes and try not to think of the mountains, focusing my attention instead on the beautiful images flickering on the dark screen of my eyelids: 14-C, 16-A, 21-E, 22-B & C, and 25-D, E & F.

When the gear wheels kiss the runway I am relieved, though I do not mention this to my colleague. If he is relieved, he does not mention it to me. (Later, the captain gives a very rational, albeit technical explanation about our approach.) We stand at the back of the plane in silence, watching as passengers deplane. There is a knock on the right-hand galley door. Airline security. A small uniformed woman enters the aircraft and asks if I locked the liquor carts. Of course I locked the liquor carts. I nod my head, she smiles and turns to frisk a catering representative who enters the plane behind her.

For obvious reasons, security is a huge issue in Colombia. Tomorrow morning, when we arrive at the Cali airport for our return flight to Miami, we will pass through three security checkpoints. At the second checkpoint all passengers are frisked by hand. Sometimes the crew is frisked, sometimes we are not. Carry-on items are subject to inspection at all three checkpoints.

The last time I was here, two security officers at the first checkpoint were playing with an automatic handgun. After my bag passed through the X-ray machine, I reached down to grab it. That's when I noticed the security officer was holding a gun in his outstretched hand. He pulled back on the slide, pulled the trigger several times and nodded approvingly to his comrade. On a previous pass through the first security checkpoint, a different officer toyed with a nickel-plated revolver. He spun the chamber once and smiled at his coworker, oblivious to the widening eyes of me and my crew.

This is what we'll go through tomorrow morning (minus the gun play, perhaps), a little more than ten hours from now. At present, the entire crew—four flight attendants and two pilots—are waiting for me in the jet bridge. I am the last to leave the aircraft. Together, we roll our crew bags down the jet bridge and past the immigration checkpoint. There, in a long queue of passengers, I notice familiar faces: the groom from Arizona, the Olympic wrestling coach, the grieving friend, the lovely occupants of 14-C, 16-A, 21-E, 22-B & C, and 25-D, E & F. I wave to all of them as we skirt immigration. They all wave back and smile.

Outside the airport, a mob of maybe two hundred people are waiting to greet their loved ones. The faces are black, white, brown, olive— the Cali region, according to my guidebook, is one of the more ethnically diverse areas of Colombia. The crowd is like a solid, multihued wall. We push through a crack in the surface, dragging our roll-aboards over shuffling feet that seem oblivious to the parade of wheels. Above the crowd, I see the curved slope of our crew van. The driver sees us and gives a quick wave. One by one, he places our bags in the van's rear compartment.

We pile in through the side door, but when the driver turns the key in the ignition, the engine fails to start. He tries again and again without success. Suddenly, the captain loses it. "This is the third damned time this has happened this month," he cries. Because the driver doesn't speak English, he fails to respond. The Spanish-speaking flight attendant chooses not to relay the captain's message.

After a few minutes, we crawl out of the van. The captain rushes into the airport, toward company operations, hoping to arrange secondary transport to the hotel. While he is gone, I mention that I can't recall a single instance when the crew van has broken down: not in Buenos Aires, Madrid or the Dominican Republic. Not in Brussels, St. Martin, Mexico City, Ecuador, Caracas, Jamaica, Boise or anywhere else. "We take van transport for granted," I say. The crew shares my sentiments. And so does the crew van, apparently. As if by magic, the engine turns over and roars.

When the captain returns, we pile into the van and pull away from the curb. He makes a few abrasive comments to the driver and tells the Spanish-speaking flight attendant to translate. Patricia, an English-speaking flight attendant, interrupts. "Why don't you learn Spanish and tell him yourself," she says. Patricia and the captain begin to argue. "He needs to get a new van," the captain exclaims. "How do you think passengers would like it if our airplane engines failed to start?"

"It happens every day," I say.

The captain disregards my comment.

For about five seconds, a peaceful silence settles inside the van. As if prompted by some unheard question, however, the captain barks at Patricia. Seems he didn't get a chance to make his point. Patricia barks back. They go back and forth, back and forth, yelling at each other like an old married couple. The other crew members ignore them. I look out the window, watching a South American moon play peek-a-boo from behind a drifting veil of clouds.

In less than thirty minutes we are in downtown Cali. There are a few high-rise office buildings and lots of neon lights. But the surrounding area is rife with stubby, one-story buildings that are beaten and shabby. While waiting for the green light, just one block away from the hotel, we hear a loud popping noise. This is followed by a protracted hiss. It's the hose to the air conditioning unit, the driver says. He'll have to fix it before picking us up tomorrow morning. And as we pull into the driveway of the Intercontinental Hotel—the kind of lodging I can never afford when traveling on my own—the captain starts bitching again. Apparently, the Cali Intercontinental does not receive the satellite television channels he prefers.

As we disembark, I notice that the lobby is bustling with people. A lot more than usual. Strangely enough, most of them are women. Most of them are beautiful, as well. They are dressed in miniskirts or provocative dresses with plunging necklines. I see Mario, the doorman. While the driver unloads our bags, Mario smiles and slaps me on the shoulder. *"Qué pasa,"* I say, not sure if I should have said, *"Qué pasó."* Mario responds, as always, with a flurry of Spanish, most of which I can't understand. But a few words are recognizable: *"fiesta," "grande,"* and *"muchas, muchas señoritas."*

After my crew receives room assignments, they walk toward the elevator. I linger at the counter and speak to the clerk. He tells me there is a big party in the ballroom tonight. He then reaches beneath the counter and shows me a business card. An American name is printed on the front of it. Beneath the name is an acronym: TLC, which stands for The Latin Connection.

Then the desk clerk gives me the scoop.

TLC is one of the largest *agencias matrimoniales* in Cali. The gathering is part of an annual event that takes place over a three-day weekend. Some seventy-five American men have paid one thousand dollars each for the privilege of attending the party. Inside, according to the desk clerk, there will be no less than seven hundred Colombian women. *"Caramba!"* I say, much louder than expected.

The desk clerk nods his head. *"Sí,"* he says with a grin. *"Caramba."* Then he gestures for me to turn around.

Angels drift in through the lobby door and turn toward the hotel ballroom. There are so many stunning women, in fact, it's difficult to focus on just one. It's like watching a parade and each passing float is more remarkable than the previous one. From where I am standing, I can see the entrance to the ballroom. I watch as the angels drift inside. There are two banquet tables on either side of the door. A group of party officials are seated at each table, checking off names and dispensing name tags to everyone. In front of the hosts are three armed guards. They are dressed in white shirts and dove-blue uniform hats. Each has a revolver hanging from his gun belt.

I remind myself that this is Colombia. Security is a very serious issue.

I take the elevator to my room, shower, change into civilian clothes and return to the lobby desk in less than ten minutes. While talking leisurely with the front desk clerk, I am secretly plotting a strategy to sneak into the ballroom. Five minutes pass. Ten. Suddenly, the three security officers hurry away from the door and I decide to make my move. A large group walks between the banquet tables and I walk in right along with them.

Once inside, I feel like I have walked into a dream. Ravishing women are everywhere. Literally. Sitting around tables. Dancing on the dance floor. Gathered in tantalizing clusters that make me dizzy when I stare. Wrapped around the ballroom is an unbelievably long queue of women—a hundred or a hundred and fifty, maybe. They are waiting patiently for a chance at the buffet.

I feel a tap on my shoulder and know instantly that I'm busted. But when I turn around, the woman standing before me has a huge smile on her face. "The young lady sitting over there would like to meet you," she says, in a lilting Colombian accent.

"Excuse me?"

"The one right there," she says, pointing to a table filled with women.

Noting the confusion in my eyes, the woman introduces herself. "My name is Anna," she says. "I am one of the interpreters."

"Ahhh, okay," I say, allowing Anna to lead me over to the table.

The rest is a blur.

I meet one woman, then another and another. All are beautiful. None speak English. Still, I am in heaven. There is another tap on my shoulder. Another introduction. I feel like a piece of meat. Happy meat. I don't mind being objectified. In fact, I rather like it. At one point, I find myself engaged in broken conversation with three of the most staggeringly beautiful women I have ever seen in my life. They are circled around me, like rock-and-roll groupies, hanging onto every butchered word I speak. Somehow, I am the life of the party. 'Da man! This is how George Clooney must feel when he walks into a room. This is what it's like to be Michael Jordan. There are so many women vying for my attention, I don't really know what to do.

There is another tap on my shoulder, but this hand is somehow different from all the rest. It seems heavier, more urgent. I turn to find a grim-faced American man staring in my face.

"Where's your name tag?" he says, his voice gruff and demanding.

"Ahh . . . I didn't get one."

"Who are you here with?"

"Well . . . I was supposed to meet a friend who—"

"I don't think your friend is here," he says, cutting me off abruptly. "You better meet him somewhere else."

I am snatched away from my lovely audience and ushered to the door. The man who has ejected me whispers into the ear of one of the three security guards. The guard nods his head and gives me a dangerous look. I remember he is carrying a gun.

26 The No-Show

Obsessed about on-time departures, airlines instill in their crew a kind of pre-flight paranoia that begins just before a flight attendant's maiden voyage and doesn't let up until retirement. *Get to work before sign-in . . . get to work before sign-in . . . get to work before sign-in, or else!*

"Sign-in" is the designated time an attendant is to show up for a flight. It's the computer equivalent of punching a time clock. Dressed in uniform and ready for battle, we're required to type a personal password into a company computer no less than one hour before departure. Hang out at the airport, near the entrance to airline operations, and you'll see hoards of flight attendants rushing toward the door, hoping to tickle a keyboard before Big Brother sets off the silent alarm. The alarm goes off immediately after the one-hour mark has expired. Thanks to the miracle of computer technology, tardiness is now recorded in nanoseconds.

A late sign-in automatically triggers a message to a flight attendant supervisor. Depending upon the length and girth of the stick wedged up a supervisor's butt, he or she will summon the offending employee at the first sign of a tardiness problem. But hey, we're only human. Every once in a while something is bound to go wrong. As is the case with employees from other industries, we get migraines and sinus infections. We break limbs, rupture appendixes, stay out all night drinking and are too hungover to function. When this happens we put in sick calls, which are frowned upon—especially when the airline suspects we're abusing the entitlement. But when one of us goes missing, it's not the end of the world. Most airlines have "standby" flight attendants waiting to pick up the slack.

Standby attendants are stationed at the airport, ready to spring into action should a scheduled crew member fail to show up. They sit in the airport crew lounge during six-hour shifts, watching television soap operas and talk shows, flipping through magazines, and talking with coworkers they haven't seen in months. The remainder of the time they sleep. There's also a group of "ready-reserve" attendants who sit at home (or move about town with a cellular phone). When Crew Scheduling calls, they drop what they're doing and report to the airport posthaste.

But standbys and ready-reserves exist only at crew bases, not at down-line destinations. If for any reason a crew member fails to show up after a layover, there's no one available to fly the trip. The flight will simply depart without him. (In the unlikely event that the FAA minimum number of flight attendants fail to show up—three on a 727, for example—the plane is grounded until a reserve can be flown in from the nearest base).

Cockpit crews are an entirely different story. It's too costly for an airline to force pilots into standby duty. Whenever they're late for work, the plane and its passengers simply have to wait. If a pilot fails to show up altogether, passengers might be waiting for a very long time.

Recently, a European airline was forced to delay a flight from New York to Geneva because the pilot failed to show up at JFK. During the layover, he had been arrested for lewd behavior in a Central Park bathroom. What kind of lewd behavior, you ask? Well . . . let's just say it was radical enough to get him arrested.

This is one of those rare situations when passengers are better off being lied to by the airline. Travelers often go ballistic when they think they're being deceived by employees. But if the gate agent makes an announcement suggesting the captain is a pervert, who knows what kind of turmoil might erupt:

Ladies and gentlemen, may I have your attention please? The flight has been canceled because our captain was caught in Central Park with his pants around his ankles. We aren't sure whether he was bending over when New York's finest walked in on him, but we do know they hauled him away. As soon as he's released from jail, we'll be on our way to Geneva.

Once, our flight from New York was delayed for two hours because the captain got stuck in a traffic jam. Another time we got canceled because the captain simply forgot he had a trip; he was out playing golf when he should have been completing the pre-flight checklist. And after a Caribbean layover that crew members would probably like to forget, the crew called the captain's room from a hotel courtesy phone in the lobby because the man was incredibly late.

Flight attendants get extra pleasure in calling a tardy captain, especially if he happens to be a jerk. Tickled to death by such a blunder from the almighty commander-in-chief, we often snicker as the stolid captain stumbles onto the bus. Sometimes he is silent; occasionally he'll mumble an apology. Often he'll say something like this: "Stupid idiots didn't give me my wake-up call." But the only true idiot is a crew member who relies on a hotel wake-up call. Most of us carry a travel alarm for backup.

Still, this particular captain never answered his phone. Perhaps he was a heavy sleeper. Maybe he had picked up a local and was right in the middle of an extra-long good-bye. Whatever thoughts crept through the minds of crew members, I assure you the thoughts were not pleasant. Passengers were waiting at the airport, for crissakes. The flight engineer needed to perform the pre-flight walk-around. Everybody wanted to get home.

At some point, the crew summoned security. A small battalion was dispatched to the captain's room. The guard knocked, but no one answered. He then inserted a master key, turned the knob and flung open the door. They found the captain stretched out between the sheets, alone, and very dead. Apparently, he had expired in his sleep—the victim of a massive heart attack.

Horrible things have happened to crew members during layovers. An unlucky few have been robbed, assaulted—even kidnapped. The grim news travels through the system as fast as one plane lands and another departs. We shake our collective head and sigh, unable to fathom the tragedy. But there's a rare breed of no-shows who deserve no sympathy. These flight attendants are not robbed, assaulted or kidnapped. They do not succumb to a mysterious illness. They fall victim to their own piss-poor judgment and suffer the disastrous consequences.

During yet another Caribbean layover, the crew gathered at the hotel pool. "Pooling," as I like to call it, is arguably the No. 1 activity among international airline crew. If time and weather permits, we change into swimwear, catch some rays and drink a few beers by the concrete pond. We do it in the afternoon. We do it at night. After all-night flights to Rio de Janeiro, there's a small contingent of diehards who—rather than sleep, like the rest of us—go straight to the pool at 10 A.M. and drink *caipirinhas* all day long.

The Caribbean crew was no less enthusiastic. They sat by the pool, drinking, laughing, trading passenger-from-hell stories that left some of them in tears. As the day wore on, their voices grew in direct proportion to the amount of booze consumed. One flight attendant, a petite blonde from Oklahoma, was completely off her face. So drunk was she, in fact, that she stumbled to the edge of the pool and dived into the shallow end. Her head smashed full-force into the concrete bottom. Suddenly sober and headachy, she resurfaced and called it a day. She went to her room, crawled into bed and slept straight through until the next morning.

When the Oklahoman woke, she could not move. Her body was paralyzed from the neck down. Worried crew members had to carry her to the bus and onto the home-bound flight. Though she remained out of work for several months, she ultimately made a full recovery. Rumor has it she tried to file a lawsuit against the hotel (perhaps the shallow end of the pool was improperly marked). I'm not sure if the airline initiated the move, or if hotel management kicked us out. But this, I do know: a few months after the incident we were laying over at a different hotel.

A few thousand miles away, at a layover hotel in London, a 767 crew prepared to fly home. One by one they emerged from the lobby elevators and turned in their keys at the front desk. They then rolled their bags toward the crew van that idled outside at the curb. As is the case after most layovers, the crew chatted about the previous day's activities. Some had gone shopping, a few may have gone out for dinner and then taken in an Andrew Lloyd Weber play.

But when pickup time came and went, the purser began to worry.

Twelve crew members had boarded the bus, but there were supposed to be thirteen. One male flight attendant was missing.

Unlike pilots, when flight attendants oversleep we often apologize profusely. After all, the captain runs the show. He can order the bus to leave (and occasionally does) instead of waiting for a tardy attendant. To thwart such action, one of us (usually the purser) will rush to the front desk and telephone the missing person. The groggy voice at the other end will suddenly come to life: "Damn! Damn! I'll be right down." A few minutes later, the flight attendant comes staggering onto the bus, unwashed, disheveled and embarrassed.

But the flight attendant in London never answered his telephone. Perhaps he had just left his room and was descending in an elevator. The crew waited. When he failed to appear they telephoned his room again. No answer. As a last resort, hotel security was summoned. The detachment of security and airline crew rode the elevator to the appropriate floor. They walked down the hallway, paused in front of the flight attendant's door, knocked. When no one answered, the guard inserted a master key. The door opened to reveal a scene that will forever live in layover infamy. I won't tell you what type of bodily fluid was smeared on the wall. I won't categorize the dark matter that had been smeared along with it. Suffice it to say the mess was so nasty, so utterly repulsive, hotel staff would later refuse to clean it. An independent cleanup service would be hired by the hotel.

Beneath the gore, face down on the bed, lay the missing flight attendant. He was bound and gagged, but very much alive. In fact, he had scarcely been injured. But the perpetrator had left a memento: a sex toy that may have been mutually enjoyed and agreed upon at the beginning of the night; a sex toy that may have later been used as an impromptu paint brush with which to create ghastly wall art. Long and cylindrical, it protruded from the young man's butt like a flag pole at the 18th hole. A dildo. How it got there, the fight attendant could or would not say. Even after the gag had been removed. The previous night he picked up a stranger at a London nightclub, he said. The rest of the evening was a blur.

Malaysia Airlines steward sentenced for biting off colleague's ear

SINGAPORE, July 17 (Associated Press) – A court has sentenced a Malaysia Airlines flight attendant to a year in jail for biting off his colleague's ear after losing an arm-wrestling match, a newspaper reported today.

James Jimbat, 30, pleaded guilty to causing "grievous hurt" to Mohamad Fadzil, 22. The incident occurred during a layover in Singapore in March.

The night they arrived in town, Jimbat and another colleague went to Fadzil's hotel room for some arm wrestling. After losing several times, Jimbat challenged Fadzil to a fight. Angered by Fadzil's refusal, he bit off his ear.

Fadzil had to undergo reconstructive surgery to have his ear reattached.

Reprinted with permission of The Associated Press, 1998.

Highly sexed: A guide to the Mile-High Club

LONDON, June 9 (London Guardian) – Felicity Lawrence –
First time:
The first in-flight sex is said to have taken place in 1916. The pilot was Lawrence Sperry, a designer of early aircraft, and he was flying a biplane over New York. He lost control and crashed, though he and his paramour survived.

Most famous exponents:
Celebrities who have claimed to have joined the Mile-High Club include Pamela Anderson and her husband Tommy Lee, pop star Brian Harvey of East 17, and actor Oliver Reed. Barbara Streisand hired a private jet to fly over Los Angeles so that she and her husband could become members.

Most powerful exponent (allegedly):
Bill Clinton was accused of trying to run a personal Mile-High Club aboard his jet during the 1992 election. The allegations of sexual harassment, uncovered by lawyers for Paula Jones, were dismissed as ridiculous by campaign advisers.

Most embarrassing coupling:
On a BA flight from Nairobi, a couple got stuck in the gap behind the last row of cabin seats; flight engineers had to be called to free them.

Most obvious coupling:
Passengers on an Air France flight from Nice to London clapped and shouted "*Vive le sport!*" when a young woman emerged from the lavatory behind her boyfriend having forgotten to put her boob tube back on.

Worst consequences:
A stewardess took Air New Zealand to court for unfair dismissal when she was sacked for being caught (while off-duty) with a male passenger in the loo. She lost her case.

Reprinted with permission of Guardian News Service Limited, London, 1999.

27 Lechery at 30,000 Feet

Relegated to yet another all-night flight from Los Angeles to New York, my bleary eyes suddenly swam into focus when two impassioned passengers, who had been cuddling in coach began kissing and groping like actors in a low budget porno flick.

Ensconced in a row by themselves, they thrashed together unrelentingly, oblivious to the sidelong glances of my colleagues who kept cruising the aisle to get a closer look. The cabin was dark save for a few passenger reading lamps that back-lit the performance like tiny, misguided spotlights. With so few passengers, most people were stretched across several seats and sleeping soundly, unaware of the escalating passion that seemed destined to redefine the concept of a "satisfying" flight.

In a display of erotic audacity, the woman threw one leg across her boyfriend's lap, straddling him with such enthusiasm that her skirt canopied like a quick-open parachute. As the couple continued to suck face, they made a mystifying attempt at camouflage by draping a blanket over their heads. The blanket could not, however, disguise the woman's sudden, mischievous movements—she began a slow grind in her boyfriend's crotch, accelerated to an equestrian gallop and in less than two minutes she was jouncing up and down at warp speed.

Peering at the action from behind the aft bulkhead, just a few feet away, I heard muffled moaning and the barely audible thwack-thwack-thwack of colliding flesh. When our female flyer arrived at her final destination—when her call-light went "ding!" when the Earth shook despite being thirty thousand feet below—she let loose a shriek that echoed through the cabin like a gunshot. She then she collapsed into her boyfriend's arms just as startled passengers sprang upright in their seats.

Welcome to the Mile-High Club.

Throughout sixteen years as a commercial flight attendant, I've witnessed numerous inductions into this infamous society of airplane passengers who engage in fellatio, cunnilingus and various forms of sexual communion at high altitude. Though in-flight copulation is often thwarted by storm-trooper flight attendants who threaten to summon security upon arrival, many of my colleagues are like me—they turn their back on passenger lasciviousness (and then find a good place from which to watch), just as long as it doesn't disturb the other passengers.

Mile-High Club liaisons are most common late at night, when lights are low, crowds are minimal, and the threat of discovery is less likely. The overtly courageous—or woefully tacky—seek membership in the comfort of their seat, cloaked by blankets and pillows and prodigious amounts of nerve. (Rumors of two-minute galley "quickies" are rife throughout the airline industry, though I've never walked in on an episode.)

Nevertheless, in keeping with a tradition that began soon after Wilbur and Orville wobbled across the skies near Kitty Hawk, most MHC wanna-bes are anointed in an aromatic airplane lavatory that only a contortionist could love.

On a recent flight from Osaka to Los Angeles, a flight attendant opened an unlocked lavatory door and got an eyeful. "One of my crew members saw a woman straddling a man on the toilet seat," she said. "She quickly closed the door and locked it from the outside." A group of flight attendants poked their heads out of the galley to watch as the Japanese couple emerged. The man returned to his seat on the right side of the plane; the woman took her seat on the left. "Later," said the flight attendant, "we noticed the woman was holding the hand of the male passenger seated next to her."

A similar tryst occurred on a flight from New York to San Juan. A male attendant was tending to first-class passengers, when a well-known sportscaster seduced a woman right in front of her boyfriend.

"After he finished his meal, the boyfriend went into the first-class lavatory," the attendant said. The woman—who was visibly inebriated and undeniably starstruck—"exchanged a look with the sportscaster. They walked to the back of the plane and entered an aft lavatory together." Some fifteen minutes later, the disheveled woman returned to her seat, followed, seconds later, by the smug-faced sportscaster. The boyfriend flew into a rage. "You screwed him, didn't you . . . you bitch!" he said. And to the sportscaster: "I know what you did to my girlfriend, punk!"

Upon arrival in San Juan, the boyfriend bolted, so did the sportscaster, leaving the woman alone and in tears.

A twenty-year flight attendant says she has witnessed every imaginable in-flight sexploit. "I've seen couples going at it in seats . . . usually the man sitting down and the woman on top. In bathrooms . . . with the woman screaming as though she was in pain and the flight attendants knocking on the door. I've witnessed a copilot and flight attendant having sex in the cockpit, guys masturbating, women too. I've seen many blow jobs, and a couple of men going down on their women. And one lucky guy had two women going down on him."

Lately, the airline industry has been besieged by more sinister manifestations of passenger outrageousness: physical assaults against pilots and flight attendants, the destruction of aircraft interiors, urinating and defecating in the aisles. While these hostile acts seem to be growing in frequency and intensity, victimless infractions like in-flight sex often go unnoticed.

But at an airline cabin-safety symposium, a Singapore Airlines official expressed great concern. "The increasing number of sexual offenses," he said, is a "particularly worrying trend." Newspaper reports suggest that at one point, a whopping one-third of Singapore Airlines' passenger misconduct cases involved sexual transgressions.

A few years ago, a South African Airways captain threatened to divert his jumbo jet due to an onboard orgy that was gathering momentum. In a two-year period at London's Heathrow Airport, fifteen passengers were reportedly detained by police because of in-flight sexual misconduct. Here in the United States, where industry disclosure about sexual activity is as likely as a lobster meal in coach, only one major airline offered cogent remarks. "Although no one is getting hurt," said a United Airlines spokesperson, "this type of activity is not to be tolerated. We treat it like any other form of passenger misconduct."

Though the FBI responds to reports of terrorism, in-flight assault, and "interference with a flight crew," local authorities are responsible for handling complaints about lewd and lascivious behavior—a misdemeanor, punishable by up to one year in prison in many states. (If a child under sixteen witnesses the act, the crime could be upgraded to a felony.) Unwilling to subject themselves to embarrassing publicity, most airlines are reluctant to pursue even the most contemptible cases.

In 1998, aboard a South African Airways flight from Johannesburg to London, a business-class couple reportedly disrobed from the waist down and began having sex in full view of other passengers. Mortified onlookers summoned flight attendants who, despite their best efforts, could not get the couple to disengage. Ultimately, the captain was forced to intervene. The high-flying exhibitionists finally geared down, but only after the captain yelled, "This is not a shag house!"

While most airlines deplore onboard "shagging," at least one major airline seems to embrace the concept. A Virgin Atlantic Airways billboard once featured the perpetually horny Austin Powers (Mike Meyers) straddling the fuselage of a jumbo jet. The caption read: "Virgin Shaglantic . . . Yeah, baby." Richard Branson, Virgin's outspoken head honcho, once exclaimed: "We're not the type of airline that bangs on bathroom doors." Claiming to have lavatories which are "larger than on other airlines," Virgin may soon develop a reputation for having lavatory queues which are *longer* than on other airlines.

But why are people so eager to have sex on an airplane these days? Especially in lavatories which are only marginally more accommodating than an outhouse? Christina Lawrence, a practicing psychologist who spent thirty years as a flight attendant for United Airlines, cites disinhibitors (drugs and alcohol), airplane density (people think they can get away with bad behavior on a plane full of strangers), and a relaxed dress code as possible reasons for mile-high mania.

"Years ago, airline passengers were more inhibited because of formal dress standards," she says. "There's a certain behavior that goes along with conservative attire." Nowadays, it's not unusual for passengers to walk around the cabin in miniskirts, shorts, see-through blouses, sweat suits, tank tops, flip-flops or no shoes at all.

I once saw a passenger traipsing around the aircraft dressed only in a slip. When the light hit just right, you could see that she wasn't wearing panties.

Mix audacious clothing with unlimited alcohol, darkness, a long flight, and smatterings of bored, sexually depraved human beings— and there's bound to be lechery in the aisles.

During a flight from Auckland, New Zealand, to Los Angeles, a flight attendant noticed "a man leaning back in his seat, eyes closed, with such a look of ecstasy on his face." The blanket across his lap was "moving up and down," she said. "Soon, the blanket fell off, showing a woman actually giving the guy a blow job."

At this point, one of the flight attendants tapped the passenger on the shoulder and said, "this type of behavior is not appropriate in business class." To the crew's amazement, "the lady giving the blow job was so into what she was doing, she didn't even notice." She continued her stellar performance until the recipient forced her to stop. They both stared up at the flight attendant who repeated her warning: "This type of behavior is not appropriate in business class." The woman, "with drool hanging out of her mouth and all (seriously now), asked 'Can we take a seat in coach?' "

Crew members are no less immune to high-altitude sins of the flesh. The problem is, when we get busted, a flying career can suddenly crash and burn. That's exactly what happened to a pilot at one airline.

While taking a scheduled break from his duties in the cockpit, the pilot retreated to his designated first-class rest-seat and, according to sources, started "smooching" with his flight attendant girlfriend. The couple then disappeared into a lavatory for "quite some time." Reports were filed, management reacted, the pilot lost his job.

Years ago, a flight attendant was terminated by her airline after being accused of prostitution. She did not perform her services aboard the plane, however. This is where she met potential Johns. While serving drinks and dinner to businessmen in the first-class section, she zeroed in on those who looked as if they wanted company for the night. Paid company. After settling on a price, the John agreed to meet in her room at the layover hotel. Once the dirty deed was done, the flight attendant went on to work another flight. But airline management soon caught wind of this lucrative undertaking. Posing as a lonely first-class businessman, an undercover airline operative caught the attendant with her skirt up. Literally. The next day her wings were clipped.

Despite the threat of dismissal—or in the case of brazen passengers, the threat of embarrassment or worse, a one-year layover in the slammer—sexual impropriety aboard airplanes may soon reach new and more astonishing lows.

British Airways was among the first to introduce a first-class seat that reclines 180 degrees—effectively becoming a six-foot, six-inch bed. Singapore Airlines, Qantas, Lufthansa, American, US Airways, Japan Airlines and others have implemented sky-beds of their own. While British Airways calls them "flying cradles," United refers to the cushy thrones as "first suites" and Singapore Airlines has adopted the magnanimous appellation, "skysuites." The industry moniker is "sleeper-seat," but no matter what you call these airborne mattresses, they're a frisky-flyer's dream come true.

The most coveted sleeper-seats are single units that slant toward the window on each side of the plane. The module's high back wraps almost completely around the passenger, creating an atmosphere of unprecedented privacy. Airline companies, in their single-minded quest to pamper first-class customers, have no idea what kind of plebian possibilities they've unleashed upon the traveling aristocracy.

But Richard Branson knows. He's even upped the sky-bed ante. Upper-class passengers on all Virgin Atlantic flights can book a seat that converts into a double bed. That's right. For around $5,500 round-trip, New York–London passengers can stretch out, roll around, even join the Mile-High Club—all this, behind the ramparts of a retractable "privacy screen."

As a courtesy to passengers and crew, let's hope the privacy screens are soundproof.

28 Miguel Mendoza: Playboy of the Skies

He's no Antonio Banderas, no Denzel Washington. No one would mistake him for Brad Pitt. For one thing he's got a crooked nose. It sort of curves toward one corpulent cheek, then suddenly, like the tip of a sickle that's been hurriedly yanked by pliers, it juts straight out at you again. On top of that, he drinks too much beer. And the ice cream sundaes—the ones he's been devouring in the first-class galley after convincing passengers not to indulge—are finally beginning to catch up with him. Despite the boxer's nose, the beer, the budding pot belly and the new flecks of gray in his hair, Miguel Mendoza is a lady killer. An airborne sex machine. He's charming and funny and he's still got that mojo working. It works on layovers, on five-hour sits between flight connections, he even gets it going on the airplane.

Chest out and belly in check, uniform shirt starched to perfection, Miguel strolls onto an Airbus as if he owns the goddamn thing. He is proud of his job and takes his responsibilities seriously. After insisting that designated crew members check all emergency equipment, he conducts a mandatory briefing in the first-class cabin. Technically, all pursers are required to perform briefings before each and every flight, but many believe the meetings are a waste of time. I couldn't agree more. After assembling the crew in the first-class section of the aircraft, the purser stands there, spouting off about passenger loads, meal allotments, weather. But before sharing this oh so critical information, he always encourages a round of introductions:

I'm Miguel.

I'm Sharon.
Marie.
Jason.
Andrea.
Doreen . . .

We grin at each other like children on the first day of summer camp. But as the names go round the cabin, Miguel grins for a different reason. Like most of us, he doesn't think pre-flight briefings are necessary. He does it, he says, so he can check out the babes on his crew. He has this uncanny knack of determining who is ripe for the plucking. And from what I know about Miguel, he plucks a lot.

Before each trip, he checks the company computer to get first and last names (even nicknames) of the female crew members. This helps foster an immediate sense of sincerity. "You must be Lizzy," he'll say, walking up to a colleague who has just entered the aircraft. Impressed that he would know her nickname—even though she has never flown with the broken-nosed Casanova—Lizzy or Sherry or Trish will almost always smile. A seed is thus planted. The groundwork laid. "It's the little things," Miguel told me, when asked why he's so popular with the ladies. "It doesn't matter what you look like, or how much money you have." He then flashed that devilish grin—the same one used to seduce half the women at the Denver base, as well as unsuspecting passengers from London to Lima, Peru. "What matters," he said, "is attention to detail."

"When Miguel looks at you," a female colleague once told me, "he makes you feel as if you're the most important person in the world." Having looked at her butt and her breasts, having calculated his chances and decided they were good, I'm sure Miguel Mendoza made her feel as important as was deemed necessary. Though most of his conquests occur at layover hotels—aided by a bottle of first-class champagne and promises of a "friendly" massage—his most daring accomplishment took place on the airplane. When it happened he was on duty and in uniform. So was the scandalous adulteress.

Miguel told the story as we downed beers at a hotel bar somewhere in the Caribbean. I can't remember whether we were in Antigua or Trinidad or Pago Pago for that matter, but I remember every detail of his sordid tale. Wide-eyed and silent, I sipped my beer and listened to Miguel Mendoza, playboy of the skies . . .

I was working first-class on a 727 with a flight attendant who had recently separated from her husband. She was new to the base. I'd never flown with her before. During the last of three legs, she sat next to me on the jump seat and complained about her husband once again. She was real touchy feely. You know how some flight attendants are. Every time she made a particularly good point she'd touch me on the arm for emphasis. Sometimes she grabbed me on the thigh and squeezed a little. Sometimes she squeezed a lot. "My husband is too insensitive," she said, for the tenth time that day. "He doesn't know how to communicate. And he doesn't like sex."

This is where my interest piqued.

We had already completed the emergency demo. The seat belts had been checked; the pre-departure cups had been collected and tossed in the trash. We were strapped in the double jump seat, our bodies pressed together like two peas in a pod.

"He doesn't like sex?" I said, hoping to keep the conversation on course.

"Nope, hardly at all," she said. "Once or twice a week and he's happy. But I need it more often than that." She glanced at me after she said that.

Before I continue, let me give you a bit of background about our trip. From the start of the first leg we had been playing an erotic game. Every time she squeezed past me in the galley she would make sure her breasts rubbed against me. She'd giggle. I'd growl. Then both of us would laugh. When it was my turn to be the aggressor, I'd sort of brush my thigh against her butt. More giggles. More growls. More laughter. It was cute and innocent, at first. Something to help make the day fly by. But by the third and final leg, we had rubbed against each other so hard and so often, I thought my crotch was going to break out in flames.

So by the time she turned to me and said her husband "doesn't like sex," I was all set to put a bottle of champagne on ice; ready to hook up the layover. You know how I am. But something in her eyes told me that she couldn't wait. She looked at me. I looked at her. We just stared at each other for a while, seeing who would blink first. The plane stopped moving, but you could feel it vibrating as the engines idled. I knew something was going to happen. I just didn't know what. She wet her lips in that quick, almost involuntary gesture that most people make before kissing somebody for the first time. I probably did the same thing. Our lips were just a couple of inches apart. I could feel her breath on my face; she had eaten some orange-flavored Tic-Tacs. I remember, because she gave me some earlier.

About this time I leaned into the aisle to check the passengers. There were only two seated in first class. And they were on the left-hand side of the aircraft, blocked from view by the coat closet and the bulkhead behind it. Whatever we decided to do, we could do it without worrying about being seen.

I kind of whispered in her ear for a while. You know, telling her what I wanted to do to her at the hotel. Then I kissed her. But about ten seconds into the kiss, I pulled back. It's a trick I learned a long time ago. You should always be the first to stop a kiss. It leaves a woman wanting more. I had no idea how much more until she put both hands on my cheeks and pulled my face to hers. It wasn't just a kiss. I damn near choked on her tongue. It started wiggling around in my mouth like a live thing. Then she started moaning. Loud. The longer we kissed, the louder she moaned. Because we were so close to the cockpit door, I worried that the pilots might hear. Maybe the passengers, too. At one point, she started grabbing at my clothes. I pushed her away a little, but that only seemed to get her more excited. For a minute there, I thought she was going to rape me. I thought I was going to let her, too. But I collected myself somehow. No use getting all wound up for nothing. We were sitting in a 727 on an active taxiway. There were three or four planes ahead, waiting to turn onto the runway. There were passengers on board, duties to complete.

"We've gotta' stop, we've gotta' stop," I said, finally. And we did stop. For a moment. But she had gone past the point of no return. I could see it in her eyes. Suddenly, and without any prompting on my part, she squirmed out of her harness and dropped to her knees. I couldn't believe what was happening. The last thing I remember hearing—after the quick downward jerk of my zipper—was the captain's voice on the P.A. system. Whenever I think about it, all I can do is smile. "Ladies and gentlemen, we've completed our cockpit checks," he said. "Flight attendants prepare for takeoff."

29 Membership Has Its Privileges

I am not a card-carrying member of the Mile-High Club. Probably never will be. Not that I haven't applied for membership, mind you. On more than a few occasions I have cruised the airplane cabin as if it were a nightclub lounge—chatting up female passengers in a dark corner of the aircraft, flirting with a colleague on my jump seat—hoping beyond hope that fantasy will blossom into real-life, high-altitude debauchery. But when I finally got the chance of a lifetime, when my MHC application received an unexpected approval, I worried about rising to the occasion.

It happened during an all-nighter to South America. Soon after take-off, I began flirting with a member of my crew. Or rather, she came on to me. Actually . . . hell, I might as well go ahead and tell it the way it really happened: She said, "I'm horny, I need to get laid." I kid you not. Those were her exact words. *I'm horny, I need to get laid.* Frisky as a sailor on twenty-four-hour shore leave, my coworker made the comment not twenty minutes after we had introduced ourselves. I've never been privy to such a blatant proposition. Lord knows it'll never happen again. She spoke with blunt, matter-of-fact swiftness that made me wonder if I'd heard correctly. At first I thought she said, "I'm hungry, I need to get paid." On second thought she might have said, "I'm happy, I'm no longer afraid." But when she stared at me in the galley of that 767, licking her lips like a Jenny Craig dropout in a chocolate shop, I realized that the woman meant business.

Tall and tanned and young and sort of lovely, she wasn't exactly the

Girl from Ipanema, but she conjured all the lust and passion of Astrud Gilberto's classic song. She stood there with her hands on her hips, five miles above the Caribbean Sea, three feet away from yours truly— gobbling me with lecherous eyes, as if I were something to be purchased, unwrapped and eaten at her discretion.

I was flattered, of course. What man wouldn't be? Since the first crotch-tingling pangs of puberty, we've all dreamed of meeting a stranger bold enough to cut to the chase; a stranger willing to acknowledge primal urges and daring enough to act upon them without feeling guilty once the deed has been done. But I was being hit on. Hard. So hard in fact, I wasn't sure how to react. The roles had been reversed so completely, the yin and yang of social discourse so thoroughly transposed, I began to feel exactly like a woman. A virgin set upon by a lustful paramour. Hungry eyes crawled over me, probing the outline of my biceps, measuring the thickness of my crotch.

I stood there, dumbfounded, unable to utter a sound.

Throughout the beverage and dinner services, she made embarrassing little comments that caused me to spill coffee on at least two passengers. "You've got the prettiest eyes," she whispered, leaning from her end of the meal cart. I grabbed a stack of napkins, apologizing to an elderly man as I wiped the spill from his armrest. "Mmmmm . . ." she said a moment later, glancing at the meal tray and then into my eyes. "The dessert looks yummy tonight." Two passengers looked up and smiled, eager to sample the cardboard crumb cake. My not-so-secret admirer was eager to sample something else.

After we completed the duty-free service, dimmed the cabin lights, started the in-flight movie and waved good-bye to the first two flight attendants scheduled for a one-hour rest break, my lusty colleague approached. I was sitting on the aft, left-hand jump seat, directly across from one of four lavatories. Unsure of how to proceed (and more than a little nervous), I waited for her to make the first move.

A copy of *National Geographic* lay open on my lap. In the photo essay, a thirteen-foot African crocodile lunged from a swamp with one powerful flick of its tail. The beast opened its jaws, exposing twin rows of jagged teeth that closed upon the throat of an unsuspecting wildebeest. Singled out from the herd which had come for a communal drink, the baby wildebeest was about to end up as crocodile chow. In blood-spurting detail that only *National Geographic* could capture, the sequence of photographs documented the poor creature's demise: 1) Wildebeest's eyeball rolls in its socket as croc bites into neck; 2) Struggling wildebeest is snatched into swamp, kicking its hooves toward the heavens; 3) Croc rips wildebeest into shreds of pink and red meat; 4) Members of herd look on—grieving for their fallen comrade, but happy as hell they hadn't been the first to take a drink.

All of a sudden, I felt a presence. I looked up from the carnage and there she was—my invitation to the Mile-High Club. Sporting the grin of a porno star who seemed ready to unleash a triple whammy, she leaned against the bulkhead with a hand on one slouched hip. The look in her eyes bore the same cold, calculating hunger apparent in the thirteen-foot African crocodile. Mesmerized by the animalistic glint in her eye, reeling from the graphic savagery of the photographs, I felt a sudden surge of emotion: blood rushed to my loins like fire down a trail of gasoline. As she bent down and whispered something dirty in my ear, the *National Geographic* shifted in my lap. Had it not been for the snug fit of my uniform trousers, the sudden arousal might have catapulted the magazine all the way to first class.

"Meet me in the lav," she said, in a soft but commanding voice. "Give me two minutes, then knock on the door three times, okay?"

Unable to speak, I simply nodded my head. She kissed me on the cheek and disappeared into the lavatory, leaving me on the jump seat with a hardening disposition.

Having never done it in an airplane lavatory, I began to worry about angles and logistics. I closed my eyes, trying to visualize all the vertical positions in the *Kama Sutra*, but in all the excitement, my brain kind of short circuited. Sexual images came at me like memories from a wet dream: long legs wrapped around a thrusting torso; wet lips pressed against the inside of a trembling thigh; my own startled face, smothered beneath the weight of a hundred bulging breasts. Staring at the lavatory door, I suddenly developed X-ray vision. I could almost see the uniform skirt falling to the floor, the regulation pantyhose peeling from around a wiggling waist, the heaving breasts, those slouching hips, a wicked tongue curling around seven lucky words: *I'm horny, I need to get laid.*

Since Adam took that first bite from the apple, never has a man been so anxious to get his groove on.

I looked at my watch. A mere thirty seconds had passed since the object of my desire disappeared into the lavatory. *Thirty-one. Thirty-two. Thirty-three.* The seconds moved like old ladies at a nursing home. But wait! Was I supposed to knock twice after three minutes, or thrice after two? I sat there, pondering the question, knowing full well that I didn't care anymore. I was going for the gusto, dammit. To hell with timetables.

I flung the *National Geographic* to the floor, stood up and raised one trembling fist to the door . . .

In all my years on airplanes, I've gotten lucky only once. But the plane was not airborne. And we didn't do it in the lavatory, either. My lover and I hooked up in the lower-lobe galley of a DC-10 as it sat on the tarmac in the middle of the night in Santo Domingo, Dominican Republic.

We had flown in from New York with a full load of passengers and landed on schedule at about 2:30 A.M. After the passengers disembarked, the crew remained on the aircraft. Because our return flight wasn't set to depart until 7:30 (a lousy arrangement, but one which had other advantages), we had about four hours in which to sleep. Somebody killed the lights. One by one we staked out our own territory and lay down in passenger seats.

After a few minutes most of the crew drifted off. But I couldn't sleep. I had an appointment to keep with a member of the crew. A week earlier, she and I had gone out on a date in Manhattan. The date went well. We had a mutual attraction that led to a slow wet kiss at the end of the night. But since then, we'd been playing phone tag. Now, at last, we were together. Before landing we came up with a plan. After our coworkers fell asleep, we would meet in the service center, take the elevator to the lower-lobe galley and see if the next kiss could be as good as the first.

When the coast was clear, I crept down the right-side aisle, past two snoring pilots who were stretched out in successive rows. With all the empty rows, I found it strange that two guys would want to sleep right next to each other. But pilots are a different breed. Perhaps the confines of the cockpit instill in them a need to stick together.

To my disappointment, the object of my desire was not in the service center. She had forgotten our little rendezvous, or so I thought. Perhaps while waiting for the crew to fall asleep, she too had drifted off. Worse, maybe she had changed her mind. I hopped into the elevator, thinking that she might be in the galley. Low and behold, I was right! When I stepped through the door, she was standing in front of a bank of ovens, filling out paperwork on a retractable counter.

She looked up at me and smiled. Locked in the awkward moment, we stood in the gauntlet of silver ovens, waiting for each other to make a move. The cargo door was wide open, revealing a sea of ramp lights that glittered like blue and white jewels. Imagine you and your lover in the kitchen of a third-floor apartment. Now imagine that one exterior wall is missing, exposing you to the stars. This is how it felt in the lower-lobe galley of the DC-10 that night. No words were spoken, no niceties exchanged. We simply fell into each others arms, guided by the moon and the ramp lights and our bubbling libidos.

She and I dated for more than a year. We buddy-bid occasionally and worked the same trips. We traveled. Watched movies. Ate out. We partied in Manhattan until the sun came up. After the breakup we remained close friends. She even invited me to her wedding.

As I prepared to enter the lavatory on the South America–bound flight, I couldn't stop thinking about that night in the lower-lobe galley. Why did we break up anyway? The woman who now waited in the lav was a stranger. There was no true attraction. Besides, what if there was an emergency, and the only two attendants in the back were actually *attending* to each other? I could lose my job. Making love with someone special on an empty DC-10 was one thing, but doing it in a lavatory in the middle of a flight? With someone whose name I had already forgotten? Despite the tingling sensation below my waist, I decided it wasn't worth it.

I looked at my watch again. Four and a half minutes had passed.

About this time I heard mutterings from the lavatory. Then there were other sounds: an elbow banging against the wall, perhaps; an angry heel driven into the floor; the faint snap of elastic popping back into place. A moment later the latch slid out of place. The door opened. My would-be lover walked out wearing a grimace that almost made my knees buckle. The eyes that once hungered for me, now held me in contempt. "I knew it," she said, spitting the words between clenched teeth. "I figured you were gay."

"WHAT? I'm not . . . look, it's just that—"

But before I could finish, she stormed up the aisle, heading for the cockpit.

I have no idea what happened up there—who am I to spread rumors. But two hours later, when she finally emerged from the cockpit, she had a big smile on her face.

Mile-high antics stun passengers

LONDON, June 1 (South China Morning Post) – Business class passengers on a South African Airways flight were treated to a brazen demonstration last week when a couple made love in full view of fellow travellers, a South African newspaper said yesterday.

"It was the most callous display of lust I have ever seen," a mother, accompanied on the flight by her husband and two young sons, told *The Sunday Times* newspaper.

Airline corporate relations manager Leon Els said the couple, a white male in his 40s and an Indian female companion, would not be charged over the incident, which occurred during a flight from Johannesburg to London.

Their names were not disclosed.

"We are not the first airline to have this sort of thing happen and it won't be the last," Mr. Els told the newspaper.

Adventurous couples who indulge in sex while airborne are said to have gained membership to the mile-high club.

Embarrassed cabin crew appeared unsure how to handle the situation.

The couple halted their love-making only when the captain was called and bellowed at them that the aircraft was not "a shag house"—by which time most of the damage was done.

"I could understand it if they covered themselves with a blanket, but no—it was wham, bam, right there in the seat," the woman's husband told the newspaper.

Permission to reprint from the South China Morning Post, 1998.

Afterword

The travel alarm is beeping again.

My right arm emerges from beneath the blanket like a creature from the bowels of the Earth. I feel it snaking toward the source of early-morning agony, limp as overcooked fettuccini, bumping against the vague shape of a table lamp, then lunging for and finally grabbing hold of the screeching, squealing, unforgiving alarm clock after knocking a hotel ashtray to the floor.

It's 4:30 A.M. local time, but I'm not exactly sure of the locale. I lay in bed—breathing the same stale air that flows through hotel rooms from Osaka to Orlando—wondering where the hell I am. Unable to gain my bearings, I mentally retrace my steps. Yesterday morning I started in Miami. The first leg we flew to Belize. We returned to Miami and, after a four-hour wait and two slices of airport pizza, I joined an Airbus crew to . . . Caracas. That's right. I'm in Caracas! Or "Crack Ass," as some of my less appreciative colleagues regard Venezuela's capital city.

I look at the clock again. It's 4:33. Time to go to work.

Eyes barely open, breath deadly enough to drop a sparrow from fifty feet, I stumble out of bed in total darkness. Last night I knew where the bathroom was. During the brief hours that I slept, however, the room layout has been altered. I open what I believe is the door to the bathroom and find myself awash in eerie light from the hotel corridor. I am naked. I am sleepy. My mind is slow to react. There is a surreal quality about the moment. The sudden juxtaposition of dream and reality leaves me wondering if I've done this before. No, somebody else has. A pilot. Capt. Sleepy. I close the door, pivot, lurch into the bathroom.

Peering at my swollen face in the mirror, the day begins to unfurl. The plane will be packed, of course. Flights from Caracas to Miami are always packed. Two hundred and fifty-one passengers in the back of an Airbus, sixteen in first-class, and a crew of seven flight attendants (a one-to-eight crew/passenger ratio in first class, a one-to-fifty ratio in coach) to give what the company calls "courteous, individual attention" in a two-hour and forty-five-minute time span. Today someone will complain about food, cabin temperature, seat pitch, lack of attention or the fact that the airplane isn't flying fast enough. It always happens. It always will.

The monotony of it all overwhelms me.

I let out a sigh, then shave, shower, pack, crawl into my uniform, schlep my Travelpro down the elevator, drop my card key at the check-out desk and wait in the lobby for my crew. The pilots will walk up, introduce themselves and stand there stiff as statues until my flight attendant colleagues show up one by one to complain about rigid pillows or too-soft mattresses or the fact that they couldn't sleep because of music from the hotel nightclub. Once inside the crew van we will make the long winding drive through the mountains, talking animatedly amongst ourselves for the first few minutes, and then settling into the grim silence that precedes most every flight. Then, like a platoon of soldiers going through maneuvers for the thousandth time, we will file into the crowded airport, toss our bags on the security conveyor belt and march toward the airplane for the start of another three-leg day.

This is going to be my last trip, I swear. When I get back to base, I'm going to walk into my supervisor's office, unpin my badge (gold wings) and slam it on his desk like a good cop in a bad movie. I've had enough of the screaming kids, the irate passengers and the lousy airplane food. I can no longer tolerate the airport crowds, the constant squawk of questions, the endless treks to yet another departure gate on the other side of Earth. Here I am, sixteen years after completing initial training and I'm still a foot soldier in the anger wars. Like a lot of my colleagues, I figured to fly a few years, see a bit of the world, then trade in my wings for something better. But flying gets in your blood. It's like malaria. Once it's in there, it never really goes away. So, I choose to keep on flying. I deal with the fourteen-hour work days and the polyester pants. I placate the cussing business fliers, sidestep the puking kids, and duck the fists of air ragers who see me as the root of all evil.

Amid the chaos, I continue to jet around the planet whenever I have a few days off.

I deal with the long lines and flight delays and missed connections because of one inescapable truth: There exists only five plausible ways to reach a distant destination. Unless you're prepared drive a car, ride a train or bus, or take a slow boat—modes of transportation that bring their own unique breed of problems—flying remains the most efficient means of travel.

The word "travel," by the way, comes from the French word "travail," which means to labor or work. When you look at it from this perspective, traveling on an airplane requires zero effort. You sit in a relatively comfortable chair while pilots fly the plane safely from point A to point B. Flight attendants ply you with drinks. The in-flight movie takes you to another world. Humming jet engines lull you to sleep.

Next time try riding a bicycle from New York to Los Angeles. When and if you reach your final destination, there might actually be something to bitch about.

Believe It or Not: ···············→

More Mind-Boggling Airline
News from Around the Globe

Couple charged after in-flight sexcapade

MANCHESTER, England, Oct. 5 (Agence France-Presse) – Two British business-class passengers were arrested after an alleged drunken sex session aboard a flight from the United States, press reports said yesterday.

A 40-year-old man and a 37-year-old woman were arrested at Manchester airport on Saturday after the pilot of their American Airlines flight from Dallas radioed ahead to complain about their behaviour.

Witnesses said the pair were strangers when they checked in for the 10-hour flight, but got friendly after making the most of the free drinks on board.

At first huddling under an airline blanket, the couple allegedly later threw caution to the wind and ignored pleas from fellow passengers and cabin crew to halt their sex session.

The pair, both married, have been charged with outraging public decency, being drunk on board an aircraft and with an offence under new "air-rage" laws for conduct causing harassment, alarm or distress. They are to appear in court in November.

Reprinted with permission of Agence France-Presse, 1999.

Pretoria air crews face sex inquiry

CAPE TOWN, South Africa, Feb. 5 (The Times of London) – Ray Kennedy – A Mile-High Club operating aboard South African Airways jets on international flights has led to the suspension of nearly 100 cabin crew and prompted a police investigation into whether they are also involved in drug-smuggling.

The airline has undergone huge changes in the six years since apartheid was outlawed and blacks, previously denied decent jobs with the state-owned operation, now make up a large proportion of cabin crews. Female prostitution is allegedly involved but senior officials say that it is the young black men working as stewards who are most in demand.

"We know from telephone conversations that have been overheard that some of our male cabin attendants are highly sought-after in destinations like Australia," Noedine Isaacs, SAA vice-president of in-flight services, said. "Women have been seen waiting for our attendants in their hotel rooms. It is an open secret among flight staff but it is difficult to prove that any money changes hands."

The suspensions come after the arrest on drug-smuggling charges of five SAA cabin crew members at Johannesburg airport after flights from South America. Ms. Isaacs said that the airline's investigations indicated that only a minority of cabin attendants were involved in the prostitution and drug-trafficking rackets "and we are determined to root it out."

The airline will begin disciplinary hearings today involving 92 cabin crew and rostering clerks, responsible for drawing up duty lists, who have been suspended.

The clerks are said to have accepted bribes of 1,000 rands (pounds 100) from cabin attendants to manipulate the duty list so that they would be allocated to destinations such as London, Miami and South America.

Branson invites Virgin travellers to join Mile-High Club

LONDON, June 8 (London Daily Telegraph) – Paul Marston – Air travellers are to be offered private double beds along with legitimate membership of the "Mile High Club" by Virgin Atlantic.

Virgin intends to install up to 10 full-sized double beds in private "cabins," separated from other passengers by screens.

Steve Ridgway, the airline's managing director, said there would be no requirement to produce marriage certificates and no bar on couples of the same sex.

Return fares between London and New York would be about pounds 6,600 per twosome, the same as two individual business-class tickets.

He did not think that the noise of love-making would be a nuisance for other passengers because there would be "quite a lot of ambient aircraft sound." Richard Branson, the airline's chairman, who launched the facility at Amsterdam airport yesterday with the help of the television presenter Dani Behr, said: "You can do it on cruise ships. You can do it at home. Why not on planes?" He said occupants would not be disturbed by prying cabin crew.

The more serious focus of a pounds 37 million revamp of Virgin's Premium class is a new seat that becomes a single bed.

This will be introduced from September, three months before British Airways hopes to start a similar product.

Virgin also displayed a new aircraft livery with Union flag wingtips and the legend "Britain's flag carrier" beneath a billowing standard on the fuselage side.

Mr Branson said prior knowledge of his new design had "panicked" British Airways into its weekend announcement of the restoration of the flag to most of its fleet at the expense of its much-criticised ethnic art tailfins.

© The Telegraph Group Limited, 1999.

Airport lovers caught by cops

TORONTO, Oct. 13 (Toronto Sun) – Tom Godfrey – Pearson Airport's Terminal 3 is not only a hotbed for sex and booze romps for frolicking bag handlers, now passengers are getting in on the act, Peel Regional Police say.

A moaning couple found making out in the handicap stall of an airport washroom had their lovemaking cooled by police.

"We broke them up and told them to move on," said a Peel officer. "They were asked politely to leave the terminal."

Police said the pair had just arrived at the airport and evidently couldn't wait to get it on. "They were making love-making type noises when we got there," the officer said.

The pair were discovered last Thursday by a woman who had just dropped off her husband to catch a flight.

"I was surprised to see that someone had stuffed toilet paper all around the spaces surrounding the door," A. Reidak wrote in a letter to the editor at the *Sun*.

"I heard what sounded like a male voice coming from inside. I decided to report the strange goings-on to an employee."

Police said the young couple weren't charged because a bathroom stall is considered a private place.

Peel Insp. John Byrne said his force has zero tolerance towards sexual acts taking place on airport property. Police are now probing a sex ring involving airport staff who use the basement of Terminal 3 for quickies.

Officers are now asking handlers and ramp workers on the tarmac for identification and are warning them ID must be worn where it's visible.

"We routinely check the clearance passes of employees," said Insp. John Byrne. "We are responding to concerns."

He said handlers whose security passes are not visible will be questioned by police.

Airport officials have installed cameras in all hallways of the terminal and police have increased their presence in areas around Terminal 3 to curb some of the shenanigans.

As well cracking down on partying staff, police have stepped up radar speed traps around the three terminals.

Reprinted with permission of Sun Media Corporation, Toronto, Ontario, 1999.

Growling woman tied to seat

MISSISSAUGA, Ontario, Sept. 13 (Edmonton Sun) – A woman on a Paris-Toronto flight got down on all fours "growling like a dog" at fellow passengers before biting and punching three flight attendants, police say.

"She was crawling in the aisle, growling like a dog at passengers and kicking in the air," said Peel Regional police Insp. John Byrne.

Police arrested a woman when the Air Canada flight landed at Toronto's Pearson airport at 2 p.m. Monday.

Staff on the flight noticed a woman drinking cognac from a bottle in her carry-on luggage, Byrne said.

About halfway through the eight-hour flight, the woman started yelling and annoying fellow passengers, then struck a 37-year-old flight attendant on the arm, Byrne said.

"(She) then returned to her seat and began an unprovoked attack on the male passenger seated next to her."

When flight staff tried to calm her down, she threw newspapers and magazines around the cabin and crawled up the aisle growling at passengers, he said.

She was tied to her seat, but not before she hit another flight attendant in the face, bit the finger of a 51-year-old male steward and grabbed another flight attendant by the throat.

Staff finally tied her arms and legs to her seat for the remaining two hours of the flight. Cops boarded the plane on arrival and arrested the woman.

Sylvaine Marie Martin-Kostajnsek, 44, a Canadian living in Paris, faces numerous charges including aggravated assault.

Police said the woman is a composer who was flying to Toronto as part of a month-long residency at Gibraltar Point Centre for the Arts. Her flight was paid for through a $1,000 travel grant by the Canada Arts Council.

Reprinted with permission of Sun Media Corporation, Toronto, Ontario, 2000.

Former official cleared in stink bombings

NEW YORK, Sept. 29 (Reuters) – The former head of New York's public hospital system was cleared on Thursday of allegations that he set off stink bombs on two TWA international flights.

Victor Botnick, 46, was cleared by a jury on federal charges stemming from incidents on flights from New York to Paris in 1998.

After the verdict he called the case "a nightmare I can't believe I ever lived through."

Prosecutors said foul odors filled the cabin during the two flights, one of which had to be canceled when passengers' eyes began to water and burn. In both incidents either a small vial or glass shards were later found under or near Botnick's seat, along with a patch of the liquid which caused the odor.

They argued that this was an impossible coincidence, and said Botnick had had a dispute with Trans World Airlines Inc. (TWA.A) a year earlier over canceled reservations and luggage delays.

Botnick's attorney said no one else was investigated and pointed to a lack of forensic evidence and witnesses.

Botnick was charged with interfering with the performance of the flight crew and lessening their ability to perform their duties.

If convicted he could have faced 20 years in prison.

Hong Kong rock star dumped in Anchorage after ruckus on jet

ANCHORAGE, Feb. 18 (Anchorage Daily News) – Molly Brown – A Hong Kong rock star caused a passenger jet to make an unplanned stop in Anchorage on Thursday after he started smoking and singing from his first-class seat, put a flight attendant in a headlock, assaulted passengers and lay on the floor screaming obscenities.

Ronald Cheng, 27, was finally subdued when the pilot of the nonstop EVA Air Flight 05 from Los Angeles to Taipei, Taiwan, handed control of his aircraft to another crew member, stepped back into the cabin and ended up hitting Cheng in the head with a flashlight, according to an affidavit filed by the FBI in federal court.

Cheng was charged with crimes aboard an aircraft, including interfering with flight crew members and assault, according to the FBI. He could face a $250,000 fine and up to 20 years in prison, Assistant U.S. Attorney Stephan Collins said.

When the EVA Air flight left Los Angeles at 11:55 p.m. Wednesday, Cheng appeared to be fine, according to the affidavit. He ordered alcoholic drinks and used the restroom. But when he left the restroom, Cheng had a hard time walking back to his seat.

Cheng, a singer known for his ballads, started crooning and smoking cigarettes and he assaulted another passenger, the affidavit said. When a flight attendant tried to quiet him and get him to put out his cigarette, he grabbed her arm and put her in a headlock until another passenger helped her get free.

A crew member turned for help from the cockpit, and the first officer headed toward the cabin to calm Cheng, who was still spewing obscenities. But Cheng attempted to choke him, the affidavit said.

When Capt. John Irving arrived with the flashlight, Cheng was lying on the floor screaming. Irving asked Cheng to return to his seat. When Cheng tried to punch him, the document said, Irving hit Cheng in the head in self-defense.

At that point, Cheng became "compliant," authorities said, and the crew used flex cuffs—plastic restraints—to hold him in his seat. They decided to divert the flight to Anchorage.

FBI agents met the plane and took Cheng to Providence Alaska Medical Center. He was treated for his injuries and is jailed at Cook Inlet Pre-Trial Facility in Anchorage. He likely will appear in federal court today, Collins said.

Anchorage FBI agent Eric Gonzalez said diverting the plane was a drastic measure but was warranted because Cheng seemed uncontrollable.

While Cheng isn't well-known in the United States, his music has topped the charts in Hong Kong. Some Hong Kong web sites call him a pop idol. One, which profiles local musicians, says that Cheng loves action movies, Elton John music and hamburgers.

Reprinted with permission of The Daily News, Anchorage, Alaska, 2000.

Passenger's bad behavior costs $10,500

OMAHA, Neb., April 16 (Omaha World-Herald) – An unruly airline passenger has been ordered to pay restitution to United Airlines for slapping a flight attendant and prompting an unscheduled landing at Eppley Airfield.

On March 13, 1999, Gail Ellen Holmes, 40, of Denver, was a first-class passenger on United Flight 410 from Denver to New York. She was the last person to board, and her carry-on luggage did not fit in the overhead compartment, according to a press release from U.S. Attorney Tom Monaghan.

The flight attendant asked her to have it checked, but Holmes began arguing with and cursing at the flight attendant, refusing to check her luggage, Monaghan said. The bag eventually was checked, but the plane was late in departing because of the incident.

Holmes began using her cell phone while the plane was still on the ground, Monaghan said. A second flight attendant asked her to turn it off. Holmes eventually complied but continued to use profanity and remained belligerent, he said.

Holmes used her cell phone again while the plane was in flight. She was asked to put it away but ignored the flight attendant, Monaghan said. Then, Holmes cursed at the attendant and slapped her with an open palm, striking her chin and nose.

He said the captain diverted the plane to Omaha, where Holmes was removed.

Holmes was ordered to pay a fine of $500 and $10,000 in restitution to United Airlines by District Court Judge Thomas M. Shanahan.

Reprinted with permission of The Omaha World-Herald Company, 2000

Air hostess "attacked" by woman smoker

MANCHESTER, England, May 20 (London Sunday Times) – Russell Jenkins – A woman who was asked to stop smoking in the lavatory of an aircraft allegedly headbutted a stewardess during a transatlantic holiday flight.

The woman, understood to have been travelling with her child, is said to have gone "berserk" on the Airtours flight from Florida to Manchester when the request was made. The pilot had to abort his landing and go into a holding pattern when the woman broke free from the cubicle where she was being restrained and ran along the gangway. She was said to have been grappled to the ground by cabin crew with the help of two passengers.

The stewardess who was allegedly attacked, Vanessa Martinez, was taken to hospital for treatment to her injuries, which included a suspected broken nose.

The pilot made a radio call to alert the authorities at Manchester International Airport. A 26-year-old woman was arrested after aircraft landed.

© Times Newspapers Limited, 20th May, 2000.

Pakistani minister in Kashmir resigns after drunken episode

MUZAFFARABAD, Pakistan, Aug. 23 (Associated Press) – Shamed after being caught drunk on Pakistan's alcohol-free national airline, a Kashmiri legislator resigned Monday, a government official said.

The public works minister in Pakistan-ruled Kashmir, Chaudhry Mohammed Yasin, was arrested last week and charged with drunkenness, a crime in Islamic Pakistan, where alcohol is forbidden.

Yasin and two cousins were arrested last week when they disembarked from a Pakistan International Airlines flight from Britain, said the official, speaking on condition of anonymity.

Throughout the flight the three men harassed women passengers, stewardesses and scuffled with the airline crew, he said.

Customs officials at Islamabad International Airport confiscated 36 bottles of liquor from the minister and his cousins. Possessing alcohol is a crime in Pakistan and carries a maximum penalty of three years in jail.

Yasin was asked by Kashmir Prime Minister Sultan Mahmood to resign as admission of his "shameful public behavior." Yasin has been released on bail, but will face charges of drunkenness and possession of alcohol.

Reprinted with permission of The Associated Press, 1999.

Controlling air rage the medieval way

LONDON, June 2 (Deutsche Press-Agentur) – Airlines are testing a body restraint device, much like a medieval torture instrument, that would pin those succumbing to air rage to their seats, *The Times* has reported.

Former police sergeant Roger Fuller had developed a body restraint package, which was being tested by a dozen airlines, including British Airways, the newspaper said Wednesday.

It is designed to be thrown around the head and shoulders of air-rage culprits and consists of an upper-body restraint, handcuffs, a waist-restraint belt and lower-arm and leg restraints.

The upper-body restraint—a large metal bar with a d-shaped strap—is swung over the back of the passenger's seat and looped just under the arms and below the chest area.

Then, it is pulled tight to prevent the offender from moving. The waist restraint, handcuffs and lower-arm and leg restraints can then be slipped on for full security.

At present, air crews are limited to handcuffs, or makeshift rope and cargo straps when dealing with disruptive passengers.

There has been a marked increase in air-rage incidents in recent months, with passengers on trans-Atlantic flights regularly succumbing to the effects of alcohol, jet lag and indifferent airline service.

Reprinted with permission of dpa, Deutsche Presse-Agentur GmbH, 2000.

Pilot's arrest delays flight to Switzerland

NEW YORK, March 28 (New York Times) – The arrest of a Swissair pilot for public lewdness in a Central Park bathroom forced the overnight delay of a flight from New York to Geneva last week, the police and the airline said yesterday.

The airline could not find a replacement pilot for Flight 139 on Thursday, so the passengers were given overnight lodging and flown to Switzerland at 8 a.m. Friday, said Jackie Pash, a spokeswoman for the airline in North America.

Ms. Pash would not confirm the charge against the pilot, who remains with the company, saying that Swissair headquarters was awaiting the police report before commenting.

The name of the pilot could not be confirmed.

The police said that usually, anyone arrested on such a charge would be given a summons to appear.

But they said that because the pilot, a 48-year-old Swiss man, did not have a New York address and there was a chance he would not appear to answer the summons, he was arrested and held.

Reprinted with permission of The New York Times, 2000.

NWA fires pilot who delayed flight when he didn't like meal

MINNEAPOLIS, Dec. 7 (Star Tribune) – Northwest Airlines has fired the pilot who delayed a flight for more than an hour because he didn't like the meal he was served and took a cab to get fast food.

Passengers on the Nov. 23 flight headed to Detroit from Las Vegas had complained that the pilot kept them waiting while he fetched a different meal.

"He got off the plane, he walked by a number of food establishments that were open and serving, he got into a cab and went off-site," Northwest spokesman Jon Austin said Monday.

The airline fired the pilot Friday for acting "to the detriment of Northwest and his fellow employees," Austin said.

The captain had worked for the airline for 22 years.

Reprinted with permission of The Star Tribune, Minneapolis-St. Paul, 1999.

Air Canada kicks 88-year-old grandmother off plane

TORONTO, July 20 (Canada Press) – Federal regulators have rebuked Air Canada for kicking an 88-year-old woman off a plane and leaving her in a snowy tarmac because she would not sit near the bathroom.

"They were very, very mean to me," Sara Brownstein said Wednesday from her home in Montreal.

Brownstein had just boarded a flight from Montreal to Washington in mid-February when the flight attendant and pilot removed her from the plane.

The attendant wanted her to sit at the back so she could be near the bathroom, according to documents released by the Canadian Transportation Agency.

Brownstein, who walks with a cane because of arthritis, said she preferred to sit at the front and would not need the bathroom.

However, the captain and the attendant decided she was "non self-reliant" and could not travel alone.

Brownstein, who claims to be a frequent flyer, said she was forced off the plane so roughly she banged her head on the way out and had to stand in the tarmac for several minutes before being taken to the terminal.

"It was snowing outside, and I became wet and I became sick like anything," she said.

In a decision released Tuesday, the transportation agency said the attendant and the pilot, who were not identified, violated Air Canada policy and "this oversight on their part had serious consequences for those involved."

The agency ordered the airline to take corrective action to ensure this does not happen again. It also ordered the airline to hand over training reports on the flight attendant and to reimburse travel expenses incurred by Brownstein's son-in-law, who had to fly in from Washington the next day to accompany her to Washington.

Brownstein's relatives have also filed complaints with the U.S. Department of Transport and the Canadian Human Rights Commission. The family is also seeking punitive damages and compensation.

Air Canada has apologized, acknowledged the attendant did not follow proper procedure and reimbursed the cost of the plane tickets held by Brownstein and her son-in-law.

But the airline also defended the attendant's actions, saying: "Mrs. Brownstein's limited mobility raised safety concerns as only one attendant would be on duty during the flight."

Reprinted with permission from The Canadian Press, 2000.

Airline alarm prankster sought

LONDON, April 26 (Associated Press) – British Airways said Monday it is trying to find the prankster who triggered a false crash alarm on a London-bound flight from San Francisco that terrified some of the 391 passengers.

The recorded announcement is kept under a plastic flap in the chief flight attendant's office near the galley and is difficult if not impossible to trigger accidentally. Someone had to lift the lid and push the button, the airline said.

The recorded announcement, played some three hours after Flight BA286 took off on Friday, told passengers that the Boeing 747 was about to crash into the sea and ordered them to put on life jackets and adopt the brace position.

"The evidence points to a tape being activated as part of a silly prank by a passenger," said BA spokesman Bruce Tobin.

The airline apologized for the false alarm, but said it was sure that the staff was not to blame. Crew members quickly realized the error, switched off the tape, and went round reassuring passengers, and the captain apologized, said Tobin.

Several shaken passengers were treated by a doctor who was on board.

Tobin said investigations are continuing to find the culprit and refused to say if an individual passenger is under suspicion.

The plane landed safely at London's Heathrow Airport.

"To be told you're about to die is not a pleasant experience," said passenger Lloyd Pople, from Reading, England.

"About 15 minutes later, the captain said, 'I understand that a false alarm sounded to the effect we were about to ditch. I can assure you that the flight is fine,' " Pople said.

Airline has stolen seat belt problem

OSLO, Norway, June 29 (Associated Press) – A Norwegian airline has run into an unexpected safety problem: Seat belts on its aircraft are vanishing because they have become a hot fashion accessory.

"What we know is that it is in fashion for the street look," Stig Martin Solberg, spokesman for Braathens airline, said Thursday. "It has been a problem for about a year and is increasing."

He said mainly young Norwegians steal the seat belts, then use them to hold up their extremely baggy pants. Solberg said the airline, which is Norway's major domestic carrier, has been losing an average of five seat belts a day.

"It is easy to spot people on the street with them," he said. Solberg did not know whether this is an international trend.

Fashion stores offer similar belts, but the real thing seems to have more status, Solberg said. He said several suspects [have] been caught and reported to the police. The airline is also making it harder to remove the belts.

Solberg said the seat belts only cost about $30 to replace but the real expense can be much higher—particularly if a passenger has to be left because they have no seat belts or if a flight has to be delayed.

Solberg said the airline is considering suing seat-belt thieves for those costs, which could make seat belts one of the season's most expensive fashions.

Gun goes off on Alaska Air flight

PORTLAND, Ore., April 25 (Associated Press) – A gun discharged in a baggage compartment on an Alaska Airlines flight while the plane was on the ground, but no one was injured.

The bullet from a .357-caliber Ruger went from the cargo hold into the passenger area and lodged in a diaper bag Monday night on Flight 101, Port of Portland spokesman Doug Roberts said.

The 737 jetliner was scheduled to depart Portland International Airport for Anchorage, Alaska, Roberts said. The crew and 86 passengers on board were transferred to another plane.

Passenger Betty Jean Smith, 66, of Eagle River, Alaska, was charged with reckless endangerment and concealing a weapon without a permit. She was released to relatives in Vancouver, Wash. The gun was one of two stored in her bag.

Air steward saves heart attack victim, 83

LONDON, Dec. 6 (London Independent) – Andrew Mullins – A tenacious senior air steward described yesterday how he saved the life of an 83-year-old grandmother after two brain surgeons considered giving up the battle to revive her.

British Airways purser Marc Harding refused to give up on Pittmanne Japal from Mauritius, after she suffered a heart attack during a family trip to Florida on Friday.

Mr. Harding rushed to the scene to find two neurosurgeons, heading for a convention, tending to the patient. "There was no breathing, there was no pulse," the purser said.

He began giving artificial respiration as the two doctors, one Irish and one Norwegian, massaged her heart. But after several minutes there was no response. "One of the doctors said 'let's stop and evaluate this,' then he said 'I don't think there is much more we can do'," Mr. Harding explained.

Using the cabin's defibrillator, which sends surges of electricity through the chest, he tried to restart Mrs. Japal's heart. Mr. Harding said: "There was an amazing jolt through her body, and all of a sudden she groaned and started breathing again and her legs and arms twitched. I was in awe."

Man stowed away aboard flight

SEATTLE, March 31 (Associated Press) – A man hid in the cargo hold of a Northwest Airlines flight Friday and traveled more than 2,000 miles to Memphis, Tenn., where he fled into the terminal and disappeared.

The stowaway settled into the heated and pressurized front section of the cargo hold, where pets are kept, as Flight 946 left Seattle on Friday morning, KIRO-TV reported.

On arrival in Memphis, he asked baggage handlers for a ride to the terminal, KIRO reported. When the handlers challenged him, he fled.

"You don't anticipate that there will be a person when you open the cargo door," said Minneapolis-based Northwest spokeswoman Kathy Peach, who said the man appeared to be in his late 20s.

The man's identity is unknown.

The Federal Aviation Administration and Seattle port police were investigating, said Scott Ingham, a Northwest spokesman in Seattle.

The FAA here referred questions to a suburban Atlanta facility, where a person who answered the phone Friday evening said FAA involvement was unknown.

A spokesman for the Port of Seattle, which operates the Seattle-Tacoma International Airport, said how the man got to the plane is unknown.

"We're very interested in learning how this individual got onto the airfield," spokesman Bob Parker said.

Memphis Airport police referred calls to Northwest.

Dreaming of Disneyland, child stowaway accidentally travels to Europe

CARACAS, Venezuela, March 18 (Associated Press) – Jorge Rueda – It's got the earmarks of an improbable movie plot: An 11-year-old boy dreaming of a trip to Disneyland slips by airport security, boards a plane and flies by mistake to Europe even though he has no ticket or passport.

Yet Venezuelan police insist the tale is true.

"We have no doubt that the case of the little stowaway was the product of a childish prank that fooled airport security," Jose Lazo Ricardi, director of the Technical Judicial Police, Venezuela's equivalent of the FBI, said Tuesday.

Officials say MacGregory Johanvar Ramos, a student at a school for children with learning problems, skipped class two weeks ago to try to fulfill his dream of going to California to visit Disneyland.

After taking a half-hour trip on a public bus to Simon Bolivar International Airport, he asked around for flights to the United States. But the boy mistakenly boarded a KLM flight bound for Amsterdam, said Ricardi. MacGregory apparently got past airline and immigration officials by acting as if he were traveling with adult passengers.

He told police he hid in a bathroom for most of the trip until a flight attendant found him. But he convinced her he was traveling with an aunt, and thus was not detained upon landing.

After a seven-hour layover in Amsterdam, MacGregory boarded a Malev Airlines flight to Budapest—apparently helped when airline workers didn't check for tickets until the flight was underway. It wasn't immediately clear how he eluded Dutch immigration and security.

When the crew discovered he was traveling alone without a passport or ticket, they notified authorities who took him into custody after the plane touched down in Budapest, Ricardi said.

He was returned to Venezuela a day later—after airline officials put him up in a hotel and gave him souvenirs and candy.

The boy's mother, unemployed nurse Belkis Coromoto Alvarez, told local media that her son may have been able to pull off the stunt because he is a charmer who easily strikes up conversations with strangers.

MacGregory was being held by Venezuelan juvenile authorities until a judge decides whether he should be returned to his mother or placed in a state facility for children.

KLM officials declined to comment.

Naked traveler arrested in Singapore

SINGAPORE, May 12 (Associated Press) – Matthew Ng was waiting for his flight when he saw men's clothing strewn on the floor of a lounge at busy Changi Airport. Moments later, he spotted the man who should have been wearing them.

"I came across a shirt. I did a double take when, 10 paces later, there was a pair of pants and then underwear," *The Straits Times* newspaper quoted Ng as saying. Then, he said, he saw a man ambling nude through the lounge among passengers who appeared "too shocked to react."

The naked man was arrested for indecent exposure late Friday, police spokesman Stanley Norbert said Saturday. The 34-year-old, whose name was not released, was believed to have been on his way from Paris to Vietnam, the newspaper said.

"He has been sent for a psychiatric evaluation," Norbert said.

Man tries to open airplane exit

AMSTERDAM, Netherlands, May 10 (Associated Press) – A passenger on board a KLM flight from Amsterdam to Newark spat on a flight attendent, threatened passengers with a cane and tried to open the emergency exit while in flight, an official said Thursday.

The 28-year-old Dutchman, whom KLM spokesman Hugo Baas described as "clearly unstable," ignored orders from flight crew to turn off his mobile phone.

He ripped up his passport and said he would hit passengers and flight attendants. He then took a seat in business class, claiming he suffered from claustrophobia.

"At 37,000 feet he decided it was time to go and tried to open the emergency exit," Baas said. However, due to the cabin pressure, it was impossible to open the aircraft's emergency door.

Eventually, the man was handcuffed by the captain and guarded by two passengers for the rest of the flight, Baas said.

Upon arrival in the United States, the man was put on the next flight back to the Netherlands under the supervision of two private security guards.

He was arrested at Amsterdam's Schiphol Airport and will face charges of attempting to endanger the lives of passengers, the spokesman said.

Cell phone spurs Saudi sentence

RIYADH, Saudi Arabia, Feb. 3 (Associated Press) – A Saudi court sentenced an army captain Saturday to 70 lashes for using a mobile phone on a domestic flight, court officials said.

The court said the man put passengers and himself at risk by using his phone during takeoff despite orders from members of the crew that he turn it off. The flight was delayed 30 minutes as a result, and airport security eventually escorted the man off the plane, Al-Eqtisadiyah newspaper reported.

It was the kingdom's first such sentence against users of mobile phones on airplanes, the court officials said on condition of anonymity.

Saudi Arabia follows a strict interpretation of Islamic law, and courts routinely order lashings and hand amputations for theft and other crimes and public execution for murder, rape and drug trafficking. Human rights organizations have criticized those penalties, saying defendants do not receive fair trials and often do not have access to lawyers.

The court did not release the cell phone user's name, saying only that he was a captain of the Saudi Arabian army.